Economic Growth, the Environment and International Relations

The ubiquity of the commitment to economic growth, which Purdey refers to as the growth paradigm, is extraordinary. National governments around the world are seized of the same objective. Major international institutions such as the UN, the WTO, the World Bank, IMF and OECD, powerful international organizations such as regional trading blocs and multinational corporations – even civil societies of all kinds enthusiastically pursue a larger economic pie.

This book examines the deep origins and rise to prominence of the commitment to economic growth. It explains why, despite the diversity of regime types, levels of development, cultures and other divisions typical of international relations, all major actors in the modern global polity pursue an identical political priority. Purdey critically examines the growth paradigm highlighting its normative foundations and its environmental impact, especially climate change. Using a neo-Gramscian approach, Purdey re-engages the 'limits to growth' controversy, identifying the commitment to growth as a form of utopianism that is as dangerous as it is seductive.

By illuminating and interrogating the history, politics and morality of the growth paradigm, this book shifts the terrain of the limits debate from instrumental to ethical considerations. It will be of interest to students and scholars of political economy, international relations, environmental studies and ethics.

Stephen J. Purdey is a Lecturer at the University of Toronto, Canada.

Routledge advances in international political economy

1 **The Future of the Nation-State**
Essays on cultural pluralism and political integration
Edited by Sverker Gustavsson and Leif Lewin
Co-publication with Nerenius and Santérus Publisher AB, Sweden

2 **Classical Liberalism and International Economic Order**
Studies in theory and intellectual history
Razeen Sally

3 **Coping with Globalization**
Jeffrey Hart and Aseem Prakash

4 **Responding to Globalization**
Jeffrey Hart and Aseem Prakash

5 **Japanese Capitalism in Crisis**
A regulationist interpretation
Edited by Robert Boyer and Toshio Yamada

6 **Globalization and Social Change**
Edited by Johannes Dragsbaek Schmidt and Jacques Hersh

7 **Multilateralism and the World Trade Organisation**
The architecture and extension of international trade recognition
Rorden Wilkinson

8 **Foreign Direct Investment, Democracy and Development**
Assessing contours, correlates and concomitants of globalization
Indra de Soysa

9 **Rethinking International Organization**
Deregulation and global governance
Barbara Emadi-Coffin

Economic Growth, the Environment and International Relations

The growth paradigm

Stephen J. Purdey

Routledge
Taylor & Francis Group
LONDON AND NEW YORK

First published 2010
by Routledge
2 Park Square, Milton Park, Abingdon, Oxon OX14 4RN

Simultaneously published in the USA and Canada
by Routledge
711 Third Avenue, New York, NY 10017

Routledge is an imprint of the Taylor & Francis Group, an informa business

First issued in paperback 2011

Typeset in Times by Wearset Ltd, Boldon, Tyne and Wear

British Library Cataloguing in Publication Data
A catalogue record for this book is available from the British Library

Library of Congress Cataloging in Publication Data
Purdey, Stephen James.
Economic growth, the environment, and international relations: the growth paradigm/Stephen James Purdey.
p. cm. – (Routledge advances in international political economy; 17)
Includes bibliographical references and index.

1. Economic development–Environmental aspects. 2. Climatic changes–Government policy–International cooperation. 3. Global warming–Government policy–International cooperation. I. Title.

HD75.6.P87 2009
338.9–dc22 2009024147

ISBN13: 978-0-415-50350-1 (pbk)
ISBN13: 978-0-415-54850-2 (hbk)
ISBN13: 978-0-203-86339-8 (ebk)

Contents

Acknowledgements

With thanks to Herman E. Daly and Robert W. Cox.

1 What is the growth paradigm?

Understanding the growth paradigm as a form of governance

International relations are shaped in large measure by the condition of anarchy. In the colloquial sense anarchy means disorder, but in the academic sense used here it means the absence of a formally constituted world government. Anarchy sets the background from which most studies of international politics begin because it stipulates immediately that there is no overarching authority, no global government, to impose order on human society as a whole. This condition – so obvious yet so important – is actually rather deceptive because it does not signify something that exists, something concrete from which people and states can take their bearings. The opposite is true: it identifies a political void at the apex of human society which provides neither rules nor goals, and which is therefore permissive of other forces that compete to fill the vacuum. And indeed, the space left vacant by anarchy is not unoccupied. Other forms of governance have intruded into it, and imposed their own kind of order on the actors and affairs of the world.

Absent a clear set of agreed policy objectives and an organized way to achieve them, such as might be provided by a world government, and given that international relations are conducted in a forum disciplined by other forms of governance which are incomplete, dissimilar and often competitive in their approach to the maintenance of order, one may ask what is the net effect of this situation on international politics. Has fragmented governance without formal oversight led to confusion and unpredictability? Or are persistent features of international relations discernible which may indicate the presence of a balance among forces, a compromise between interests or even a consensus that effectively displaces anarchy? It seems clear that many such persistent features do exist. World affairs are, in the main, conducted in an orderly fashion and, in fact, identifying the source or sources of that order has long been a particular objective of the academic discipline of international relations (IR), not only as a matter of scholarly interest, but because understanding order can lead to its improvement, if not to a world government as such; and because where order is improved, so security may be enhanced as well. The present study follows this tradition. My interest, however, is not to catalogue various forms of governance, to situate them on a hierarchy of importance, to compare their relative merits, or to examine the ways in which they interact. Instead my interest is to identify, amidst the welter of possibilities, the particular form of governance that most powerfully shapes the present conduct and perhaps the future evolution of international relations; to discover its origins and path to preeminence; to reveal the form and substance of its normative foundations; and to determine the extent to which that governance structure may be germane to the security of human society as a whole.

It would be naïve to conclude that, in the rush to fill the void of anarchy, only those ordered systems that are disabused of coercive elements, or that represent a thoughtfully considered normative consensus, have prevailed over other systems of a less benign nature. Many forces with various characteristics co-exist simultaneously on the international stage, vying for authoritative status. Some offer legitimate, if partial, governance of world affairs, such as the United Nations and other international organizations which promote an evolving corpus of international laws and regulations. Others look less like structures of governance and more like self-interested regional actors – hegemonic states, for example – which seek to impose order coercively by extending their influence over ever-wider swaths of territory. Still other contenders may promote a distinct ideology instead of national or regional interests. The Cold War confrontation between the United States and the Soviet Union, for example, was a contest of strength, but it was also an argument about the relative benefits of capitalist and communist socio-economic systems. Each was advertised to better serve the common good, and each was offered to the world as the normative core around which global governance should evolve. In more recent times, conflicts between religious beliefs, or even between civilizations – 'the West against the rest', to express a simplistic example – also highlight ideological clashes springing from disagreement about values, and about the merit of their respective contributions to the mix of global governance systems. And, predominantly in contemporary world politics, the purportedly self-regulating mechanics of commercial activity offer yet another alternative to disorder by generating equilibria in economic relations, thereby helping to stabilize social and political affairs.

Globalization – the modern trend to tighter worldwide integration and the de-territorialization of authority – has spawned a fresh wave of new kinds of ordered systems which also contribute to governance in the emerging global arena. Typically transnational in scope and complex in structure,[1] these systems vary in type from formally constituted international organizations and regimes to policy networks and public–private partnerships which function in new political spaces which globalizing processes have created both above and below the state. Like the pre-existing systems of rule already mentioned, however, these new entities are all partial; they do not constitute, singly or collectively, truly global governance as such. '[T]here is little evidence', write Grande and Pauly, 'of the emergence of a fully integrated global political system'.[2]

In fact, not all patterned human behaviour is intended to induce political order, though it may do so inadvertently. The preferences of individual buyers and sellers, for example, give rise to an orderly marketplace without a shared intention of accomplishing that end, and the prevention of particular instances of abuse by Amnesty International may unexpectedly contribute to the construction of a human rights regime; but according to James Rosenau, systems that most closely represent governance are those that are 'suffused with intentionality'.[3] This is so because governance, as opposed to mere order, has purpose. It embodies a conscious and systematic effort to compensate in part for the absence of government, to help fill the void with structures responsive to what people need or want, to create and maintain some degree of stability and predictability based on shared expectations. On this view, governance can be summed as 'order plus intentionality',[4] and it will be effective as a surrogate or partial government only to the extent that agreement with its premises and intentions can be sustained.[5] I endorse this understanding of governance. In addition, I note that the inclusion of a purposive element in its definition implies that objectives chosen will conform with a given value set, so this conception of governance unavoidably includes a normative dimension. To the extent that international relations are guided by systems of governance, then, they are also shaped fundamentally and necessarily by a collective sense of what purposes should be pursued, and what kind of morality should prevail. 'Norms are at the heart of all governance structures',[6] as one analyst has succinctly expressed this important point.

The most salient and influential form of governance in international relations will be identifiable in the first instance by the extent to which its premises and purposes are agreed and sustained; the wider the support for it, the more closely it will approximate truly global governance.[7] The United Nations (UN) and its associated family of agencies and institutions is certainly the most institutionally sophisticated world body extant today, and its diverse purposes – from maintaining peace and security to resolving economic, social, cultural and humanitarian problems – are laudable and widely endorsed. On the other hand, however, like the League of Nations before it, the UN represents liberal ideals which do not necessarily hold sway in the gritty world of international relations. It seems as likely that those relations are dominated by the exercise of power and the overriding pursuit of national interest. The tension between liberalism and *realpolitik* is palpable on the world stage, in the various personalities and policies of state leaders, and among IR scholars whose analyses cannot categorically determine whether right or might rules international political behaviour.

Despite these controversies and a plethora of candidates, the first question raised by this discussion – what is the form of governance that most powerfully shapes contemporary international relations? – can in fact be answered straightforwardly. Despite the remark by Grande and Pauly that a fully integrated global political system does not exist, I argue that it does. Whether international relations are fundamentally conflictual or cooperative in nature, and notwithstanding key roles played by powerful states, institutions and ideologies, a single shared purpose clearly reveals the presence of one dominant ordered system with which all major actors voluntarily comply, and with which all major international institutions willingly conform. I refer to this form of governance as the growth paradigm. Its central feature is a common commitment to economic growth.

The ubiquity of the political – and, I will argue, normative – commitment to growth as a policy priority is unique in international relations. It encompasses all types of state government, and remains constant despite variations in domestic policies which reflect divergent opinions about how best to achieve it. Without important exception, all national governments of North and South, East and West, share the commitment. International organizations whose objectives are to promote social development, such as the UN, recognize the dependency of development objectives on robust economic growth;[8] and interstate alliances whose objectives are to enhance military security, such as the North Atlantic Treaty Organization (NATO), are at least tacitly constrained to support growth by the close association of wealth and power. More explicitly, major institutions such as the World Bank, International Monetary Fund (IMF), and World Trade Organization (WTO) strive to optimize economic growth. As well, the G8, the Organization for Economic Cooperation and Development (OECD), and informal organizations such as the Trilateral Commission and the World Economic Forum, endorse and encourage growth. All regional trading blocs in the Americas, Europe and Asia were constructed to enhance the potential for growth. Multinational corporations pursue growth as a formal responsibility and *raison d'être*, and civil society itself, whether conceived as a national or transnational entity, is not indisposed to its crucial role as consumer in a growth economy.

If governance can reasonably be understood as order plus intentionality, then one may say that order within the growth paradigm is provided by the structure, common orientation and collective influence of the various organizations named above, and intentionality is indicated by the shared commitment to pursue economic growth. The normative dimension of this form of governance is implicit in the fact that growth is intended to improve social welfare by elevating standards of living and, in the general case, to ensure a safe and prosperous future for all. I note further that safety, prosperity and betterment of the human condition are the quintessential goals of enlightened government. Given the uniquely preeminent status of the commitment to economic growth and its conformity with these same goals, I begin from the premise that the growth paradigm represents the most salient form of global governance, and the most powerful surrogate of world government, in the anarchic domain of international relations.

It remains to determine how and why this particular form of governance gained its uniquely preeminent status, and to assess the moral legitimacy of its normative foundations; much of what follows will address these questions. Before outlining the approach I take to them, however, I return first for a closer look at the purpose to which the paradigm is oriented. Of the three broad goals listed above, the first is safety. This goal identifies the primordial obligation of any government or system of governance to answer the needs of security, defined in terms of the preservation of human life and the orderly continuation of social systems through time. I noted before that scholarly interest in discovering the source or sources of order in international relations is motivated in large part by the fact that understanding order can lead to its enhancement (through the construction of new institutions, for example). I also alluded to the fact that the growth paradigm includes an inherent security dimension. Directly, economic growth generates revenue to pay for the military power which underwrites traditional forms of security in international relations; and indirectly, growth ostensibly leads to improved living standards which, in turn, are widely thought to reduce the motivation to go to war, at least from a liberal point of view. It will be a central contention of this book, however, that the growth paradigm is ultimately destabilizing to international relations: that its monolithic structure actively excludes alternative and perhaps better forms of governance, that its constant forward motion is disruptive to the social systems which structure human society, and moreover that its processes of production and consumption pose a lethal threat to the viability of natural systems which ultimately sustain the human population on Earth. I will argue that, when seen in the larger context of the planetary biosphere, the growth paradigm is unsafe: it threatens and does not enhance international security.

This threat arises because order is a necessary but not sufficient condition for security. Ordered systems may or may not enhance security, depending on how they are sustained, and on their compatibility with other entities they may impinge upon. The organized expansion of the sphere of influence of a hegemonic state, for example, may enhance the security of its citizens but at the expense of conquered or otherwise coerced neighbours. And, like an expansionist state enlarging its domain within the world's society of states, the growth paradigm enlarges the sum total of economic activity generated by the human population relative to Earth's singular ecosystem. In each case the process of enlargement may not be mutually beneficial. Security may be enhanced for the smaller part, but compromised or diminished for the whole. A prima facie assessment of the relationship between economic activity and the planetary ecosystem suggests a potential incompatibility because, while the political commitment to economic growth is open-ended – it does not include a provision to eventually halt growth – the biosphere in which growth occurs is finite in size. The result of this apparent incompatibility may be environmental degradation with a correspondingly negative impact on planetary habitability, and on the security of human society as a whole.

To raise the issue of ecosystemic stability and the durability of social systems *vis-à-vis* the growth paradigm, however, is to raise once again the 'limits to growth' debate which flared and subsided some 30 years ago. Seminal to that debate was research commissioned by the Club of Rome[9] and undertaken by a team at the Massachusetts Institute of Technology (MIT) to examine in detail the impact of steadily increasing human activity on natural systems, and to extrapolate the trajectory of that impact into the future, assuming no major changes in the activities being investigated. The researchers did not foresee, at the conclusion of their project, a hopeful future, but their work was challenged on substantive and methodological grounds and their gloomy prognostications were subsequently dismissed by professional analysts and political practitioners alike. Indeed, within ten years of their publication date, a new 'neoliberal' ideology had taken root in the United States and in Britain that supported the notion of ever more rapid growth of the global economy unconstrained by public ownership or regulatory intervention. The debate about limits to growth had by then been decisively resolved in favour of the pro-growth faction, and supporters of the contrary view were relegated to the sidelines of international politics, a position they continue to inhabit today.

Despite this situation, however, the relationship between growth and the environment remains problematic. Disagreements about the Meadows et al. report notwithstanding, it seems clear that aggregate human activity on Earth is bumping up against certain structural constraints of the planet's biophysical systems. The human population has evidently become a force of nature, and as such is now a new and important variable in the functionality of the biosphere – significantly but not exclusively with regard to the atmosphere. The prospect of continuously increasing economic activity, continuously increasing production and consumption, seems reckless and suggests that a closer look at the premises and objectives of the growth paradigm as a form of governance might be prudent. On that basis, it is a strategic objective of this book to re-engage the currently sidelined limits to growth debate, and to help construct a suitable disciplinary forum in which that debate might continue.

Environmental issues in general, and environmental security as a particular political problem, have not yet found a conducive or permanent home in IR.[10] To some extent these issues have been addressed from an institutional point of view as problems of environmental governance, or they have been gathered under the broader rubric of political ecology,[11] but this latter, nascent subdiscipline does not yet comprise distinctive subject matter or endorse a clearly defined research agenda. Moreover, the notion of environmental security represents, for some, an unwelcome intrusion into what is arguably the core concern of IR, namely, national security. Daniel Deudney, for example, has argued that including issues of environmental degradation under the general heading of security muddies the term and reduces its analytical utility,[12] but I take the wider view that any serious anthropogenic threat to society may reasonably be construed in such terms. This position follows naturally from the premise that the most important responsibility of political leaders is to protect life, and to ensure the durability of social systems through time. If the successful engagement of that responsibility presupposes a stable planetary environment, and if that stability is somehow threatened by excessive economic activity, then understanding the growth paradigm must necessarily include consideration of its environmental context, and its effect on security.

Given its preeminent status in international relations, my primary objective in this book is to explain the rise to dominance of the growth paradigm, especially in light of its implications regarding ecological safety. I will ascertain how and why the political commitment to economic growth became the centrepiece of a form of governance that has evidently imposed its own terms of reference and functional parameters on the otherwise anarchic condition of international relations, and I will assess the political durability of the paradigm in the face of tensions that may be inherent to it. Or, to put this differently, I am interested to discover whether this hegemonic system of rule has generated, as hegemony often does, counterforces sufficiently powerful to induce transformative change.

Prominent features of the growth paradigm

Because the governance of modern international relations puts economic growth at its core, this study is logically situated in the analytical domain of international political economy (IPE). In order to develop an approach to understanding the paradigm in that context, it is useful to list some of its key features, beginning with a working definition of economic growth as such. Modern economic science is a technical, heavily mathematized, and complexly rigorous discipline in which causes, processes, measurements, even definitions of growth are routinely contested. I do not engage with the details of that debate here, but rely instead on the relatively simple but commonly used notion of growth as an increase in Gross National Product (GNP),[13] which offers a broad measure of the total of all economic exchanges in a given country. Somewhat more exactly, economic growth refers to 'an increase of the transactions made on markets (goods, labour and capital markets), measured in monetary terms'.[14] The GNP of individual states can be summed to yield an approximate measure of world economic product.

The terms 'economic exchanges' and 'market transactions' do not make clear the extent to which economic growth is or is not a physical process reliant on resource input. Much of the limits to growth debate mentioned earlier circles around the contentious issue of whether economic growth can occur without a continuously increasing input of material and energy. This issue is crucial because, if growth could somehow be decoupled from Earth's ecosystem, then presumably it would no longer pose a threat to the environment. A useful approach to a better understanding of this problem has been developed by Herman Daly and John Cobb, who unpack economic growth into two closely related but ultimately dissimilar parts, namely growth and development. Daly and Cobb use these terms separately to refer to quantitative enlargement and qualitative improvement, respectively. Specifically, '[g]rowth should refer to quantitative expansion in the scale of the physical dimensions of the economic system, while development should refer to the qualitative change of a physically non-growing economic system in dynamic equilibrium with the environment'.[15] Given this dichotomy, one may readily conceive of continuous improvements in the quality of health and education services, in sciences and engineering, in arts and culture, without radically increasing material and energy throughput in the global economy. On the other hand, it is much harder to imagine continuous increases in the quantitative production of consumer goods – cars, for example – without major increases in resource dependency. Advocates of growth tend to conflate it with development by, for example, stipulating that growth is a necessary precondition for development to occur, or by defining it in terms of increases in GNP per capita, which answers the normative requirement for growth to benefit everyone, which in turn may be construed as an improvement in social welfare. I side with Daly and Cobb's interpretation, however, and support their contention that qualitative improvement of the human condition is not necessarily tied to the quantitative enlargement of the global economy; that bigger is not a prerequisite for better.

Further to this issue I will show in Chapter 5 that, despite a trend in some advanced economies to service industries instead of manufacturing, no significant dematerialization of economic activity has yet occurred. Industrial production around the world has benefited from improvements in processes and technologies which have substantially reduced the resource input and waste produced per unit of GNP, but relative decreases in input/output levels per unit will not lead to absolute decreases if total production climbs continuously, as dictated by the terms of the growth paradigm. Indeed, no significant decoupling of the global economy from Earth's ecosystem is likely to occur any time soon, especially with respect to the linkage between growth, energy consumption and carbon dioxide emissions. As indicated, I will expand on this issue in subsequent chapters. For the present, I return to an enumeration of the most prominent features of the growth paradigm as such.

First, the breadth and depth of the paradigm – which comprises all major actors in international politics from the UN and WTO to domestic civil societies – indicate that it is unusually inclusive. Participants in the paradigm have evidently agreed to or acquiesce in a set of axiomatic expectations that are so deeply embedded as to have become what may be called an immanent feature of world culture. The paradigm is thoroughly implicit in all aspects of the socio-economic and political life of modern human society, and as such is so transparently normal that its presence, character and consequences rarely provoke critical scrutiny.

Second, it follows closely from the inclusive nature and global scope of the paradigm that it can usefully be conceptualized in holistic terms. Given the willingness of consumers to endorse national policies that encourage growth, for example, it is reasonable to surmise that the 'state–society complex'[16] might be a more relevant unit of analysis than the state alone; that reference to transnational civil society (which crosses state borders) may be pertinent; that, in fact, one may usefully speak of human society as a whole with regard to the paradigm. And moreover, given the impact of human activity on the biosphere, it also seems reasonable to recognize the linkage between economic growth and that larger set of dynamic entities and processes that compose Earth's ecosystem, such as the atmosphere, oceans and freshwater systems, and life in its many forms and relationships. The biosphere is ultimately a single functional unit within which our population is embedded, and in this respect understanding the paradigm will be more completely accomplished if it includes an acknowledgement of the holistic relationship between human society and the planet.

This second characteristic of the growth paradigm is key to the discussion which follows, and is thematic to the central argument of this book, so I elaborate briefly here in order to establish a clear understanding of my point of view. The 'holistic relationship between human society and the planet' introduced above constitutes what I refer to as a socio-natural continuum, a term intended to convey the intimate bond between people and planet; but within this whole one may readily distinguish between physical and non-physical realities. Schematically, the continuum is bracketed at one end by the natural world, by the material substance of Earth itself, and at the other end by the emergent property of human consciousness – the immaterial, ineffable world of ideas. This basic dichotomy indicates that the holism embodied in the socio-natural continuum can, for analytical purposes, be parsed into a mind/matter duality. Reflecting this, I will characterize the growth paradigm as having two fundamental components – ideational and material. The dialectical tensions that join these parts will shape and drive much of the discussion which follows.

One such thematic tension, as I will argue throughout this book, arises from the fact that the ideational component of the paradigm – namely, the shared belief in the efficacy of economic growth – has gained overwhelming ascendancy over the material component with the result that the relationship between the two has become unbalanced and disharmonious, the consequences of which pervade economic, political and environmental practices and expectations throughout modern human society. The ascendancy of the ideational component notwithstanding, however, I grant ontological priority to the natural world as the physical context from which all life forms, including human, evolved, and of which ideas are emergent phenomena. Earth can and did exist long before the ideational and social attributes of humans appeared in history, but neither humans nor their unique attributes can exist without propitious material preconditions provided by Earth. The prior ontological status of the natural world suggests that ideas must ultimately be accountable to or in some sense commensurate with their material context, but that is not the case with respect to the growth paradigm.

The dichotomy just described is straightforward, but a host of intractable epistemological and ontological issues arise between the end brackets, where mind and matter are intimately engaged. In this intermediate domain it is often difficult to distinguish the ideational from the material and, in fact, the two are sometimes mutually involved in ways that make any such distinction arbitrary and problematic. This is the case, for example, with institutions such as state governments, and with invisible structures such as shared values or interests which are clearly ideational, but which nonetheless can shape and predetermine social practices as ineluctably as physical constraints. Increasingly, analysts have turned to social constructivism as a way to better understand modern experiences in this intermediate domain, especially when those experiences seem to be dominated by powerful intersubjectively shared beliefs and commitments, including the commitment to economic growth as a political priority. Poststructuralism is a particularly effective mode of constructivist inquiry in this respect because of its focus on discourse analysis – the analysis of dominant ideas – but, problematically for present purposes, poststructural analysis begins from the premise that the Cartesian distinction between mind and matter is fundamentally misleading; that the two are inextricably engaged with each other, significantly through language and symbologies. This approach is useful when the objective of research is to untangle the social complexities that inhabit the domain between the end brackets of the socio-natural continuum, but I reject the claim that extradiscursive reality is ultimately of secondary importance, and may in fact not be knowable at all. The utility of discourse analysis diminishes, in my view, the closer one approaches the 'natural' end of the continuum; each step from words to action is a step further removed from signs, symbols and the discursive production of meaning. Eventually one encounters ecological realities whose extradiscursive features are brutish and much more physically potent than any social artifact, no matter how elaborate. As J. Magnus Ryner, an analyst sympathetic to but critical of the poststructuralist point of view, has drily observed, ecological reactions to inept human behaviour, such as climate change, desertification and so forth, 'clearly indicate that something more than Lacanian semiosis is at work'.[17] I will show in subsequent sections of this chapter that a neo-Gramscian variant of critical theory, which is mindful of both social and material realities, and of the tensions between them, is the approach better suited to engaging with the dual structure of contemporary realities, and with the environmental challenges now confronting human society in its relationship with Earth.

The point to be made here is twofold. First, notwithstanding the holism of the socio-natural continuum, I will deploy a thematic distinction between the ideational and the material in order to better highlight the features of the growth paradigm, and I will consistently grant ontological priority, and therefore a fundamental and inescapable importance, to the natural world. Second, I also note that between these poles the distinction is often moot, and that the term 'material' may also be applied to constructed entities such as social relations, social practices and institutions which shape individual and collective behaviour. I will have occasion to refer to materiality in both senses – as the social relations of economic production and, more concretely, as the physical reality of the natural world. The form of usage of the term will be evident from its context.

With these clarifications in mind, I reiterate that the growth paradigm comprises two basic components, namely, an ideational and a material element, both of which have perceptibly evolved over time. The former element is made manifest in the political commitment to economic growth as a policy objective and, more generally, in the intersubjectively shared belief in the desirability of growth, and in its efficacy with respect to the improvement of social welfare. The latter refers to the fact that ideas must ultimately be grounded in the material world – in the institutions and organizations previously mentioned, in people and their social relations, and in the natural world that sustains them. Beliefs and preferences can only subsist in the minds of real people in real historical circumstances, and they can only be instantiated through an engagement with their physical context: thus the material and ideational components of the paradigm are necessarily linked. It is a core contention of this book, however, that a radical disarticulation of the ideational from the material elements of the paradigm constitutes one of its most distinctive features, and one of its deepest anomalies.

The third basic characteristic of the growth paradigm is that, its present status as a globally pervasive phenomenon notwithstanding, it did not emerge from history fully formed. Discovering its origins, tracing its evolution and understanding its ascent to preeminence will be a particular goal of this book, and a historical perspective will be required to accomplish that. I will develop that perspective in due course, noting for the time being that I will call on the notion of 'temporal frames' to guide my investigation. Derived from the *Annales* school of historiography, to which Fernand Braudel is the best-known contributor, these frames refer to short-, medium- or long-term points of view, each of which illuminates a particular socio-political ontology, which in turn has some bearing on the choice of appropriate methodological tools. I will show that a long-term temporal frame is best suited to the problem at hand, and that historicism – or, more specifically, historical materialism – offers a useful set of tools to investigate the emergence of the paradigm from its roots.

A fourth feature of the paradigm is that, despite its wide endorsement in theory and in practice, it harbours tensions – and, in some cases, contradictions – the resolution of which is not readily foreseeable. The most basic of these tensions arises from the duality between the ideational and material poles of the paradigm; specifically, the entrenched expectation of perpetual economic growth on a materially finite planet remains problematic. In Chapter 5 I will examine several other tensions in order to determine whether they might collectively presage or directly induce the displacement of the paradigm by an equally robust but less contradictory – and more environmentally benign – set of beliefs and practices.

Finally, I note that the prospect of a paradigm change suggests the possible presence of dissident social actors (individuals and/or organized groups) whose agency, animated by the tensions just mentioned and guided by an alternative set of goals, might somehow cause such a shift to occur. Their agency would necessarily stand opposed to an established array of social actors who actively support the existing paradigm, who populate a variety of existing political and economic institutions, and who continuously reconstruct and legitimate the growth-oriented practices of those institutions. The respective roles and the relative power of these sets of opposed actors are key to an assessment of the stability of the paradigm over time.

With the important exception of political agency, all of the features of the growth paradigm listed above can be mapped directly onto the general concept of paradigm as first articulated by Thomas S. Kuhn, which is why I employ that terminology here. Kuhn introduced paradigms in the context of the natural sciences so the concept is thoroughly grounded in material realities, which also serves present purposes, but ultimately Kuhnian paradigms are limited as heuristic or explanatory devices because they are not specifically attuned to the social sciences; they do not illuminate social actors or the roles they play in the maintenance or disruption of existing paradigms. In the following sections I discuss more precisely the pertinence of the notion of paradigm, and I show how a link can be forged between paradigms and critical theory in IPE, which in turn will furnish the social scientific perspective lacking in Kuhn's work. In particular, I will indicate that a neo-Gramscian variant of critical theory provides a useful analytical lens through which to bring to focus the history, the social construction, and the normative foundations of the growth paradigm; and that a neo-Gramscian addition to Kuhnian paradigms affords a more realistic understanding of the socio-natural continuum than other modes of inquiry less attuned to the brute facts of nature.

Thomas Kuhn's paradigms

The notion of a paradigm was first brought to professional and popular attention by Thomas S. Kuhn in 1962,[18] but the meaning of the term has been contested, and its relevance to science challenged, since then. Margaret Masterman, for example, claims in her analysis of Kuhn's book that he uses the word paradigm in not less than 21 distinguishable ways,[19] and this imprecision has clearly contributed to the absence of any consensually agreed meaning. Rather than attempting to construct an amalgamated definition then – one perhaps not intended by Kuhn – I offer a generic account of Kuhnian paradigms below, and show how this account can be applied to an understanding of the widespread political commitment to economic growth.

Paradigms are not just scientific interpretations of the material world; they are socio-cultural too. They include, among other things, 'the entire constellation of beliefs, values, techniques and so on shared by members of a given community',[20] and these attributes cultivate and promote what Kuhn called a domain of normal science. Normalcy, he argued, is a necessary attribute of any paradigm. It establishes a common framework for analysis and action, and it stipulates the contextual parameters that define the acceptable and exclude that which is not. An Earth-centred universe exemplified the domain of normalcy imposed by the Catholic Church in medieval Europe, for example, and the heliocentrism professed by Copernicus was, for some time, opposed to it. In a similar vein, an axiomatic predisposition to economic growth and a rejection of alternative priorities are the distinguishing features of the normalcy of the growth paradigm. During periods of paradigmatic hegemony, normal science research 'is directed to the articulation of those phenomena and theories that the paradigm already supplies;'[21] or, as Kuhn puts it somewhat differently elsewhere, 'bringing a normal research problem to a conclusion is achieving the anticipated in a new way'.[22] Normal science is like a crossword puzzle, for which the solution is guaranteed. Only the ingenuity of the puzzle solver is being tested. Success leads to personal satisfaction and affirmation of the paradigm; failure reflects not on the paradigm, but on the individual.

Normal science may be characterized as fine-tuning within a given set of expectations, or as 'mopping up', but Kuhn is careful to point out that it is, in fact, 'a highly cumulative enterprise, eminently successful in its aim, the steady extension of the scope and precision of scientific knowledge'.[23] The rapid evolution of scientific methods and technologies during the regime of Newtonian mechanics, for example, or the explosion in econometrics characteristic of the present era, speak directly to the positive side of normal science. But, paradoxically, by extending the domain of knowledge, normal science also prepares the ground for 'extraordinary' science because '[t]he more precise and far-reaching [a] paradigm is, the more sensitive an indicator it provides of anomaly and hence of an occasion for paradigm change'.[24] This is so, writes Margaret Masterman, because '[a] fully extended paradigm reaches a point where further extensions of it produce diminishing returns ... if stretched too far, [it produces] conceptual inconsistency, absurdity, misexpectation, disorder, complexity and confusion'.[25] Kuhn calls these unwanted results anomalies, and concludes that when a profession 'can no longer evade anomalies that subvert the existing tradition of scientific practice – then begin the extraordinary investigations that lead the profession at last to a new set of commitments'.[26] Such episodes are scientific revolutions, typified historically by radical shifts to heliocentricism, or from Newtonian to relativistic physics. In the present context it is not unreasonable to speculate that the growth paradigm, having at last encountered the material constraints of Earth's biosphere, is beginning to generate its own stream of tensions, contradictions, complexities and confusion.

Kuhnian paradigms comprise both ideational and material elements. In the natural sciences, the ideational element is manifested in prevailing beliefs about the nature of the world, and those beliefs are embodied in educational institutions and professional associations which add legitimacy to them. The material element is the objective world of empirical reality. The positivist approach typical of natural science links the two by requiring that the veracity of observations and the cogency of conclusions meet the criterion of truth as correspondence: that which is believed to be correct will correspond accurately with material reality, and will be reliably testable on that basis. In the social sciences, the two components of paradigms are also linked, though the relationship between them may not be as straightforward given the changeable nature of social realities. Here, a wider variety of methodologies are useful, including the poststructuralism previously mentioned because of its orientation to the analysis of dominant discursive practices that produce particular paradigmatic worlds. In both the natural and the social sciences, however, the examination of hegemonic worldviews carries with it an explicit interest in systemic change. Poststructualism tends to collapse the epistemological distinction between the material and the discursive on the grounds that any such distinction would be arbitrary, and moreover would necessarily (and purposively) marginalize or exclude certain sectors of society; the change it seeks is therefore one informed by an illumination of existing structures of power which must be destabilized and replaced.[27]

This orientation to emancipation from oppression is typical of post-positivist critical theories and methodologies, including the neo-Gramscian variant of critical theory which I introduce later in this chapter. Kuhnian paradigms lack the element of agency which is inherent to the post-positivist enterprise, but Kuhn nonetheless was fundamentally interested in how paradigms change over time. I elaborate briefly in order to bridge the gap between natural and social scientific approaches to systemic change.

At pivotal times in history when normal and extraordinary science overlap, researchers turn to philosophical analysis and speculative hypotheses. A 'proliferation of competing articulations, the willingness to try anything, the expression of explicit discontent, the recourse to philosophy and to debate over fundamentals, all of these are symptoms of a transition from [one paradigm to another]',[28] says Kuhn. And, notably, the transition is not necessarily welcomed. New paradigms test the ontological foundations of knowledge, challenge epistemological truth claims and try on new methodologies, but wholesale upheaval is resisted by practitioners of normal science – not because they are obdurate, but because robust beliefs should be defended with a certain dogmatism so that their relevance and utility can be fully explored; or, as Kuhn puts it, '[b]y ensuring that the paradigm will not be too easily surrendered, resistance guarantees that scientists will not be lightly distracted and that the anomalies that lead to paradigm change will penetrate existing knowledge to the core'.[29] Indeed, penetrating existing knowledge to the core suggests that choosing between competing paradigms is a fundamentally normative exercise; it involves 'a choice between incompatible modes of community life [for which] there is no higher standard than the assent of the relevant community', according to Kuhn.[30] Empirical measurement still has a role to play in this choice – a new paradigm may answer practical questions, or improve living standards – but, other things being equal, the choice of a new paradigm must ultimately rely upon an assessment of modes of community life, and this phrase clearly implies a normative evaluation.

R. J. Bernstein has criticized Kuhn for calling upon norms, persuasive argumentation and philosophy to describe the process of paradigm change, arguing that Kuhn 'sees the scientific community less as one with an impartial interest in the quest for truth than as a political community where authority is imposed, and novelty and deviance suppressed'.[31] Instead of referring to 'the assent of the relevant community' Bernstein suggests that 'What is required is a more comprehensive and subtle understanding of rationality, to let us grasp the complex argumentation processes involved in adjudicating among competing paradigms'.[32] This latter point of view, however, would steer the discussion in a decidedly poststructuralist direction by focusing attention on the complex micro-conditions that underlie dominant beliefs and practices and that determine the mechanics by which one discourse supersedes another. This is unnecessarily analytical and is not, in my view, Kuhn's intent. Deconstructing the rationality of and power relations embedded in complex arguments may answer 'how' questions, but it cannot answer 'why' questions, and it adds little to the more inclusive meaning of Kuhn's phrase 'modes of community life'. The broad sweep of this concept calls for a more holistic process of evaluation, though Kuhn himself did not propose a method for doing so. I understand his intent in this regard as reflecting the view that a socio-cultural commitment to dominant beliefs, whether derived from the natural or the social sciences, necessarily entails a collective value judgment about the world, as was the case with the Ptolemaic tradition, which in turn supports a particular social order. Extending this point of view, I conclude that any cultural project that encompasses the global polis, as the collective effort to achieve sustained economic growth does, entails the specification and maintenance of a particular global order, to the exclusion of others, that is oriented by a set of values on the basis of which it is susceptible to normative interrogation and evaluation by the community at large.

Linking Kuhnian paradigms more explicitly with the social sciences, and with IPE in particular, can be accomplished by noting that 'normal versus extraordinary science' is directly comparable to, if not entirely congruent with, a similar duality expressed by Robert W. Cox in terms of 'problem-solving versus critical theory'.[33] The purpose of problem-solving theory is conservative, to maintain the status quo, and 'to arrive at statements ... which appear to have general validity but which imply ... the institutional and relational parameters assumed in the problem-solving approach'.[34] Problem-solving theory, says Cox, serves 'particular national, sectional, or class interests, which are comfortable within the given order'.[35] Critical theory, on the other hand,

> stands apart from the prevailing order of the world and asks how that order came about ... [it] does not take institutions and social and power relations for granted but calls them into question by concerning itself with their origins and how and whether they might be in the process of changing.[36]

Its purpose is to illuminate a range of alternative possible futures, and to allow for 'a normative choice in favour of a social and political order different from the prevailing order'.[37] Both Kuhn and Cox are interested in better understanding the historically contingent origins of dominant belief systems, the ideas and relationships that sustain them, and the factors that precipitate episodic change. Extraordinary science and Coxian critical theory are both nourished by a stream of unresolved problems and anomalous data, but Cox's work is alive to the agency of social actors who respond purposively to those anomalies. In other words Cox is interested not only in what social forces dominate hegemonic systems, but also in how opposed social forces might perceive and react to tensions and contradictions in those systems, which may in turn lead to structural transformations in international relations.

Essentially, Cox does not understand hegemonic systems in the same terms as Kuhn because his theoretical orientation and historical analyses pertain to the discipline of international political economy, not the natural sciences. For him, 'paradigms' are conceived in terms of 'historical structures' – relatively long-lasting historical configurations such as the Pax Britannica – which are constituted by particular (but ultimately changeable) sets of ideas, institutional arrangements, and material capabilities.[38] These entities are similar to paradigms, significantly with respect to the fact that they include ideational and material elements, but with the crucial difference that historical structures (which are international in composition and scope) are constructed through the complex interplay of (sometimes transnational) social groups – or social forces, in Coxian terminology – rather than on the basis of a particular or novel mode of discovery.

This concept of historical structures, and the critical theory that underlies it, offer by analogy a useful extension of Kuhnian paradigms into social science, and I will rely heavily on Cox's work in what follows – but I do not explicitly adopt historical structure as a heuristic device for present purposes, that is, with respect to the history and political (and environmental) impact of the shared commitment to economic growth. I summarize briefly my reasons for preferring the term growth paradigm. First, Coxian historical structures are, in Braudelian terms, conjunctural, or medium-term, episodes – as mentioned, the nineteenth-century Pax Britannica is a prominent example – and as such do not map congruently onto the much longer timeframe of the modern age, which encompasses that period of time from the feudal/modern juncture to the present and which, I will show in Chapter 2, is the effective temporal domain of the growth paradigm. Second, historical structures do not, in my view, allow sufficient room for the exploration of the ideational and normative components of hegemonic systems. Coxian structures are constituted by particular sets of ideas, institutions and material capabilities: those sets are historically contingent because they are the collective outcome of conflict and compromise among unique social forces, and because they are inevitably riven by inherent tensions which ultimately cause profound change in the extant world order. Coxian theory reveals that the actual mix of ideas, institutions and capabilities will vary over time as structures change, and that one or another may be the most influential of the three at a given historical moment. The discovery of how historical structures are actually constituted is a matter for empirical historical analysis. However, Cox's work suggests that social forces – particular groups with particular capabilities, and the institutions they form – play a significantly more prominent role in practice than ideas do in the construction of historical structures. Paradigms, on the other hand, although likewise embedded in and reflective of historical material settings, tend in the main to draw more heavily on the ideational component of their hegemony, and tend also to be somewhat more long-lived, as the Ptolemaic and Newtonian traditions suggest. Because the commitment to growth is approximately congruent with the *longue durée* of the modern age and because, as I will argue, its hegemony is primarily ideational and normative in nature, the term paradigm provides a more conducive image. It is evocative without being misleading, and it is amenable to interpretation because of the flexible manner in which Kuhn introduced the term to science. However paradigms are construed, though, it is clear that they must be joined with critical theory to bring to sharper relief the social dimension of their hegemonic power.

Having established the sense in which I employ the term growth paradigm, and on the basis of the premise that it represents a particular form of international governance, the following two sections will serve to introduce the approach I will take to discovering its historical trajectory, and to understanding how it ascended to political dominance. First I will show how the neo-Gramscian variant of critical theory is best suited to analysis of the growth paradigm. I also clarify the general analytical orientation which is associated with neo-Gramscian analysis, namely, historical materialism. In the second section to follow, I discuss the particular interpretive methodology which is appropriate to this study. A concluding section of this chapter will present an overview of how my analysis of the growth paradigm will proceed.

Critical theory and its neo-Gramscian variant

The origins of critique[39] lie at the European Reformation, when religious revolutions of the sixteenth century challenged the authority of the Church of Rome. Its purpose was to delegitimize the claims and assumptions (in the Bible and other ancient texts) which supported the established power and privilege of the Church. By the time of the Enlightenment, however, critique had shed its strictly religious cast, and had come to be associated more generally with the exercise of reason. In keeping with the new Enlightenment commitment to uproot false beliefs and debunk irrational thinking, the 'critical' approach to truth called for the discovery of the foundations of and conditions for reliable knowledge, as opposed to truth as revelation.

Early empiricists such as John Locke and David Hume argued that inquiry must be restricted to deciphering data acquired through the senses, but Immanuel Kant believed that consciousness was more than a passive receptor of impressions; he emphasized the creative rationality of the human mind, a role that enabled the perception of the world as an ordered realm. Kant did not, however, theorize the origins of this creative capacity, assuming that all subjects had access to it, and that it was unchanging through time. G. W. F. Hegel's contribution to the evolution of critique as the search for reliable knowledge was to argue that rationality was a historically contingent social product, not a transcendental constant. As such, the exercise of rationality could be impeded by socially constructed constraints on human autonomy, and thus Hegel broadened the notion of critique to include the need for emancipation from those constraints. Critical theory came to involve more than questions of epistemology; it now took on the rational critique of forms of social life. Karl Marx, following Hegel as a social critic, saw the latter's work as too theoretical and abstract. For Hegel, social and political life was of secondary importance to the evolution of *Geist* (spirit) as the creative force in history. Marx replaced 'spirit' with real human subjects who must make their own history, and secure their own emancipation. Real people engage in a material exchange process with nature to build their worlds, and real freedom, he argued, would require fundamental change to the way society was organized. For Marx, the capitalist mode of production and the social strata that imposed it were the new targets of critique.

Since Marx's time, the tradition of critical theory has diversified to the point where its status in IR is neither simple nor clear. Critical theory now embraces a broad range of post-positivist research which has challenged, among other things, the dominance of neorealism and neoliberalism during the 'Third Debate' of the 1980s,[40] and the alleged relationship between these modes of theorizing and the manner in which they were reflected in the structuring of international affairs; a relationship that was implicated, for example, in the persistence of conflictual Cold War institutions and inequitable global economic relations.[41] More generally, though, all modern forms of critical theory reject the rationalist/positivist orientation of contemporary social scientific analysis. They disavow the early Enlightenment pursuit of dispassionate reason, and reject value-neutral theorizing in favour of an explicitly normative commitment to the exposure of structures of domination.[42] Critical theory retains its original historical focus on emancipation from oppression, but its modern objective is to open new avenues for both theory and political practice by highlighting the obstacles to, and the possibilities for, transformative change toward a more just future.

Among many others, two important intellectual strands which may be loosely described as neo-Marxist have emerged from the evolution of critical theory, both of which have divorced themselves from the scientism and historical teleology associated with classical Marxism. The first of these strands was developed by the Frankfurt Institute of Social Research, most notably during and immediately following the Second World War, under the leadership of Max Horkheimer, Theodor Adorno and Herbert Marcuse and, more recently, Jürgen Habermas. Now known as the Frankfurt School, these writers laid down a fundamental challenge to the orthodox Marxist vision of a progressive march of history, arguing that the increasing application of instrumental reason, and the increasing mastery of nature through development of the forces of production, would lead to less freedom, not more.

The Frankfurt School broadened Marx's critique of political economy to a critique of ideology in order to explore issues of domination and exploitation beyond the economic sphere.[43] The School is critical of totalitarianism, instrumental or technological rationality, mass culture and consumerism, and it acknowledges the dwindling revolutionary potential of the working classes; but it has been criticized for its unrelenting pessimism,[44] its rarefied language and concomitant weak link to policy relevance. The Frankfurt School is more interested in the dominant role played by instrumental reason than in social actors as such – it sees social movements as merely defensive (that is, resisting 'colonization' of the 'life-world' in Habermasian language), not as historic bearers of emancipatory ideas – and for this reason its general orientation is less well suited to an exploration of the social forces that sustain or challenge the growth paradigm. The second stream of neo-Marxist critical theory, more explicitly attuned to the emancipatory potential of social actors, is referred to as the Italian School, originating with the work of former Italian Communist Party leader Antonio Gramsci, and imported into IR and the domain of international political economy by Robert Cox. I locate the present study in this stream.

* * *

Antonio Gramsci was a political activist and theorist. A founding member of the Italian Communist Party (PCI), he became its leader in 1924 and was subsequently arrested and imprisoned by Mussolini's fascist regime in 1928. During this period of incarceration he produced his major opus, a 4,000-page manuscript called the *Prison Notebooks*. Gramsci wrote broadly in the Marxist tradition of historical materialism and hence is associated with the point of view that posits a dominant class and social order whose power derives from control over the mode and relations of economic production. For the most part, his work focused on Italian national politics; his objective was to explain why a revolution of the proletariat failed to materialize in post-First World War Italy despite the apparent fact that the 'objective' socio-economic conditions for it (subsequent to the Russian Revolution of 1917) were in place. His explanation led him to propose that a new form of cultural hegemony was at play which attenuated or otherwise mollified the revolutionary zeal of the proletariat.

It was Robert Cox who first 'internationalized' Gramsci (hence, *neo*-Gramscian analysis). He recognized that Gramsci's political observations, stemming from a socio–cultural interpretation of hegemony, could be applied to a wider arena, that the state-society complex could usefully be taken as a basic entity of international affairs, and that power relations among those entities were shaped by more than the relative size of accumulated material capabilities. By recognizing that certain structures and processes could be profitably examined using the methodological tools and historicist conceptions developed by Gramsci, Cox has added a new dimension to the field of critical IPE – though not without controversy. Some critics[45] have maintained that no such extrapolation can be derived from a political theory developed for a particular place and time, and that too much has been 'read into' Gramsci by those who wish to apply his thinking to international relations. Cox has countered that these criticisms miss the point. It is not a question of attempting to infer or deduce what Antonio Gramsci may have thought about political affairs beyond his immediate ken, but rather of applying his insights in new ways, to new situations. As Cox concludes (referring to himself), 'The concern should be with the adequacy of Cox's understanding of the world rather than with the adequacy of his understanding of Gramsci'.[46] I adopt the same conclusion, and on that basis seek to extend the neo-Gramscian project still further.

Like the Frankfurt School, the neo-Gramscian approach to IPE rejects the economic determinism of orthodox Marxism. That kind of determinism is now referred to as historical economism (or simply economism) by critical theorists in order to distinguish it from historical materialism, a tradition now under renovation, and to which I will return later in this chapter. It follows from the rejection of economic determinism that the relationship posited by Marx between the 'base' and the 'superstructure' is also rejected. For Marx, the base, the socio-economic foundation of society, was prior to and in large measure determined the content of the political, ideological and cultural superstructure of society. Gramsci problematized and reformulated that relationship as much more fluid and interactive. For him, ideas and socio-economic foundations function together as an organic whole. To put this differently, the neo-Gramscian approach to IPE joins Marxian materialism with social constructivism to produce a broader and more integrated picture of political society.

Gramsci's new conception of hegemony called upon a holistic interpretation of dominant social forces and their interaction with subordinate strata, and Cox has seized upon this conception to develop an approach to international politics that highlights the hegemony of historical structures. Both analysts were motivated by the prospect of achievable social change and, indeed, the Italian School differs significantly from the Frankfurt School with respect to the role of intellectuals. The latter saw them as, essentially, observers disengaged from social processes already beyond repair; the former sees an activist role for 'organic intellectuals' fully engaged with civil society, from which change for the better might emerge. Neo-Gramscians take seriously Marx's admonition that 'Philosophers have only interpreted the world, in various ways; the point is to change it'.[47] As a starting point for such change, these analysts take a fresh look at the unmet promise of historical materialism.

Like realism or liberalism, historical materialism is a mode of theorizing, not a methodology. As a distinctive approach to the study of international political economy, however, historical materialism has limited credibility. Its roots in classical Marxism (and in the seminal works of Engels and Lenin) tend to emphasize its limitations, especially its association with the dead-end failure of the Soviet Union. Totalitarian state power in several dictatorial countries has also brought the Marxian tendency toward dogmatism and intolerance into sharp relief. In turn, that intolerance was derived from the sense of rectitude engendered by its teleology, that is, by the belief that historical events will unfold in an inevitable and ultimately emancipatory, and therefore correct, direction. Historical materialism in its classical form therefore closely constrains the realm of desirable futures, and it also limits the range of antecedent conditions which might explain the march of history. It relies too heavily on economic factors to support its contentions; its reductionist proclivities are well known. Moreover, historical materialism has evidently failed to explain major features of international relations. Nationalism, for example, has consistently proved itself superior to class loyalties in mobilizing mass action, and capitalism has only rarely provoked a seriously revolutionary reaction by the proletariat. Capitalist democracy, as Fred Halliday notes, 'has secured the loyalty or at least the acquiescence of the mass of the population in the more developed capitalist countries … with resort to only limited coercion and intimidation on the part of the ruling classes'.[48]

Having noted these shortcomings, however, the rehabilitation of historical materialism, by neo-Gramscian analysts in particular, has taken this mode of theorizing into a new and more relevant contemporary context, while retaining certain key concepts which are inherent to the original works of Marx and Engels. For example, the level of industrialization (forces of production) and the prevailing systems of ownership and control (relations of production) continue to play key roles in the evolution of society, but are now understood to be contingencies, not deterministic. Teleology, in other words, has been jettisoned from contemporary versions of historical materialism, but the belief that the character of and events within any society can only be understood in historical context, remains. The fact of historical contingency is taken to mean that social forms and evolutionary trajectories are not inevitable; that alternatives are possible, given appropriate agency, within the constraints of time and place.

A friendly reading of Marx might suggest, as Halliday has done, that a distinctively useful feature of his work was the portrayal of society as 'a totality, a composite within which each element [is] ... governed by the character and tendency of the whole'.[49] Marxian analysis emphasized the importance of these larger social formations within which ideas, institutions and events reacted interdependently, and which, by the same token, could not be properly understood in abstraction from the underlying mode of production. Contemporary historical materialism retains these features of holism and interdependence. As Cox puts this point, 'ideas and material conditions are always bound together, mutually influencing one another, and not reducible to one another'.[50] The observation that these social components are 'not reducible to one another' affirms the rejection of materialist economism, and it also opens the possibility that, depending on historical circumstances, material factors may dominate ideational factors, or the reverse may be true. I will show that this latter arrangement is in fact a defining characteristic of the growth paradigm. A hegemonic belief system, or ideational superstructure, now dominates the modern landscape in its socio-political aspect, and literally as well.

Contemporary historical materialism also retains a focus on social strata (classes) as actors, and highlights the occurrence of conflict between them. The emphasis on conflict – how it is generated, conducted and resolved – underscores its importance as a source of change; it also characteristically differentiates historical materialism from the mainstream IR focus on security and stability. For the latter, conflict is a recurring phenomenon in need of constant resolution. In the dialectical context of historical materialism, conflict is the progenitor of change.

In sum, then, historical materialism is the mode of theorizing that is preferred by critical theorists of the Italian School. Materialism refers to the production of goods and services, which in turn implies the reciprocal engagement of human society with nature. Production is understood to be of universal significance. 'Production creates the material basis for all forms of social existence', writes Cox, 'and the ways in which human efforts are combined in production processes affect all other aspects of social life, including the polity'.[51] Historical materialism is also oriented to the discovery of contingencies and dialectical tensions that shape evolving social formations within the polity. In this respect it is a mode of discovery that is conducive to the interpretation of events changing during the course of history, without laying claim to foundational knowledge. It is not, however, a methodology as such. The next section of this chapter takes on the task of outlining the interpretive methodology which will be deployed for the remainder of this study.

Methodology

Two incommensurate modes of knowledge acquisition, characterized by Robert Keohane as rationalist and reflectivist approaches,[52] co-exist in IR. Various other terminologies, such as positivist/empirical and constructivist/interpretive, have been applied to this division. The terms Robert Cox uses are positivism and historicism. An important feature of the former mode of knowledge acquisition is its separation of subject from object, and its quest for universal or ahistorical laws of social science. Its task is to discover regularities in human activity, to develop theories that explain why those regularities hold under certain objective conditions, and to test those theories with reference to empirical evidence. In contrast, interpretivist accounts of human behaviour are concerned to explore and understand reasons for actions that derive from sets of interests which are shaped by characteristics of personal or social identity. An interpretive methodology is a search for meaning, not data. Reasons for actions, like interests and identities, are thoroughly embedded in social relations, often taking the form of intersubjective beliefs which guide and legitimize behaviour. These beliefs, or collectively held meanings, are deemed 'social facts' with real causal power, but their embeddedness, unobservability, historical contingency and evolution over time all conspire to conceal their presence from empirical inquiry.[53] The ineffable nature of human motivation and the unpredictability of human behaviour give rise to the notion that social science can be more profitably served by the pursuit of holistic and integrated knowledge than by the generation of more information.

Historicism is a form of constructivist/interpretivist methodology that, as its name implies, is used to understand historical events; indeed, historians turned to narrative description and interpretation as tools to develop knowledge long before the Enlightenment shifted the emphasis of inquiry to the rationalism of the scientific method. As with interpretive methodologies more generally, historicism does not separate fact from value, or subject from object. It allows that

> human institutions are made by ... collective responses to a collectively perceived problematic that produce certain practices. Institutions and practices are therefore to be understood through the changing mental process of their makers. There is, in this perspective, an identity of subject and object.[54]

And, because the practices of human interaction change over time it is fruitless, on this view, to seek transcendent laws which stand outside of history. One may, however, discern particular historical eras during which regularities do occur, and it is the business of historicism to reveal the structures characteristic of those eras, and to explain transformations from one set of structures to another. Doing so may be called an exercise in historical sociology but, more generally, it is an exercise in interpretive social science that attempts to move beyond rational-actor models toward a broader approach in which the roles of transnationally constituted collective actors are highlighted.

Drawing on formative work by Donald E. Polkinghorne,[55] John Ruggie refers to this interpretive or historicist methodology as narrative explanation. As he puts it,

> [t]he narrative explanatory protocol comprises two 'orders' of information: the descriptive and the configurative. The first simply links 'events' along a temporal dimension … The second organizes these descriptive statements into an interpretive 'gestalt' or 'coherence structure'. These operations rest on … the successive adjusting of a conjectured ordering scheme to the available facts [which] allow them to be grasped together as parts of one story … [which is] believable to others looking at the same events.[56]

This methodological model will be deployed in subsequent chapters, in which I trace the historical evolution of the political commitment to economic growth. Events will be described and linked along a temporal dimension. The interpretation of those events as the evolution of a growth paradigm is, in effect, the 'configurative' element of the narration that bonds events together as one 'story' which unfolds during the span of one historical era. This approach to methodology, however, is not particularly common so a few additional words of clarification may be useful.

As noted above, Ruggie's description of a narrative explanatory protocol draws on earlier work by Donald Polkinghorne. The latter asserts that narrative is important because it renders human experience meaningful. 'Narrative meaning', he says, 'functions to give form to the understanding of a purpose to life and to join everyday actions and events into episodic units'.[57] But importantly, Polkinghorne identifies two different kinds of narrative. The first is an implicit, shared understanding of how history is unfolding. For example 'the narrative of progress' is a phrase that portrays a widely understood conception of the modern world, and that carries with it a clear set of shared beliefs, values and expectations. The second kind of narrative refers to the process of making a story; it refers to the construction of a narrative overlay which is imposed on history by the storyteller. It is, in other words, an act of interpretation, a methodology intended to reveal a particular aspect of meaning, and to put a particular purpose in human affairs on display. This second kind of narrative, as Ruggie said, configures a sequence of events into a unified gestalt in which they take on significance as having contributed to a discrete historical episode.

Narrative in this methodological sense is distinct from a chronicling of history because the latter simply lists events according to their place in a timeline, whereas the narrative protocol 'can retrospectively alter the meaning of events after the final outcome is known'.[58] An example offered by Polkinghorne reveals that a historical chronicle would simply indicate that Edward Hallet Carr was born in 1892, whereas a narrative might say 'In 1892 the author of *The Twenty Years' Crisis* was born'. This latter formulation is the beginning of a story about the evolution of the theoretical school of realism, which allows the retrospective application of meaning to a historical event. Similarly narration can identify, retrospectively, the Enlightenment (among other historical events) as the origin of the growth paradigm, in the context of the story being told here. The story of the evolution of the paradigm is the 'plot' or interpretive gestalt that transforms mere events into a schematic whole.

Plots are not invented fully formed. They are constructed in a process Polkinghorne calls emplotment, and which Ruggie referred to above as the successive adjusting of a conjectured ordering scheme. 'The reasoning used to construct a plot', notes Polkinghorne, 'is similar to that used to develop a hypothesis. Both are interactive activities that take place between a conception that might explain or show a connection among the events and the resistance of the events to fit the construction'.[59] It follows from this that a conjectured plot may not work well to order events; or, on the other hand, more than one plot might provide a useful integration of and meaningful overlay for the same set of events. For example, the evolution of the modern commitment to economic growth could be embedded in an ecological story which emphasizes the natural propensity of all species to maximize their consumptive and reproductive potential; in a feminist story which highlights the role of patriarchy in the pursuit of economic power and the subjugation of nature; or in a story which features complexity theory, the role of entropy, and the descent from order into chaos as economic growth fractures and degrades the planetary environment. Each of these storylines is useable, and each may bring to light different aspects of the underlying, socially embedded 'narrative of progress'. Indeed, if more than one plot converges on the same conclusion, then that conclusion is more strongly substantiated. For present purposes, however, a single plot derived from a neo-Gramscian perspective will be employed here.

The fact that multiple interpretive overlays can be constructed, and that not each will work as effectively as others, raises the question of which validation criteria are pertinent. For positivism, the fit between hypothesis and empirical reality provides the relevant measure of success. Ruggie admits that narrative forms of explanation may seem to be 'arbitrary, subjective and soft'[60] compared to the deductive-nomological (law-seeking) explanatory scheme, but argues nonetheless that modes of epistemology and methodology in research must conform, or at least somehow be commensurate with, the ontological phenomenon at issue.[61] Though the imprint of the growth paradigm on international institutions, and on economic and political policy-making, is evident, and its impact on the environment is palpable, the paradigm itself is predominantly ideational; it is a belief system and set of norms the existence of which is not possible to categorically affirm in a positivist moment of truth as correspondence. Alternative validation criteria of the interpretive mode must therefore include such elements as plausibility, which is derived from a reasonable number of relevant events along the plotline and logical linkages among them; conformity with empirical evidence within the context of the plot; the presence of key structural elements in the narration, such as agents, motives and goals; the internal coherence and credibility of the overall framework of human desires and purposes; and the progressiveness of meanings exposed, or conclusions reached, with respect to contributions made to the larger IR research programme.[62] Explanatory credibility may also be affected by the temper of the socio-scientific milieu, and by the body of community interests which sustain it; credibility can be affected, in other words, by the paradigmatic commitments of the day.

The discovery of contradictions, or anomalies, inherent to the growth paradigm is key to the narrative process. Each contradiction sets up a dialectical tension which forms the basis for dialogue between opposed positions, and this tension moves forward the process of narrative. Dialectics figure prominently in Ruggie's description of narrative explanation, they are a necessary ingredient in Kuhn's paradigm shifts, and they are part and parcel of the neo-Gramscian version of historical materialism employed by the Italian School. In that regard, Cox distinguishes between dialectic at the (conceptual) level of logic, and at the (empirical) level of real history. In the former, dialectic means 'a dialogue seeking truth through the exploration of contradictions ... the continual confrontation of concepts with the reality they are supposed to represent and their adjustment to this reality as it continually changes'. At the level of real history, it means 'the confrontation of opposed social forces in any concrete historical situation'.[63] Significantly, whether social change provoked by conflict will be for the better or worse cannot be predetermined.[64] The outcome will depend on the nature of the conflict, the power differentials between competing factions, and the strategies and objectives of the actors involved.

I have portrayed the paradigm as a form of governance, as the foundation of normal international political economy, and as such it is structural in nature. But, like the realm of meaning itself, the paradigm is also a dynamic system which is extrapolated by social forces through time and space, and which maintains its pride of place against opposition through the constant and active interplay of coercion and consent, which serve to resolve (temporarily and incompletely) inherent tensions. The paradigm, in other words, is both structure and process, and in this sense is susceptible to a historical, and dialectical, interpretive methodology. More importantly, this methodology allows an approach that is sensitive to deeply implicit socio-cultural conditions which can shape and legitimize public policy. As Thomas Homer-Dixon has put this point, neo-Gramscianism 'helps explain why [the political commitment to economic growth] is largely invisible ... and how it permeates, defines and informs so much of our social and economic being (from personal identities to corporations to economic policies) ... [T]he growth paradigm has so saturated our perception of social reality that to question it is to render oneself almost incomprehensible'.[65] It will be thematic to this study that the invisibility and taken-for-granted status of the commitment to growth can be attributed in large part to its abstract character and disassociation from the material world. These features allow it to take on any shape or proportion and, I will show, also allow it to take on the appealing but ultimately illusory appearance of a social, political, economic and environmental panacea.

Overview

This book begins from the observation that contemporary international relations, though complex and diverse, are unified by a common commitment to economic growth as a policy priority. This commitment is shared among all major actors, and as such forms the ideational core of a form of global governance which I have labelled the growth paradigm. My primary objective is to determine how and why this paradigm rose to prominence. In light of the possibility that continuous economic growth is not compatible with a finite planetary ecosystem, a second objective is to determine whether counter-hegemonic social forces could conceivably induce a paradigm shift to a new form of governance which is environmentally benign.

I will show in Chapter 3 that the origins of the growth paradigm can be traced to a particular confluence of events which occurred at the time of the European Enlightenment, approximately 300 years ago. At that time, many transformational changes, from radical religious reforms to the Industrial Revolution, combined to bring an end to the feudal era and usher in modernity, the chief characteristic of which was the new idea of progress.[66] The rapid accumulation of knowledge and its practical application to the material world engendered for the first time a shared expectation that life and living conditions could be progressively improved, instead of being merely endured at the whim of natural exigencies and seasonal fluctuations. The dominant collective social perception about the way of the world – what John Ruggie has called a social episteme – shifted at the feudal/modern juncture from one which was essentially cyclical to one which was linear, oriented in a forward direction toward the prospect of continuous improvement. This new episteme, I will show, has since been imprinted on contemporary international relations as a collective commitment to economic growth.

In general terms, one may conceive of progress as an idea that originated in and was propagated across the European landscape, and from there spread in ever-widening and more inclusive circles until all major political and economic actors accepted its precepts and objectives; and until civil societies were won over, coercively, by concession, or by voluntary compliance, to become important participants in growth-oriented economies. When the rulers and the ruled finally formed, in effect, an intersubjectively coherent coalition oriented by the same set of beliefs and to the same set of goals, a Gramscian hegemony may be said to have been achieved. That condition obtains today; it represents the culmination of a single historical episode of some 300 years' duration.

Gramscian hegemony is the outcome of an evolutionary process that gradually incorporated the interests and expectations of civil society into political and economic decision-making, but at its earliest stages the commitment to progress is best understood in terms of the material benefits – namely, wealth and power – which accrued to the elite strata of the industrializing world, from the eighteenth to the early twentieth century. In other words the growth paradigm was, at its origin, an elitist project. It was propagated through time and space not because it represented an exercise in the extension of enlightened knowledge, or because it improved the welfare of ordinary people, but because it served the interests of political and economic leaders who, I will show, gradually coalesced to form what may be called today a transnational managerial class. In a similar vein, civil societies also gradually coalesced, beginning in Europe, into a collection of discernible and significant social forces, and eventually – though the process has been desultory, less complete and less coherent – into a nascent transnational civil society which is increasingly evident today. This latter group forms the socio-cultural foundation, and provides the political legitimacy for the hegemonic structure of the paradigm in its modern form. Both sectors, the transnational managerial class and transnational civil society, participate in the paradigm because it conforms with – indeed, defines – their beliefs, and serves their respective material interests. Contemporary rulers who preside over prosperous economies are likely to enjoy power, social stability and electoral success; and those who are ruled are likely to enjoy enhanced prospects for personal security and steadily increasing opportunities for improved standards of living.

Neo-Gramscian analysis, however, by providing a wider interpretive lens, allows for the possibility that an interest-based explanation for the domination of the growth paradigm may be incomplete. As emphasized in preceding sections of this chapter, the neo-Gramscian approach marries materiality with an ideational element, and grants equal status to each; their respective influence on particular hegemonic structures is a matter for historical research. In the present case, I contend that the latter element is more salient. The ideational superstructure of the paradigm – which, in essence, embodies a belief in the socio-political efficacy of economic growth – endows the paradigm with specific meaning, and orients it toward the promise of a better future on the strength of which current problems, shortages or challenges may be more easily borne. Thus the paradigm is perceived not only as desirable and useful but also, in light of its progressive teleology, as the right way to improve the human condition. Governments' common pursuit of growth strengthens their hold on power even as it serves the will of the people, which in turn affirms the legitimacy and rectitude of their policy-making.

This book will illuminate a collectively held belief which warrants that growth will offer all the modern benefits of progress to whomever participates in it, and that the process of continuous economic growth is neither constrained nor limited. I will also argue that what makes growth the right thing to do – what makes growth normatively legitimate – is not only its progressive teleology but, more specifically, its close association with political and economic freedom. Freedom is commonly perceived to be intrinsically good, so if growth is linked to freedom, then the pursuit of growth becomes tantamount to the pursuit of freedom.

Progress is made manifest in the material benefits generated by economic growth, but it has also, from its inception at the Enlightenment, included a notion of freedom – freedom from domination, oppression and exploitation, and freedom to pursue desirable goals and a better life. Thus progress has always comprised both a quantitative and a qualitative dimension; the two are mutually involved and, arguably, progress is best achieved when these dimensions are balanced or harmonious. An increase in knowledge, for example, will be most salutary if it engenders or facilitates improvements to the physical security and material welfare of people, or to the ecological viability of Earth. A process of abstraction, however, traced in Chapter 3, has de-linked the qualitative (ideational) from the quantitative (material) aspect of progress, such that the mutual relationship between them has been radically disengaged. The belief in progress and in the expectation of continuous improvement of the human condition is no longer accountable to material considerations. And the notion of freedom, embedded in the idea of progress but now also relieved of accountability, has been reimagined to mean freedom to pursue a limitless and cornucopian image of the future.

The open-endedness of perpetual growth, and the adoption in international relations of an unconstrained notion of freedom, endow ruling elites and the collective psyche of modern civil society with privileges they do not intrinsically own. I will argue in this book that the conflation of growth with freedom has permitted a rejection of the political obligation to redress inequities. It has displaced the moral injunction to redistribute resources between rich and poor, to husband them for the prosperity of future generations, and to share them between humans and other life forms on Earth. By facilitating this moral defection without incurring the revolutionary wrath of civil society, the paradigm binds rulers and ruled together in common cause. Political expedience, moral convenience and the promise of a bounteous future, all help to explain the dominance of the growth paradigm in international relations.

A neo-Gramscian interpretation of the paradigm will proceed as follows. Chapter 3 will focus on the evolution of the ideational superstructure of the paradigm, showing its origins and the process by which it became abstracted from the natural world. Bearing in mind that ideas are carried forward through time by particular social actors in particular historical circumstances, Chapter 4 will focus on the evolution of what can now be recognized as a transnational managerial class. Drawing on Gramsci's conception of the phases through which classes are thought to develop, I apply his insights to the gradual coalescence of a ruling stratum of economic and political leadership, from the era of pre-capitalist mercantilism to the present day. It is this stratum in particular which exercises the coercive and concessional power that has served to incorporate civil society into the paradigm. Chapter 5 turns toward the parallel evolution of transnational civil society. Given its diversity, and given the democratic impulse to allow wide scope for freedom of political expression, this sector – even though it is evidently thoroughly imbued with a culture of consumerism – cannot be uniformly or completely incorporated within any hegemonic structure. For that reason primarily, opposition to the growth paradigm, drawing on tensions and contradictions inherent to it, may arise from that sector. This chapter will explore the stream of anomalies generated by the paradigm, and determine the extent to which transnational civil society has seized upon those anomalies to justify and motivate social pressure for transformational change, in order to assess the prospects for a different form of governance and for an ecologically sustainable future.

A neo-Gramscian interpretation the commitment to growth is illuminating, but it does not lay claim to exclusivity; other explanations are also accessible and useful. With that in mind, in Chapter 2 I examine alternative approaches drawn from the three traditional levels of analysis in IR. I show there that structural, functional and psychological factors, drawn respectively from systemic, state and individual points of view, all offer important contributions to the explanatory matrix.

2 Systemic-, state-, and individual-level contributions to understanding the paradigm

Introduction

Given the divisions and stratifications characteristic of international politics, and the diversity of histories, cultures, levels of development and strategic objectives among states, it is curious that economic policies, both domestic and international, have settled uniformly on a commitment to growth. I introduced in Chapter 1 a neo-Gramscian approach to understanding this puzzle; it will be the purpose of the present chapter to incorporate alternative perspectives, drawn from traditional approaches to IR, into the explanatory matrix. Though none is as sensitive to socio-cultural background conditions, or to the ethos and tensions that animate those conditions, three such perspectives offer important contributions to understanding the ubiquity of the growth paradigm.

These perspectives can be usefully categorized according to 'levels of analysis', by which the relative importance of causal factors at different levels of aggregation can be assessed.[1] In IR these levels are typically identified as systemic, state and individual. Each yields a unique set of plausible explanations for the commitment to growth, and each set in turn reflects a particular type of explanatory mode. Specifically, systemic factors are structural in nature, constraining or enabling state behaviour in a top–down fashion; state-level factors tend to be of a functional type, that is, they reflect policy decisions purposely taken to serve particular needs; and individual-level factors are either genetic or socio-psychological in origin, bringing bottom–up pressure to bear on policy-making. Using this approach one may then hypothesize, for example, that free market capitalism is the systemic force that drives growth; or that domestic pressures for a continuously improving standard of living push state policy toward economic growth; or that the penchant for growth is more deeply engrained in the human psyche, a psychological, even genetic, predisposition made manifest in political decision-making. I discuss these possibilities in the following sections.

Systemic factors

Reflections from IPE theory: realist, liberal, and 'world system' perspectives regarding economic growth

Robert Gilpin has defined the sub-field of international political economy (IPE) as a study of 'the reciprocal and dynamic interaction in international relations of the pursuit of wealth and power'.[2] The simplest explanation for the hegemonic status of the growth paradigm rests on this 'reciprocal and dynamic interaction'. If states are concerned about their own interests, and if the successful pursuit of those interests in the anarchic forum of international politics requires the exercise of power, then each state, irrespective of how it may be structured politically, must extract as much as possible from its economy to guarantee survival in a dangerous world, and to gain its strategic objectives. A growing economy means steadily improving opportunities to achieve, and widen the ambit of, national interests. It follows from these tenets of neorealism that all states will inevitably adopt policies and programmes that maximize economic growth, as is the case today.

Though perhaps useful as a first approximation, however, this explanation does more to conceal than to reveal. It does not illuminate the meaning of national interest, an ill-defined term which could include anything from the protection of vital resources in distant lands to domestic welfare issues. Nor does this explanation clarify the nature of power relative to the attainment of interests. Though understood in its most general sense as the ability to influence outcomes, the specific meaning(s) of power vary widely according to type (hard or soft), the issue-area at question, and fungibility across issue-areas, among many other conditioning and contextual variables. Perhaps most importantly, the power/wealth equation glosses over a tension between what Gilpin calls 'two fundamentally different ways of organizing human relationships', namely, states and markets. '[T]he state', writes Gilpin, 'is based on … territoriality, loyalty and exclusivity, [but] the market is based on … functional integration, contractual relationships, and expanding interdependence of buyers and sellers … The logic of the market is to locate economic activities where they are most productive and profitable; the logic of the state is to capture and control the processes of economic growth and capital accumulation'.[3] These observations emphasize the problematic relationship between wealth and power, and, moreover, they raise vexing questions about where preponderant power really lies, and which systemic factors are determinative. The influence of the world market versus that of states with respect to the global distribution of wealth and power constitutes one of the most divisive issues in international political economy studies today.

Three main system-level explanatory frameworks are available in IPE, each of which conceives the state/market dichotomy differently, and each of which has a distinctive point of view regarding the structural characteristics of the commitment to growth. Realism (also known in IPE as economic nationalism or, originally, mercantilism) asserts the primacy of politics over economics. Liberalism sees politics and economics as inhabiting separate but complementary spheres. Marxism and Marxist offshoots tend toward systemic analyses that privilege economics over politics, frequently in a deterministic fashion. I briefly discuss these different frameworks in the following paragraphs.

Economic nationalism conforms most closely to the scenario described at the beginning of this section, in which wealth was portrayed as an essential means to power, whether for security, aggression, or aspirations to hegemony. By the same token, power is essential for the acquisition or protection of wealth, and thus the two are closely linked, and both are common objectives of national policy. According to this point of view, 'the struggle among states – capitalist, socialist or whatever – for economic resources [is] pervasive and indeed inherent in the nature of the international system'.[4] Many such resources, once acquired, are funnelled into industry. Industrialization is part and parcel of the realist enterprise because the construction of military capabilities depends upon the extraction and development by industry of material resources from the state's economic system, and because it tends to develop an entire economy (which facilitates the pursuit of interests) through spillover into non-industrial sectors. On the other hand, economic nationalism turns a blind eye to the possibility that industrialization, especially for military purposes, may not generate net social benefits. The simultaneous pursuit of wealth and power may be contradictory if industrialization entails costs to society which undermine overall economic productivity; if, for example, a state's comparative advantages in trade remain underdeveloped even as militarization proceeds unchecked. Arguably, the former Soviet Union committed this miscalculation.

Economic nationalists also tend to perceive international relations as a zero-sum game in which relative gains are of paramount importance, but this perception is contrary to the widely held belief that the market system can function to the benefit of all, and contrary to the liberal claim that equal attention should be afforded to the 'low politics' of finance and trade.[5] During the 1970s, against the backdrop of the American defeat in Vietnam which degraded the perceived utility of military interventions, traditional realist canon was recast to reflect new economic realities caused by two oil shocks and emerging trade problems with Japan, all of which engendered a perceptible shift in international relations to the global economy. Liberal analyses also evolved during the 1970s in reaction to such new factors as the rise of OPEC, former US President Nixon's unilateral abandonment of the Bretton Woods agreements on monetary stability, and the growing importance of interdependent economic relations in international affairs. Robert Keohane and his collaborator Joseph Nye, in particular, developed a liberal counterpoint to economic nationalism by focusing on the role of institutions in a world characterized by complex interdependence.[6] A number of common benefits, they argued, such as the reduction of uncertainty (by revealing others' preferences and intentions) and lowered transaction costs, ensure that institutions can facilitate cooperation among rational self-interested states. Moreover, they can encourage the pursuit of absolute gains, not just relative advantage, at least in the three issue areas (trade, oil and money) which served as case studies for subsequent empirical analyses.[7]

There ensued from this parallel development of realist and liberal schools a vigorous theoretical confrontation in IR about the weight that should be accorded to absolute versus relative gains in states' foreign policy,[8] but lost in this debate was any sustained focus on the nature or purpose of economic growth itself. The neorealist emphasis on survival, power relations and distributional conflict forced economic issues into an inherently secondary role: the importance of economic activity could only be defined with reference to the political power it could support. The liberal approach, on the other hand, though more concerned with economic issues as such, and with the cooperative resolution of market failures, did not problematize the commitment to growth. The pursuit of greater wealth was assumed to be desirable, and achievable through rational behaviour.

Notwithstanding the realist move to acknowledge the importance of trade and finance, the distinction between state and market as two distinct modes of social organization is a fact more compatible with classical liberal doctrine than with realism. The liberal preference for a separation of state and market into relatively autonomous spheres arose from the conviction that it is inherent among humans to truck, barter and trade; that 'humans are by nature economic animals, and therefore markets evolve naturally without central direction';[9] that the market and the price mechanism are sufficient to the task of organizing economic relations; and therefore that state intervention should be minimized. Further still, 'liberals believe economics is progressive and politics is retrogressive. Thus they conceive of progress [defined as an increase in wealth per capita] as divorced from politics and based on the evolution of the market'.[10] The market, according to liberal doctrine, not only benefits its immediate participants; it also tends to unite the modern and traditional sectors of human society as the latter adapt to, or are incorporated within, the former. Underlying this vision of progress is the normative belief in a harmony of interests among all societies, and a commitment to *laissez-faire* to maximize the growth of wealth. These characteristics have all been incorporated into the neoliberal ideology dominant in international relations today.

Liberalism in IPE, however, like its realist counterpart, is susceptible to a number of criticisms. Its vision of progress, for example, arose at that time of European history when momentous change and rapid material improvements were pervasive. The processes of modernization and harmonization of interests around notions of industrial development were canonized in liberal doctrine as if they were universally appropriate, when if fact they were regionally and temporally specific. And characteristics later ascribed to economic actors and the market, such as rationality and equal access to information, were very narrowly drawn, raising the suspicion that the separation of the economy from social and political realities may be artificial and potentially destabilizing. Today that separation is manifest in the tendency for the (neoliberal) market to remain aloof from issues of distributional justice or environmental sustainability, a criticism I will return to in later chapters. For present purposes, however, the point to be made is that liberalism simply assumes the desirability and efficacy of the pursuit of economic growth, and in this respect is not immediately helpful to an exploration of its origins or current status as a political priority.

The third theoretical theme in IPE that may be called upon to help explain the preeminence of the commitment to growth offers a more explicitly deterministic account of international political economy. Immanuel Wallerstein is perhaps the most prominent exponent of the world system thesis, which posits an underlying domain of social and economic forces which are prior to states and markets.[11] As its name implies, world system theory begins from the premise that the world is an economically unified whole. This is distinct from the liberal perception of modern and traditional sectors, and distinct as well from the Marxist assertion that capitalism will spread across the globe and help to develop an otherwise unproductive hinterland. For Wallerstein, the world is already and has been for centuries an essentially capitalist system which benefits the rich and oppressively underdevelops the poor. The most important feature of this type of economy, according to Wallerstein, is an international division of labour between economies designated as core and periphery. The former controls international commerce and extracts economic surplus from trade; the latter countries are dependent on coerced (not wage) labour, and export raw materials to the core. Importantly, Wallerstein perceived a semi-periphery as well – both exploiter and exploited – that functions as a crucial buffer between core and periphery, and that prevents what otherwise would amount to extreme polarization and political instability. A world economy could, argued Wallerstein, function with a multiplicity of regime types providing that their domestic economies were integrated into the larger tripartite whole.

The systemic perspective adopted by Wallerstein is not without explanatory interest. For example, it permits a revisioning of the Cold War era such that the Soviet Union is not cast as a superpower on equal footing with the United States. The era was not, on this view, bipolar; instead, the Soviet Union occupied a semi-peripheral location in the international division of labour.[12] Its internal resources and military grip on Eastern Europe supported its aspirations to global power, but its dysfunctional domestic economy made it weak. Relative American economic strength, as well as its military muscle, meant that the United States was a core state which could control the international economy in ways that the Soviet Union could not. Communism, on this view, is just a collectivist form of semi-peripheral capitalism which is inherently weak, which accounts for the marginal position of Communist states in the international economy.

Wallerstein's world system draws attention to the commitment to growth by positing a universal capitalistic political economy of which growth is an intrinsic feature, but his elision of different socio-economic systems and his uncompromising structural-functionalism make the theory vulnerable to the same determinist criticisms that classical Marxism endures. Nor can world system theory account for the influence of local conditions on the changeable status and strength of participant states. It minimizes or neglects the importance, in other words, of political and strategic relations among states, and cannot explain major structural changes which have occurred over the centuries as the international division of labour evolved. These and other criticisms have been taken up by, among others, Theda Skocpol[13] and A. L. Stinchcombe.[14]

In sum, contributions from mainstream IPE theory to a structural explanation of the commitment to growth are useful, but not decisive. Economic nationalism emphasizes the important link between power and wealth, but runs foul of the state–market dichotomy and cannot explain the rise of a global economy and the 'retreat of the state'.[15] Liberalism is more attuned to the potential for a harmony of economic interests, but focuses on the achievement of and obstacles to the evolution of conducive institutions, not on the underlying assumption of progressive growth which it treats as exogenously given, and unproblematic. Finally, Wallerstein's structural approach is too rigid and formalized to account for historical change. Its benefit, however, is its explicit focus on an economy of worldwide proportion, which in turn brings into sharper relief the role played by capitalism; and it raises the question of the extent to which capitalism may be determinative of the commitment to growth. I examine this in the next section.

Systemic factors continued

Capitalism and the market system

The key attributes of capitalism are the private ownership of the means of production and waged labour. Its motive force is provided by the drive to accumulate and reinvest capital, by the maximization of profits to firms and the maximization of utility to consumers. The market, on the other hand, implies the existence of competing buyers and sellers among whom goods and services are exchanged on the basis of negotiated prices. Capitalism and the market system are both premised on, and seek to maximize, economic growth.

The history of capitalism begins circa 1500 CE, but 'its origins', writes one representative author, 'extend far into the human past; the complex logic of capitalism is rooted in the ancient logics of possession and power, of enrichment and exchange'.[16] Grafting these atavistic impulses onto the production process gave the latter an enormous boost. The surplus acquired through production, and through trade, was applied to expanding the field of profitable activity in order to extract additional surplus. This expansionism, stimulated by entrepreneurial innovation, by competition, and by a quest for monopolistic power, is a fundamental fact of capitalism. It has generated (albeit unevenly) such improvements in standards of living worldwide that it seems unsurprising that '[g]rowth has in fact become the supreme goal of . . . contemporary societies'.[17]

The market system likewise has deep roots, once again reaching into the turmoil of early European history. Its emergence depended on bringing political arbitrariness to heel: irregular levies, confiscations and other heavy-handed interventions by mercantilists stood in the way of a new, quasi-automatic system that self-regulated through the price mechanism.[18] For Karl Polanyi, the decisive turning point in the evolution of the market system came with the increasing complexities of industrial production, and the need to safeguard the major elements of industrial supply, namely labour, land and money. 'In a commercial society', Polanyi writes,

> their supply could be organized in one way only: by being made available for purchase.... The extension of the market mechanism to ... labor, land and money was the inevitable consequence of the introduction of the factory system in a commercial society. The elements of industry had to be for sale.[19]

Like capitalism, the market system is dynamic and expansionary. Its generalization beyond produced goods and services to include labour, land and capital reinforced its tendency to incorporate every aspect of society into itself, a process which dissolved and displaced traditional societies accustomed to other forms and purposes of exchange. The market also tended to expand geographically. Pulled by the growth of demand, and pushed by new productive technologies, efficiencies of scale, and by the quest for lower costs of labour and resources, more and more of the nonmarket periphery was engulfed by the market mechanism.[20] It is difficult to underestimate the impact of these transformative changes. For North and Thomas, they account for nothing less than the rise of the West.[21] Efficient economic organization was the key to new growth, allowing the West to break free from centuries of poverty and to begin to enjoy a new quality of life made possible by relative abundance. In fact, increased trade and a new focus on competitiveness may have given rise to the state system itself. Hendrik Spruyt elaborates this argument, developing the thesis that territorial states were more efficient and responsive to new market pressures than were alternative, concurrent forms of social organization such as city-states and city-leagues.[22]

In the remainder of this section, I explore three key features of market capitalism which have contributed to the commitment to growth. First, its path-dependency, that is, the tendency of capitalism to lock in its own competitive criteria to the exclusion of other socio-economic systems. Second, its apparent ability to induce a convergence of economic policies among states despite wide variations in states' histories, cultures, levels of development and so forth. And third, I look briefly at the process of convergence through a sociological lens in order to better discern its cultural dimension.

Given its transformative power, it is not unreasonable to suppose that market capitalism may also have the capacity to lock in its own characteristics such that alternative socio-economic arrangements become increasingly inaccessible. Joshua Cohen and Joel Rogers explore this hypothesis – that capitalism creates its own path-dependency – in the context of democratic polities. They suggest that 'the calculation of economic interest ... is especially encouraged by [capitalist democracy], and its pursuit tends to reproduce that system over time'.[23] The approach developed by these authors is keyed to class relations between capitalists and workers, and it is their objective to account for and redress the (undemocratic) power asymmetries between these social groups. Their argument with respect to path-dependency pivots on two central contentions: that the interests of workers are structurally subordinated to those of capitalists, and that any ensuing struggle with respect to that subordination will logically reduce to a struggle over short-term material gain.

Cohen and Rogers argue that the general interests of capitalists have come to be seen as congruent with the common good of society, and prior to the particular interests of all other actors, because 'the satisfaction of the interests of capitalists is a necessary [though not sufficient] condition for the satisfaction of all other interests within the system'.[24] Without profit, investment will not be made, employment will not be provided, and earned money will not be available for workers to pursue the many other goals of life, most of which require material resources which must be paid for. The welfare of workers is dependent on, and thus subordinate to, the welfare of capitalists.

Whether or not workers agree in principle with this arrangement, they acquiesce in it because the labour market is vulnerable to the independent investment decisions of capitalist owners.[25] Given this vulnerability, workers may be uncertain about the security of their employment, which means they might be uncertain about their continuing access to wages and the material resources they need. It follows that it is economically rational for workers to push for increased wages in the short term in order to lessen uncertainty in the longer term, and in this way capitalism tends to structurally limit the parameters of class conflict, reducing it to a struggle over short-term material interests, many of which can be readily satisfied in the form of better wages and other benefits for workers, and increased production and profits for owners. Notably, rising wages also bring cost-push pressure to bear on the production process, which forces (locks in) a heavier reliance on growth (in the form of increased output, higher productivity, or both) to absorb the higher price of labour.

While orthodox economists would suggest that workers voluntarily choose to pursue their own hierarchy of interests, one need not rely on an assumption of ordered preferences to explain economic behaviour because that behaviour, according to Cohen and Rogers, is more plausibly a structural artifact of capitalism itself. They write that

> capitalist democracy can take many different people with diverse motivations and effectively bend them to engage in certain shared patterns of consensual behaviour with which they will at least partly identify and which they find at least in some measure rewarding.[26]

Workers are allowed to win, in other words, exactly what capitalism can deliver – short-term material gain – and are thereby persuaded to grant their consent to the reproduction and continued operation of the system.

Workers could use their political rights in a democracy to secure other, longer-term benefits through the formation of trade unions, or by pressing through political parties for social programmes such as improved pension schemes or health care programmes, but this participation in the democratic process will ultimately fail to instigate a more fundamental shift in power relations. The intrusion of private interests into deliberative processes,[27] and the mobilization problems associated with collective action, are bound to constrain outcomes to those that favour private over public or sectoral interests. And, elements of labour that may wish to engage in democratic struggle for radical economic change – to worker-dominated socialism, for example – are effectively blocked. Capitalists have several formidable advantages, such as ownership of fixed and liquid assets, access to strategic economic information and to political decision-makers, and low coordination costs because of their relatively small numbers. Labour, on the other hand, would face unknown costs and benefits, as well as the inevitable defections and free-riding which would ensue from such an undertaking. It would appear to be irrational as well as structurally prohibitive for workers to attempt to dismantle or radically reform the very system and institutions that are the source of their current and immediate gain.

Cohen and Rogers offer a lucid account of the structural domination of capitalism,[28] and its tendency to persist once established, but their argument is, ultimately, too narrowly drawn to provide a robust explanation of the commitment to growth in international relations. Capitalist–worker relations are identified as the key structural attribute of a democratic polity, but this belief, if held too closely, artificially diminishes the importance of the state with respect to its domestic responsibilities, and its role in international affairs. For these authors, the state is not an autonomous entity; it is an outcome and an expression of material conflict between capital and labour. Its role is to organize and enforce a compromise which reflects the balance of power between these social forces such that labour will not make unmanageable wage demands on capital, and capital will continue to invest, ensuring continued employment for workers. But this portrayal of the state's role pushes the structural position too far: little room for policy autonomy is admitted under the oppressive constraints of capitalism. Neither political analysts, in the main, nor state leaders charged with maintaining the well-being of their citizenry, would accept the proposition that choice is so delimited by class conflict. In a similar vein, Cohen and Rogers portray international politics as reflective primarily of relations between capital and labour. Foreign policy is 'set by the nature of the [domestic] accord or compromise that the state is presently enforcing',[29] and 'the content and aims of foreign policy reflect the goals of dominant domestic actors'.[30] Given the condition of anarchy, those dominant domestic actors – that is, capitalists – will also hold sway on the international stage, and the parameters of international compromise and order will be set by the relative power of those actors.

Again, this argument is too deterministic, and too much influenced by Marxist canon. The struggle for power between classes is so sharply presented that the authors are obliged to offer an equally extreme remedy to capitalism which, they say, is inherently unjust and incompatible with long-term planning. Having stripped the state and all international institutions of the capacity for transformative leadership, they turn instead to activist elements of civil society whose objectives are shaped by ideals of social justice, equality and democratic pluralism. These elements, we are told, will one day disengage capitalism, and the preponderant power it accords to the private sector, from the democratic process and the fair consideration of public issues which the latter ostensibly entails.

For present purposes, then, only three features of the Cohen and Rogers study will be retained and blended into subsequent discussion of the growth paradigm. The first of these is the structural power of capitalism itself. Their account clearly reveals the dominant role of private interests, which I will show to be a formative element in the evolution of the paradigm and the deepening commitment to economic growth. The second feature to be retained is that of consent. Classical Marxism has been hard pressed to explain why the proletariat, within particular polities or in the international domain, has not (with few exceptions) taken up arms against their capitalist oppressors. Cohen and Rogers have illuminated the structural reasons why this is so, but emphasize also that capitalism 'delivers the goods', at least in the short term, and for this reason workers acquiesce in, give their consent to, or are otherwise co-opted by their capitalist masters. This consent is an indispensable ingredient in paradigmatic hegemony as described by Antonio Gramsci, a point I take up later. Third, Cohen and Rogers draw an important distinction between *calculation* and *choice* on which, they contend, any escape from capitalism must depend. The former refers to the processes of economic rationality by which costs and benefits are evaluated. No rational calculation by workers, or by the state, can give logical or reasonable preference to anti-capitalistic behaviour, as previously discussed: this is the key to capitalist path-dependency, and the tool by which class asymmetries and short-term materialism are locked in. Choice, on the other hand, refers to decision-making based on longer-range factors, or principled and ethical criteria, where utility is of secondary importance. Though they did not express it in these terms, these authors were tacitly distinguishing between utilitarian and deontic reasoning, the latter of which can provide the intellectual foundation for social change which otherwise would be precluded by the prospect of prohibitive cost. The opportunity to choose, so defined, is the indispensable core of political freedom and proactive agency.

Structural explanations of the political commitment to economic growth can draw on more than relations between capital and workers; they may focus instead on the instrumental causes of convergence of states' economic policies in the international domain which effectively exclude alternative forms of economic development. For example, the internationalization of production, and in particular the commodification of finance capital, has led to the present-day phenomenon of massive and virtually instantaneous capital mobility across state borders. David M. Andrews has argued[31] that this flow of money constitutes a structural variable in international relations (insofar as the threat of capital flight constrains state behaviour) the effect of which is to reduce state autonomy, and to push and/or pull state policies toward meeting the competitive criteria of capitalist investment. This argument has been advanced by others[32] as part of a larger debate in IPE which explores the diverse features of globalization, the central problematic of which (notwithstanding its reputed social, cultural and political dimensions) is the apparent convergence of state policies toward similar patterns of economic management. The key question posed in this debate is whether the pattern is imposed exogenously, or is the result of purposive choice by individual states. The debate is wide-ranging and controversial,[33] raising fundamental concerns about who or what motivates the process, what purposes or interests are served, and what shifts in power relations, if any, may be anticipated.

With respect to the particular issue of capital market integration, the conversation is polarized between those who retain a state-centric point of view, such as Goodman and Pauly,[34] and those who perceive structural forces as decisive independent variables. For the former, systemic forces, though formidable, can be explained largely in terms of the unintended consequences of unit-level changes: convergence to capital decontrol is driven, on this view, by a combination of technological innovation in communications and information technologies, the development by the private sector of new instruments to facilitate capital flow, and by the removal of technical and legal barriers by the public sector, all of which could be reined in, if states were so inclined, albeit not without cost. The structural position advanced by Andrews, on the other hand, emphasizes that competition between states for capital, the exponential growth of financial markets and foreign direct investment, and the socialization of international monetary authorities around a common ideological commitment to liberalization, among other factors, all point to the conclusion that systemic factors are indeed forcibly narrowing the choice set of states, committing them ever more closely to monetary policies over which they have no independent control.

Neoclassical doctrine certainly fosters the expectation that, under the influence of international competition and the deregulation of capital markets, convergence to policies which maximize the potential for growth will be accentuated. As Suzanne Berger observes, '[n]eoclassical conceptions of trade, competition and growth [sustain] an expectation of convergence, understood in a general way to mean the spread across the world of the same patterns of economic life'.[35] This assertion from theory is neutral with respect to the means by which convergence will occur – purposive choice or external imposition – and is therefore compatible with both bottom–up and top–down points of view. The common commitment to growth is, no doubt, encouraged by forces both external to and within individual states; it is not my intention necessarily to prefer one point of view over the other, but to make the more general point that both neoclassical theory and the particular pressures imposed by the movement of money both contribute to the task of explaining the uniformity of the commitment to growth, even if they are somewhat indeterminate regarding the direction of causation.

It is also true, in any event, that capital mobility is a relatively recent addition to international affairs, so cannot explain the historical continuity of economic growth as a policy objective among states. Capital decontrol may be more constructively conceived as a recent effect of prior political preferences, rather than as a cause of the commitment to growth. And the same holds true with respect to the wider issue of globalization. While mobile capital offers a comparatively simple example of a structural push to economic growth, in response to which convergent monetary policies are fashioned to suit capitalist investment, globalization cannot be so readily categorized with respect to either cause or effect; indeed, no distinctive set of dependent variables has been identified and consensually agreed to be the primary or decisive indicator of such a process. Globalization may refer, for example, to the wide diffusion of markets and the internationalization of production; the spread of democracy (which ostensibly adds political to economic freedom); the creation of a new transnational space which supervenes upon state territoriality; or, perhaps, the Americanization of global culture. It is not possible to infer from these speculations the presence of a structurally driven propensity to economic growth which can account for the ubiquity of an identical political priority across the global polity. And, as with capital mobility, economic globalization (depending on its definition) is usually construed as a relatively recent phenomenon which is as likely a result of the neoliberal ideological revolution as a primary cause of growth in the world economy.

It is perhaps not surprising that, in light of its transnational character, the growth paradigm can be approached advantageously from several quite different systemic points of view. Before leaving this section, it is useful to look briefly at Western modernism from one other perspective – through a sociological lens, as Martha Finnemore has done,[36] because that perspective illuminates certain cultural determinants of transnational change. She deploys an explicitly constructivist approach, sociological institutionalism (SI), which is sensitive to historical change and is therefore more relevant to the longer-term perspective adopted for this study. On the other hand, SI falls squarely on the holist/structural side of the agent–structure debate (so that structure is ontologically prior to and generative of agents), and therefore undervalues the importance of choice in the evolution of international relations.

Finnemore sees a set of world cultural rules that constitute actors – states, organizations and individuals – and that define legitimate or desirable goals to pursue. This system-level theoretic framework generates hypotheses which predict 'similarities in behaviour caused by common global culture, where realism or liberalism would expect differences in behaviour by differently situated actors with different interests'.[37] More specifically, SI grounds (an expanding and deepening) global culture in Western Christendom and early capitalism, arguing that this culture 'emphasizes Weberian rationality as the means to both justice, defined as equality, and progress, defined as wealth accumulation'.[38] The conventional wisdom which arises from these roots is that rationalized bureaucratic structures are 'the only way to divide labor, specify responsibilities, and institutionalize coordination and decision-making' in efficient and effective ways.[39] Finnemore has documented the diffusion of cultural norms among otherwise radically different states such that those states then express identical policy preferences, or establish similar institutional arrangements.[40] The norms are diffused from core to periphery in the international system, and embody the bureaucratized rationality typical of Weber's modern state.

The precise mechanisms of cultural diffusion are not yet well understood by SI[41] and in any event this approach treats progress by assumption, which is not helpful to the present study. Progress is conflated with growth and is defined in material terms – increased personal wealth for individuals and increased GNP for states – and its origins are not examined. Of more importance to SI are the cultural sources of the transnational preference for rational action as an effective and efficient way to achieve (given) objectives. Markets and bureaucracies are the putative means to progress and justice, respectively, and they are culturally legitimated in terms of equality, namely, equal opportunity in the marketplace, and equal access to government services. For my purposes, two things are of particular interest here: first, the emphasis that SI brings to bear on the role of culture in international society and, second, the functionalist nature of that culture. I elaborate briefly.

The expansion of Western-style bureaucratic management to all corners of the world suggests, says Finnemore, that a cultural overlay has been superimposed on otherwise dissimilar states. 'The modern bureaucratic state', she notes, 'has become the sole legitimate form of political organization in the world.... Empires, colonies, feudal arrangements, and a variety of other forms, have become extinct and, perhaps more important, unimaginable in contemporary politics'.[42] Because states exist at different stages of development, sometimes that overlay is inappropriate (for example, when a state with no scientific capability nonetheless establishes a science ministry), but takes root anyway because that bureaucratic form is an expected part of what is perceived to be a modern country. Bureaucracy as a preferred mode of organization, in effect, spread faster than some states were being developed economically and technologically. This indicates that bureaucracy does not spread only because of its functional virtues, but because it is 'externally legitimated'. This, says Finnemore, is the 'entry point for culture. The content of this external environment is cultural'.[43] Thus, for sociologists, the most formative of systemic influences which pertain to contemporary international politics is culture, the content of which is specifically characterized by the structuring of purposive action in terms of means and ends,[44] that is, in terms of the rational pursuit of progress and justice. Though I do not emphasize to the same degree the structural role played by culture, it is appropriate to take note of the importance of culture with respect to hegemonic international processes, as this will reoccur in subsequent discussions of certain aspects of Gramscian hegemony.

The second point bears more directly on the next section to follow. Weberian bureaucratic rationality is task-oriented; its pervasiveness and legitimacy among states imply that this form of organization has been endorsed and incorporated by states because it is perceived to be useful, serving a set of important functions. This in turn opens the possibility that the political commitment to growth may be explained in functional terms at the state level, without recourse to structural determinants, because all states claim the right to reject external pressures outright if they wish, costs notwithstanding. This constitutes the non-negotiable core of the state-centric position, which arises from the fundamental proposition that states are and will remain sovereign even in the face of transnational phenomena. In the next section I explore the possibility that states, in the acknowledged presence of a common instrumental culture, have purposely selected economic growth as a means to achieve an explicit set of objectives.

State-level factors

The spread of bureaucratic rationality as a preferred form of state; the concomitant structuring of purposive action by states in terms of means and ends; the utilitarian ethic that supports rational calculation; and a shared neoliberal ideology that gives precedence to the mechanics of economic intercourse: all these characteristics of modern societies underline the importance of tangible results of policy. Modern states are, above all, task-oriented, and governments are elected to perform specific functions. It follows from these (contentious but plausible) assertions that a functional analysis of state behaviour with respect to economic growth may be illuminating.

The consequences of action, rather than their causes, are at the focal point of functional analysis. This approach does not trace, therefore, the origins of societal change, such as the emergence of a popular demand for social welfare and commensurate pursuit of material advancement. State-level explanations of the commitment to growth are best pursued not by asking 'What is the cause of the commitment to growth?', but, 'What functions does the commitment serve?' A distinctive feature of this type of consequentialist analysis is its premise that form follows function. A state, for example, is a social system that seeks to maintain internal cohesion, and to reproduce itself through time. These are its most rudimentary functions; to fulfil them requires that certain formal arrangements be adopted. As philosopher of social science Martin Hollis expresses this point, 'Whatever meets [systemic needs to survive and flourish] is *functional* for the system and occurs *because* it is functional'.[45] Economic growth, on this view, embodies a preferred set of practices (form) because the preservation and enhancement of state life (function) are deemed to require it.

Functional analysis has its origins in biology, and was pioneered in the social sciences by Emile Durkheim in France, and Herbert Spencer in England.[46] It was imported into IR and most fully developed in that context by David Mitrany. His 1940s classic, *A Working Peace System*,[47] envisaged the development of new transnational institutions which would arise in response to change brought about by the scientific and technological innovations characteristic of Western modernity. These changes – in production, transportation and communication, for example – are broader in scope than the geography of any one state; they generate, therefore, new transnational challenges which in turn create opportunities for joint problem-solving among states. Solutions take the form of new institutions of international governance – task-oriented agencies, that is, of various purposes, scope and membership. The end result of this process, Mitrany argued, could be a transformation of the dilemmas of balance of power and self-help in international politics into a working peace system of technocratic agencies and associative security.

Functionalism has not found a permanent place in the study of international relations. The seminal and ascendant role assigned to science by this approach engendered a sense of technological determinism, and Mitrany's hopeful expectations that functional agencies, run rationally and consensually by experts, could mark the way to greater freedom and justice, proved elusive. The approach resurfaced briefly during the behaviouralist era of the 1960s and 1970s as neo-functionalism, which stressed technical cooperation among states and the construction of institutions whose success would spill over into other areas of interaction.[48] The emerging community of closely integrated states in Western Europe provided the testing ground for this updated version of functionalism but, like its predecessor, it underestimated the political nature of knowledge production within epistemic communities, and foundered on the unwillingness of states to subordinate their sovereignty to a global technocratic social democracy.

As an explanatory framework for international relations, then, functionalism has passed its zenith, but a functional approach to political study – less deterministic, less utopian and more pragmatic – can still be useful, by simply posing the question 'Which policies work, and why?' This approach fits well with the means/ends rationality of bureaucratized state actors, the instrumental (even apolitical) ethos of neoliberalism and with modern scientism, as expressed by the heavy reliance within both private and public spheres on the objectivity and legitimacy of science, and on the productive potential of practical technologies. And, this approach suggests a straightforward, state-level explanation of the common commitment to growth: it may be no more than a reflection of the aggregated policies of individual states – growth-based policies, that is, which have been endorsed and implemented because they work.

In the first instance, then, a functional explanation for the propensity among states for economic growth would seek to link the need to meet popular demands for improved living standards to growth as an appropriate political response. This linkage is readily made, in that growth in GNP is (more or less) directly proportional to consumption, so states encourage growth through appropriate policy commitments. Below I identify several other state-level policy concerns that may be satisfied by the persuit of economic growth, including optimizing employment, reducing poverty, securing peace at home and abroad, and protecting the environment. Subsequently I will show, however, that the functionalist approach does not capture the full scope of the paradigmatic commitment to growth.

Mitrany recognized that better standards of living are closely tied to improvements in technology, but technological change has other less positive social ramifications which also incline state policies toward economic growth. Of particular importance in this regard is the displacement of segments of the labour force by production machinery and streamlined production processes. Displaced workers are obliged to seek similar work in other industries, or to retrain for new employment in more technologically advanced sectors. The absorption of displaced labour is, arguably, most easily accomplished by a growing national economy which generates a continuous stream of new opportunities for work. Unemployment, on the other hand, may be exacerbated not by mechanical displacement, but by population increase, for which growth also provides a ready answer. This problem is not of great concern in developed states with more or less stable populations, but it is of critical importance in developing states whose numbers are rising rapidly. No Third World country expects to absorb these new people – in the sense of offering them healthful and efficacious lives and a productive role in society – without proportionate increases in GNP.

Relatedly, growth is linked to poverty reduction, both at home and abroad. Growth-oriented public policies are intended to raise average per capita income, to reduce disparities between rich and poor segments of the national population, and to redress underdevelopment abroad through the mechanism of liberalized trade.[49] Neoliberal doctrine is explicit in this regard: the competitive interplay among states of their respective comparative advantages will lead to a progressive levelling of disparities in the international political economy. By adopting trade policies premised on growth, rich states need not ameliorate North–South economic disparities by subsidy, or by compromising living standards at home. By the same token, the need for potentially contentious or divisive domestic policies, by which wealth is extracted from the rich and distributed to the poor, may be radically reduced.

Growth is also linked to peace. It was integral to Mitrany's original argument that conflict will be less likely between states whose populations are materially sated. This may or may not be empirically true, but it resonates anyway with the still commonly held opinion (reflected in neoliberal doctrine) that, as economic disparities among states are reduced, the motivation to redress inequities by violent means will be reduced proportionately. To put this in more distinctively functionalist terms: securing peace is a task to be met by national governments; material abundance may reduce conflict, and is desired by society in any event; therefore, growth-oriented policies and practices (pulled by the need for peace, and pushed by social pressure) constitute the form that follows. Under conditions of sustained growth in world production and trade, an ever-broadening field of play can readily accommodate competition between states, as each seeks to develop and expand its market share based on comparative advantage. Without growth in the global economy, however, the international struggle for new markets could generate conflict as more, and more powerful, actors confront the same set of fixed assets.[50]

Domestically, a wide range of tasks have likewise evoked growth-based responses. Most states still support substantial military budgets, for example, but defence spending must compete for funds with other governmental responsibilities, such as the provision of public infrastructure and utilities, or education and health care, all of which must be adequately met without limiting the availability of rewards for personal initiative and achievement. And, governments everywhere must have the financial resources necessary to intervene in the economy, as required, to respond to economic downturns, to prevent stagnation, recession or depression; to control inflation, or smoothe over boom–bust tendencies in the business cycle; or to repay debt, or fund future budgetary demands such as old-age programmes: all of which are easier to accomplish in a growing economy. Good management with respect to these tasks draws approbation from the private sector too, as many businesses face similar challenges. And when governments and industry agree on the efficacy of growth, and on its embodiment in public policies, then the private sector can enjoy the sense of stability, predictability, rationality and continuity upon which new investment depends.

Finally, it bears repeating that state policies respecting environmental issues are also keyed to and almost wholly reliant on economic growth. Despite the sustainable development rhetoric which seeks to merge economic with environmental concerns, the former retains its priority status: environmental protection initiatives are, in the main, not permitted to stunt growth, block job creation or diminish material living standards. Solutions to environmental problems are more often demanded from technology – fuel efficiencies, or carbon capture and storage, for example – than from lifestyle changes such as reduced consumption, and these solutions will not be available without investment by both the public and private sectors, which depends in turn on a viable tax base and profitable production respectively.

These linkages drawn between economic growth, the various policies which embrace growth and the functions served by those policies, are all common currency in contemporary politics and international relations. A survey of industrialized and industrializing states' behaviour undertaken by J. K. Galbraith[51] supports the conclusion that economic growth represents the ideal and most efficacious of political practices for any state, because it is the best of all social lubricants. Not only does it (at least potentially) deliver the quantifiable outcomes enumerated in the foregoing paragraphs, but it does so on grounds with which all major actors and social sectors – public and private, employer and employee, rich and poor – can agree. Economic growth benefits them all, and no one need be penalized.

The argument in favour of a state-level explanation of the growth paradigm is particularly cogent given the instrumental nature of the commitment to economic growth by policy-makers. It may very well be true that those policy-makers, if asked, would identify a long and specific list of tasks the completion of which would be facilitated by growth; but it may be equally true that a more basic and unexpressed objective underlies the ends identified publicly, namely, political stability. Galbraith's argument implicitly endorses this possibility, and the relationship between growth and stability has been taken up more recently, and more extensively, by Homer-Dixon.[52] Using the phrase growth imperative, he shows how the propensity for growth and the instrumental advantages facilitated by it are relevant not only to modern societies, but historically to (among others) the Roman Empire, the stability of which depended directly on ever-widening access to (agriculture-based) energy supplies. The need faced by any ruler, at any time, to underwrite social stability can be met in large measure by relying on a steady stream of new goods and services – by a continuously increasing throughput of matter and energy, in modern terms – to absorb the otherwise potentially incompatible expectations of diverse social groups.

The imperative to grow persists today, though the commitment to growth underwent a metamorphosis at the feudal/modern juncture. Before modernity, the accumulation of wealth tended to follow the exercise of power. After, however, and particularly with the commodification of the means of production, power began to follow wealth in the new and rapidly expanding market society. And, significantly, the benefits of growth in the modernizing world spread beyond power-seeking elites: ordinary people were gradually incorporated into the market too (as I show in subsequent chapters) and new, popular ideas about progress and freedom came to be closely linked to economic growth as a means to realize them. The growth paradigm as such began to emerge at the dawn of the modern age, rising from the deeper roots of the political imperative to counteract the centrifugal forces inherent to any social structure.

State-level explanations for the ubiquity of the growth paradigm centre on the delivery of practical results. Growth generates tangible benefits, so it can be readily sold to the people of any state. The pursuit of growth also diminishes and contains conflicts between competing claims to national income, so it works to maintain social stability, thereby serving the needs of those who rule. The growth paradigm is, in short, politically expedient, and this conclusion speaks powerfully to the cogency of the state-level point of view. Nonetheless, this perspective is inadequate. I show below that the application of functional analysis to the growth paradigm reveals an element of illogic, even irrationality, in state behaviour which eludes explanation; and, significantly, the distinctively normative content of the paradigm remains unaccounted for by this genre of analysis.

The problem-solving orientation of functionalism carries with it the implication that, in any given system, a set of equilibrium-seeking dynamics is at play.[53] States solve problems because they intend to (re)establish stability. In the present case, states' preferences for socio-political stability over time have, ostensibly, been met by equilibrium-inducing conditions generated by growth-oriented practices. To put this somewhat differently, all of the problems discussed above – from international struggles over market share to domestic poverty reduction – are potentially destabilizing, both to individual states, and to the international system they compose. Economic growth works to assuage tensions, and to maintain or regain stability, and on that basis is said to constitute an effective way to move toward a condition of equilibrium.

Conceiving state behaviour in terms of the pursuit of equilibria offers a useful heuristic for better understanding the political attractiveness of the growth paradigm, but it also exposes an element of illogic in state behaviour which can be clarified with reference to the distinction between functionalism as practice, and as theory. As theory, functionalism is intended not only to discover workable solutions to problems, but also to inquire whether other means to other, perhaps quite different, equilibria, might also be available. Failure to evaluate alternative solution sets would represent a breach of the rationalism which is central to the functional approach: due attention to alternative means improves the prospects for efficiency, and reduces the risk of pursuing unstable, or even dysfunctional, equilibria. In practice, however, it cannot be said with any assurance that all states which now embrace economic growth as a political priority do so after having evaluated and rejected other ways to achieve their objectives. Cost–benefit calculations, if undertaken rationally, cannot preclude in advance the possibility that the costs of growth may outweigh its benefits,[54] yet no-growth or differently attuned policies are ignored or given short shrift, and consequently have no political currency whatever. Poverty reduction, for example, is an ethical concern the resolution of which does not depend only, or even primarily, on growing economies.

Rationalism requires that various means be compared, but equally it requires that various ends be examined too in order to avoid the problem of illusory or dysfunctional objectives; but no evidence supports the conclusion that such comparisons have been undertaken. Beyond a generic orientation among states toward 'peace and prosperity in our time', no clear and detailed exposition of alternative long-term equilibria has been articulated by any modern leader, even though it is not possible to know which outcome is preferable – which equilibrium is most desirable – without evaluating the merits of all plausible candidates. Even the relatively stable state system, for example, is not necessarily the best of all outcomes, though it is commonly thought to have evolved in response to functionalist considerations such as security concerns, centralized tax collection and so on. As Martha Finnemore has suggested (in her previously cited work on the spread of bureaucratic rationality), self-determination in the modern world effectively requires having a state, which creates an all-or-nothing dynamic in international politics which forecloses other organizational forms that may be more conducive to societal development, or to conflict resolution. The state system, in other words, may be in some important respects dysfunctional, but it cannot be improved upon without first admitting the possibility of other political arrangements. Of more immediate interest to this study is the fact that no-growth alternative equilibria, such as that embodied in the concept of a steady-state economy, are not considered in any important political or economic forum, indicating that a full range of development trajectories is not being discussed. This inappropriate, even irresponsible behaviour by state leaders in their pursuit of economic growth is left unexplained by functionalism.

State-level expositions of the growth paradigm are also limited because functionalism does not explicitly problematize the emergence of a popular demand for continuous improvements in personal and social welfare, and commensurate pursuit of material abundance. Neoclassical economic theory treats consumer insatiability as a historical constant, but in fact the widespread public expectation of continuous improvements in welfare is of relatively recent origin. Prior to the emergence of modernity, life was conceived primarily in terms of cyclical, not linear, change. Absent the historical contextualization of this transformation in the collective psyche of human society, subsequent state behaviour with respect to growth cannot be said to have any substantive foundation, or starting point. Nor can this shortcoming be redressed by simply building in historical antecedents to a functionalist point of view. Functionalism is a needs-based approach which directs our attention to the evolution of policy shaped by those needs, not by the historical contingencies from which they may have arisen. To shift the analytical terrain in that way would be to evince a different kind of reasoning which in turn would bring to bear a different, and wider, set of interpretive possibilities. Historicization and the development of a wider frame of reference are more compatible with the neo-Gramscian approach.

As emphasized throughout, neo-Gramscianism directs analytical attention to the normative foundations of hegemony, and here too functionalism misses an important aspect of state endorsement of growth. Not only is the pursuit of economic growth politically expedient, it is also aggressively portrayed by policy-makers as the right thing to do, and it is this portrayal in particular which focuses attention on the moral underpinnings of the international political economy. What makes growth 'the right thing to do' – what makes it normatively legitimate – is its close association with the idea of economic and political freedom. The idea of freedom is hugely important in the global polity; this is best exemplified with regard to American foreign policy, which encourages people everywhere to seek freedom. The 2006 version of George Bush's National Security Strategy, for example, asserts that 'All free nations have a responsibility to stand together for freedom because all free nations share an interest in freedom's advance'.[55] This militant call to action highlights the well-known American attachment to freedom, and the National Security Strategy articulates many ways to advance freedom in the world, one of the most important of which is to encourage economic freedom because, as the document goes on to say, 'Greater economic freedom [through free markets and free trade] is ultimately inseparable from political liberty'.[56] This assertion clearly echoes Milton Friedman whose work is neatly summarized in Bush's manifesto. 'Economic freedom', it says quite bluntly, 'is a moral imperative'.[57] Limits imposed on growth mean limits imposed on liberty. These limits, we are told, are counterproductive, illegitimate, and wrong. I will return to this important point respecting the normative foundations of the growth paradigm in later chapters, but note for the present that the state-level explanation does not address the source or implications of this 'moral imperative'.

Analysis of the task orientation of state behaviour indicates that the commitment to growth reflects a tactical preference for immediately available solutions to pressing problems and a tacit propensity for political stability. While the fact of paradigmatic conformity may be attributable in large part to the short-term exigencies of political management, however, it may also be the case that the ubiquity of the paradigm arises from much deeper origins; from characteristics that are innate to the human psyche, and to the psycho-social propensities of large groups. I explore this possibility in the following section.

Individual-level factors

The general argument from an individual level of analysis suggests that large-scale characteristics of human society may not be the result of systemic factors such as power relations under anarchy, or the shared preferences of capitalist policy-makers. Instead of top–down, a bottom–up process may be at play, by which the behaviour of individual people sums to large-scale patterns which may or may not be intended by those individuals. The study of the relationship between the behavioural characteristics of individuals, and of aggregates, has been undertaken in some detail by Thomas C. Schelling.[58] His analysis begins from two assumptions: first, that people's behaviour is rational and purposive, and second, that it is contingent. The latter assumption simply refers to the fact that people impinge on and adapt to others. What people do depends on what others are doing.

While Schelling examines a wide variety of examples of patterned behaviour which are directly attributable to the aggregated motives of individual people, the one of most pertinence here is economic. 'In economics', writes Schelling, 'it often appears that … unmanaged and unguided individual activity leads to aggregate results that are … about as good as could be expected if somebody took command and figured out what ought to be done'.[59] This familiar characterization of the market system reflects the original observation of Adam Smith, some 250 years ago, that the system works as if an unseen hand had imposed or directed its coordination. Individuals motivated by the rational pursuit of their own interests, and influenced by only a local part of the larger pattern, comprise a system they need know nothing about, but that works nonetheless to the mutual benefit of all participants. Individual preferences for maximized utility lead to the macropatterns of market behaviour, of which continuous expansion is an inherent part because utility increases with consumption. Public policy that supports economic growth merely codifies this outcome.

Given the size, diversity and complexity of human societies, it is not surprising that the market system as a useful but unintended epiphenomenon does not work to perfection. For markets to function as best they can, private and public authorities must intervene to establish rules of ownership, regulations and standards, a host of institutional arrangements and, not least, a normative foundation that secures a common commitment to order and fairness. These interventions are so much an intrinsic part of social structure, however, that their existence modifies and otherwise obscures what may be the underlying operation of a pure market system. The middle ground, in other words, between individual preferences and public policy supporting economic growth becomes so thickly populated with rules and obligations that the direction of causal arrows becomes less clear, and the bottom–up mechanisms described by Schelling become less compelling. Macrobehaviour begins to look more like a social construction shared by consenting parties, than a (relatively) simple pattern of aggregated individual decisions. Moreover, the premise of rationality of individual motivations does not stand up well to close scrutiny. Problematic assumptions typical of neoclassical economics, such as utility maximization, freely available information, consistent sets of ordered preferences, or, importantly, the insatiability of consumer demands, do not provide a secure foundation from which to extrapolate broad commitments at the level of economic policy-making.[60] The rationalist explanation for the growth paradigm assumes a kind of pre-socialized self-interest that privileges characteristics such as possessiveness, competitiveness and individualism without identifying the source or cause of those characteristics. For these various reasons, this account of the paradigm is interesting but, ultimately, not persuasive.

Schelling is careful to eschew any appeal to human nature in his analysis of various patterns of macrobehaviour, preferring instead to call upon the logic of aggregation as it plays out in various situations, and calling for the construction of institutions – planned forms of social organization – to deal with outcomes or externalities that are unwanted, inefficient or deleterious to the common good. Another approach to micromotives as a possible explanatory source of the commitment to growth, however, focuses on non-rational foundations of behaviour; causes, that is, rooted in genetics.

The most radical argument from biology disregards rationality and sociality of all kinds. Echoing the deterministic teleology of (early forms of) functionalism, it posits genes as ontologically primitive units whose sole purpose is reproduction. Each unique type of DNA (technically, genotype) interacts with its environment, builds a body (phenotype) from found resources, and uses that body to replicate itself. All life forms, including people, are survival machines for DNA, and each tries to maximize its own reproductive success.[61] The propensity for economic growth could be traced to this biological imperative, insofar as a more robust economy works to support a larger species population.

An advantage this approach brings to bear is that it seems to cut neatly through the fog of cultural and socially constructed variables which would otherwise overrule a role for nature in the behaviour of human beings. Irrespective of our ability to reason, or our morality, or any other feature of higher consciousness, people are, like any other life form, intent on survival and propagation. We are unique, certainly – not because of our higher features, however, but because we are a superspecies, 'a superior competitor … [which] is predicted to competitively displace all other species no matter how heterogeneous the habitat may be'.[62] And from this point of view, the maximal exploitation of resources and resultant destruction of non-human habitat is neither mysterious nor unexpected. Given the extraordinary versatility of human life, both individually and collectively, limits imposed by external constraints (such as geography, climate, competition, predation and so on) and by internal constraints (essentially, genetic limitations to adaptability) are far removed from those imposed on all others. This leads inevitably to expansionary pressure and resource appropriation which is paid for with the lives and living spaces of species less invasive and adaptable than our own. The notion of growth and its major environmental implications are, arguably, entirely congruent with this explanatory framework.

Several disadvantages afflict the genetic model, however. First, none of it can be proved. The problem in this regard is that learning, culture and other socially constructed intervening variables cannot be so easily dismissed. They are unavoidably interposed between putative biological causes and behavioural effects such that measurements of genetic influence are not directly possible, except in trivial cases such as simple biological functions. This methodological conundrum explains why opinions range from one extreme (all behaviour is a cover for genetic propagation) to the other (human behaviour is in no way predetermined). These opposed points of view reflect familiar tensions that emerge in any discussion of agents versus structure, or, in this case, nature versus nurture. The genetic model offers no guidance with respect to which specific political programmes or policies may be affected by behavioural predispositions, and which ones might be a matter of independent choice, so the degree to which human agency is constrained is not clear. It is also the case that not all human societies clearly demonstrate an imperative to maximize their populations, even though all states pursue economic growth.

The body of literature from which this discussion is drawn is referred to as sociobiology or, more recently, evolutionary psychology. A long-standing debate about genetic determinism was given new impetus in 1975 by E. O. Wilson with the publication of *Sociobiology: The New Synthesis*.[63] His sustained effort (and that of many subsequent writers) to isolate biological causes for a variety of human behaviours was not well received, nor were his conclusions clearly substantiated, because of impenetrable intervening variables. There is no current consensus in the social sciences regarding this problem, and I do not pursue it here. Having said this, however, it is not unreasonable to suppose that our biological and evolutionary heritage does play at least some role in behaviour formation. Though usually rejected (and excoriated) as a form of social Darwinism, evolutionary psychology today begins from the plausible premise that the effect of genetic predispositions is greater than zero; and even this minimalist position leaves open the possibility that socialized behaviour constructed by purposive agents can overwhelm and redirect these predispositions. We may be naturally inclined to violence, for example, but may deliberately choose compassion instead. The point is not that the commitment to growth can be fully explained by resort to biological first principles, which it clearly cannot. Appeals to genetic predispositions are controversial, and only suggestive at best, but human psychology still plays an acknowledged and important role in the social sciences, including IR. Notions of territoriality, competition, predation, symbiotic cooperation, status hierarchies and so on are all instinctual characteristics of many species, and they all have clear analogues in international relations; thus, the impulse to explore connections between the domains of human social behaviour and nature is strong. My purpose in this section is to follow that impulse, to examine the possibility that the ubiquity of the commitment to growth may be somehow attributable to, or a reflection of, shared characteristics of the human psyche. I have found Reinhold Niebuhr's work particularly helpful in this regard. Writing in the tradition of classical realism, Niebuhr posits an inherent expansionary tendency rooted in human psychology, and he contextualizes that tendency within a hierarchical social system of class relations. His perspective suits my purposes by serving as a kind of psychological prelude to the neo-Gramscian discussion to follow, which likewise will emphasize social stratifications, and the power differentials between them.

Niebuhr's *Moral Man and Immoral Society* is a treatise on individual and collective psychology, on the tensions between atavistic impulse and rational morality at these two levels, and on the implications that those tensions have for international relations. He argues that individuals have a moral cast which engenders love, altruism and a sense of justice, and that individuals have the capacity to overcome native impulses in order to serve the larger community. The 'tragedy of the human spirit', however, lies in 'its inability to conform its collective life to its individual ideals'.[64] Groups are 'less subject to internal moral restraints. The larger the group the more difficult it is to achieve a common mind and purpose and the more inevitably will it be unified by momentary impulses and immediate and unreflective purposes'.[65] Reason cannot transcend these impulses because it has no impartial perspective from which to view human action, so there are 'elements in man's collective behaviour which belong to the order of nature and can never be brought under the dominion of reason or conscience'.[66] A Niebuhrian interpretation of the commitment to growth sees it as an 'immediate and unreflective purpose' of group behaviour which has achieved the status of codified policy. It is an impulse that originates in part from the instinctual drive to survive, but also in part from a psychological need. Expansionism in the human psyche is, says Niebuhr, a 'note of protest against finiteness'.[67] Self-consciousness 'recognizes the ego as an insignificant point amidst the immensities of the world', is not comforted by this recognition, and rebels against it. This rebellion 'makes the universal character of his imperial dreams inevitable'.[68]

Niebuhr's observations resonate with key features of the growth paradigm. Though it may be debatable whether or not expansionism is a 'note of protest against finiteness', it is certainly true that the notion of continuous growth is grounded somehow in the expectation that no material limits can constrain human behaviour. The full breadth of Niebuhr's argument presents a series of conjectures which are valuable to the present study because, taken together, they serve as a kind of group-psychological profile of the social context of the growth paradigm. As previously mentioned, these conjectures are consistent with, and form a useful backdrop for, the neo-Gramscian approach to international relations which I develop in the next chapter. With this in mind, I elaborate briefly on Niebuhr's analysis.

Niebuhr's consistent theme is that individuals are rational and morally sentient and can therefore, at least potentially, rein in their rooted proclivity to expansionism. His major thesis, however, is that the efficacy of reason and morality diminishes from individual to group, and diminishes further as group size grows larger. This thesis is intuitively appealing, and it has been demonstrated persuasively by, for example, Mancur Olson, that large groups will not act cohesively to achieve their collective best interests, absent coercion or special incentives.[69] The fact of anarchy in international politics also speaks to the relative weakness of the human capacity to self-organize at large numbers, and also (perhaps) to the diminished moral drive to do so. The mind, says Niebuhr, restrains immoral or amoral impulses in individual life, but a collective mind exists only in very inchoate form in large groups. Ethical action requires self-criticism, and self-criticism requires the rational capacity of self-transcendence, but 'the feeble mind of the nation'[70] cannot achieve this higher-order perspective so common impulses are left unexamined, and unrestrained.

Niebuhr does not disallow the liberal contention that people can cooperate and construct institutions under anarchy, some of which have important ethical dimensions, but he does argue that relations between groups will always be predominantly political rather than ethical, because collective minds are ill formed, weak and susceptible to common impulse. Rational or moral appraisals of competing claims will always be slanted by the proportion of power each group brings to bear. As Niebuhr puts it, 'Politics will, to the end of history, be an area where conscience and power meet, where the ethical and coercive factors of human life will interpenetrate and work out their tentative and uneasy compromises'.[71] On this view, then, cooperation between any but the most intimate of social groups will always require a measure of coercion. To the extent that cooperation between groups, or within a single group, requires the exercise of power, that power will reside with a dominant stratum. Inequalities in power relations become the basis of class divisions, and dominance by one class over another leads inexorably to inequalities in social privilege. Inequities of social privilege arise because the group that organizes society, however solicitous or beneficent its intentions may have been, will be inclined to claim an inordinate reward for itself. Even if differentials in rewards are functionally useful (to attract competent people to positions of responsible authority, for example), those rewards will tend to be higher than warranted by services rendered because people 'will always be imaginative enough to enlarge [their] needs beyond minimum requirements and selfish enough to feel the pressure of their needs more than the needs of others';[72] and because 'no impartial [adjudicator] determines the rewards. The men of power who control society grant these perquisites to themselves'.[73]

It may be that Niebuhr's realism overstates the case here, and yet one sees inordinate rewards more and more commonly in the corporate world, which has claimed for itself (or has been granted voluntarily) an increasing share of power over public policy-making, and over the evolutionary path of society as a whole. Indeed, Niebuhr asserts that commercial/industrial society (characterized by its embrace of capitalism) has been ascendant since the fall of feudalism; that economic, not political, military, or religious power has become the most potent coercive force of the modern age; and that moreover 'the creeds and institutions of democracy have never become fully divorced from the special interests of the commercial classes who conceived and developed them. It was their interest to destroy political restraint upon economic activity'.[74] In this latter comment, one sees a reflection of the Cohen and Rogers thesis regarding the untoward relationship between capitalism and democracy, and a similar complaint that economic activity has somehow escaped the political control of the people it is intended to serve.

Niebuhr's socio-psychological contributions to an understanding of growth can be summed as follows. First, individuals everywhere are motivated by self-serving and expansionist material interests. This trait provides the foundation for what has come to be a political expression of it, namely the commitment to economic growth. Second, people are also endowed with the capacity for moral reflection, and can therefore effectively contain or redirect self-serving impulses. This capacity is weaker, however, in groups, and weakest at the aggregate level of human society as a whole. It follows from this that, third, relations within and between groups tend to be uncooperative, riven by the tension between ethics and power. Fourth, those groups with greater power will impose order on others, and in doing so have established the class relations which obtain today, within all societies and, by extension, within human society as a whole. Finally, the greater power is wielded by commercial/industrial classes which have eclipsed political, military and religious sectors, and that (as Cohen and Rogers would add), structurally subordinate those sectors through their private control of capitalist enterprise.

The individual (or, perhaps more appropriately in this case, the group-psychological) level of analysis, clearly offers an incomplete picture of the roots and branches of the growth paradigm, and yet the subliminal stratum unearthed by this perspective begins to reveal, unlike the previous levels already discussed, how values important to individuals can lose their salience, vitality and relevance in the context of group behaviour; indeed, it hints at how those values can be distorted into caricatures as they are diffused through ever-larger populations. Self-regulation among individuals may be ethically informed and effective, but self-regulation for the common good, defined, for instance, with reference to normative criteria of fairness, is weakest at the level of human society as a whole, which is precisely the context in which normative criteria are most important.

Conclusion

Pressures emanating from large-scale socio-economic systems such as capitalism push and pull human society inexorably toward growth. The structure of capitalism generates a kind of path-dependency which tends to lock in the pursuit of short-term material interests, and the competitive nature of international trade and mobile capital constrains actors to endorse growth by making it too costly not to play by the rules of the game. Systemic pressures of this nature provide compelling reasons for the political preference for economic growth. Sovereign states, on the other hand, retain both the right and the responsibility to filter and shape those pressures to the best advantage of their citizenry, which implies that states may not settle upon identical economic policy priorities, instead following demonstrably different developmental trajectories. Variation among national priorities and trajectories is in fact evident, but these differences are uniformly consistent with an overriding commitment to economic expansionism. If sovereignty has not been engulfed entirely by transnational forces which promote and require growth, then state-level reasons for voluntary compliance with the growth consensus must also be taken into account.

States are concerned primarily with policies that work to ensure stability and prosperity at home, and peace abroad. The voluntary pursuit of growth by states may be desirable and useful because many practical political issues related to stability, prosperity and peace can be solved or ameliorated through the benefits engendered by growing national economies, so states may have gravitated individually and collectively toward economic growth irrespective of national differences or exogenous pressures. And, given the short-term efficacy of growth-based policies, it may not be surprising that states would embrace the growth paradigm despite its apparent strategic or normative deficiencies. Moreover, among national policy-makers there is no compelling reason *not* to pursue growth. The expectation of benefits, from military security to national health, is deeply engraved in their collective psyche and no alternative means to those ends is mooted in any national or international forum today. One of the most salient social costs of the global economy – distributional inequities within and between states – is thought to be resolvable by the continued application of neoliberal doctrine, which is premised on a notion of equality of opportunity, if not equality of outcomes, and on more rapid growth. An even more important cost of growth, at least from the vantage of the present study, is its environmental impact, but here too no compelling reason motivates a move away from the commitment. Growth is considered to be a necessary part of the solution to environmental degradation inasmuch as new technologies, clean-up, adaptation, protection and enhancement programmes are all thought to depend on the profitability of growing economies.

Structural pressures by definition suffuse whole systems, shaping the historical circumstances of a given time, and are therefore granted a degree of causal priority (from the systemic point of view), but the state-level demand for sovereignty – for national self-determination – stands opposed to any such exogenous imposition. No state will easily compromise the legally granted and normatively valued principle of freedom of choice. Freedom of choice is also in tension with individual-level factors regarding economic growth. At this level of analysis, speculations from Niebuhrian psychology suggest that the drive to compete, to accumulate, to expand and to exercise the social power derived from the success of those pursuits, are all atavistic impulses built into the human psyche, but few would disagree that biological or psychological propensities can be overridden by personal force of will, so those impulses cannot be determinative. For personal freedom to have any meaning, individual agency must necessarily have the potential to at least partially overcome subliminal predilections. Like state autonomy, even limited individual freedom is an undeniable feature of the political landscape, so it must be granted an influential role in the construction of that landscape. Notwithstanding personal freedom and state autonomy, however, the uniformity of the growth paradigm remains in place. It has evidently coerced or attracted the consent of all major actors in international relations over a period of at least 300 years; it has eroded or bent to its requirements the freedom to choose an alternative developmental path, regardless of the level of social aggregation examined. Choices have been made at both the individual and the state levels to voluntarily comply with paradigmatic axioms.

Marx has said, in paraphrase, that people can construct their own destiny, but only within the constraints of historical circumstance. This observation succinctly captures the tension that subsists within any agent–structure relationship and, indirectly, it reminds us that absolute freedom may be illusory and possibly pathological. Individual behaviour is shaped and constrained by social contexts, including the state, just as state behaviour is limited by the society of states in which it is embedded. These contextual factors constrain but they also enable action, both individual and collective, which might otherwise be unachievable by an independent agent. This observation, which reflects the importance of duty, responsibility and shared endeavours, is hardly new. It does, however, provide the normative referent against which the unconstrained, unlimited conception of economic freedom can be measured. In the next chapter I will begin the construction of a neo-Gramscian narrative that shows how the commitment to economic growth became abstracted from its socio-natural context; how it became dissociated from the political and ecological foundations which would otherwise keep it grounded. In doing so I will emphasize in particular the political expedience of the pursuit of growth, and the moral convenience spawned by an unconstrained conception of economic freedom, which are the two cornerstones of the growth paradigm in international relations.

3 The ideational superstructure of the paradigm

Introduction

A paradigm can be defined in terms of two component parts, namely, discourse and process. The former is its ideational aspect, which legitimates and gives direction to the paradigm. It embodies axiomatic beliefs that express common values, interests and goals, that prescribe appropriate means to realize them, and that, in general, define a domain of normalcy typical of paradigmatic eras. Cox has described this type of historical occurrence as the 'temporary universalization *in thought* of a particular power structure, conceived not as domination but as the necessary order of nature'.[1] The second part of a paradigm is its material component, which in this case is instantiated in the process of economic production. Brought into focus through the lens of critical theory, this element comprises social classes, the social relations of production, and the physical artifacts of production as such. The material component of the paradigm links human society necessarily to the natural world.

The present chapter focuses on the ideational component, because it is a key contention of this study that the core and leading element of the growth paradigm is a collectively held belief in the efficacy of growth, a belief which has remained constant for some 300 years. This ideational theme, or superstructure, joins the growth era into a single historical entity, even though the story of growth and the actors involved have changed over time as progress transformed the physical and political landscape inhabited by human society. The objective of this chapter is to illuminate the genesis and political import of the ideational superstructure of the growth paradigm, and to show how an incremental process of abstraction has disarticulated the superstructure from its social context, and from its material foundations.

As the preceding sentence implies, the ideational superstructure co-exists with a substructure of social relations and material objects. This co-existence – a reflection of the socio-natural continuum – will be explored in more detail in the next section of this chapter but for the moment I note that, because the major part of the paradigm is ideational, and because that component may be characterized as a dominant discourse, it would seem to follow that a form of discourse analysis might be appropriate to the content of this chapter. In fact discourse analysis and neo-Gramscianism overlap in important ways and can be mutually beneficial as compatible modes of inquiry but, as adumbrated in Chapter 1, I prefer the latter for reasons which I describe below.

John Dryzec offers a simple definition of the term: a discourse is 'a shared way of apprehending the world', resting on a set of assumptions, judgments and contentions.[2] Somewhat more helpfully, Jim George defines it as a 'matrix of social practices that gives meaning to the way that people understand themselves and their behaviour. A discourse … generates the categories of meaning by which reality can be understood and explained'.[3] Capitalist discourse, for example, specifies roles, expectations and norms associated with economic behaviour and as such facilitates communication between people, which in turn increases the incentive for others to adopt the discourse as well.[4]

An important feature of discourse is that these social practices and categories of meaning are not value-free. The process of discursive representation is never neutral; it is 'always imbued with the power and authority of the namers and makers of reality – it is always knowledge as power'.[5] The function of discourse analysis is to explore this 'knowledge/power nexus' and to expose the exclusionary practices that privilege one type of knowledge over another, and that actively block critical thought and action. For example, such analysis may emphasize the oppressive nature of a contemporary metanarrative, both dominant and exclusive, at the core of which a secular, rational-scientific individual is confronted by a single, empirically accessible reality. On this view, Western modernism appears as a dominant discourse oriented to the search for instrumental control of the real world, and for material progress within it. The modernist era is contrasted to pre-scientific, pre-Enlightenment traditionalism, grounded in myth and superstition.

Perhaps the most illuminating aspect of discourse theory is its emphasis on productivity. Discourse is said to constitute the identities and interests of actors – it is (re)productive of the things and relations it defines – and it is a major objective of analysis 'to explain how power is constituted and how its premises and givens are replicated at all levels of society'.[6] The replication of discourse through time and social strata creates a 'regime of truth'[7] that identifies those individuals or institutions authorized to speak and to act; it defines the practices that determine the propriety of actions taken by authorized individuals; and it constitutes the public on whose behalf actions are taken, endowing that public with the common sense by which they justify their acquiescence. Discourses are understood to define, and to enable, but this mode of productivity is also selective. It silences and excludes, as Jennifer Milliken notes, 'by limiting and restricting authorities and experts to some groups, but not others, endorsing a certain common sense, but making other modes of categorizing and judging meaningless, impracticable, inadequate or otherwise disqualified'.[8]

This insight is helpful, inasmuch as the growth paradigm may readily be conceived as a regime of truth in which economic and political policy-makers speak authoritatively about the need for growth. And the extent to which growth is accepted by civil society as common sense is easily discernible in everyday vernacular and the mass media, where rapid growth is portrayed as healthy but slow growth is worrisome. Public acceptance is a key characteristic of a dominant discourse, just as it is under conditions of paradigmatic hegemony; indeed, as Steve Smith has observed, '[d]efining common sense is ... the ultimate act of political power'.[9] Against the bedrock of public opinion and the leadership of authoritative policy-makers, alternatives to growth are rendered, as Milliken has said, meaningless, impracticable, inadequate and disqualified.

Notwithstanding the heuristic benefit of these general features of discourse as applied to the growth paradigm, however, poststructuralist discourse theory is ultimately inadequate to the purposes of the present study, not least because of its anthropocentrism. Its field of study is restricted to human constructions, bracketed on one side by the sociological extremity of a rigid overarching discursive structure, and on the other by the individual agent who 'can will anything into existence through an appropriately articulated discourse'.[10] Much is at stake between these extremes but nonetheless this brand of constructivism asserts that the material world itself conveys no meaning, and therefore has no independent role to play in human affairs; instead, people construct the meaning of things, as they construct social realities, using (primarily linguistic) systems of signification. This pushes the constructivist project too far. Of course much of international politics, and human society in general, is socially constructed and therefore changeable – but this approach undervalues the significance of the natural world. The environment is much more than a neutral backdrop waiting to be assigned a meaning; it is the systemic whole by virtue of which social realities may be constructed in the first place. Poststructuralism is unrelentingly anthropocentric, a characteristic that blinds it to a fulsome appreciation of the material precursors to social constructions, and to the real causes which may issue therefrom. Undervaluation of the material world restricts the methodological tools available to poststructuralism to, for the most part, textual analysis. The natural sciences have no role to play here.

Relatedly, a sustained focus on the discursive practices associated with the production of hegemony leads inevitably to the microphysics of social constructions. As Miller and Rose have said in their analysis (and extension) of Foucauldian governmentality, understanding the foundations of hegemonic 'mentalities' requires an examination of

> the little engineers of the human soul, and their mundane knowledges, techniques and procedures – psychologists, psychiatrists, medics, accountants, social workers, factory managers, town planners and others ... it was only because of the work of [these] small figures, with their own aspirations as well as those foisted on them, together with their little instruments, that rule could actually occur.[11]

This is not to say that poststructuralists are uninterested in the strategic codification of power relations which underlies macro-social order, but it does suggest that discursive analyses are more concerned with the mechanical details of *how* questions than with more elusive *why* questions. Uncovering the normative foundations of the growth paradigm requires more emphasis on the latter.

Another problem with discourse analysis is its rejection of metanarrative in principle on the grounds that it carries with it the potential for abusive domination and because, in any event, no metanarrative can gain credence from (nonexistent) foundational knowledge. It should be avoided, therefore, because only closure and the suppression of difference can follow. But this is wrong-headed: metanarrative may be oppressive but there is no a priori reason to suppose that it could not as easily be liberating, or function as a source of guidance, metaphorical or practical. For example, Daniel Deudney (while stopping short of a fully developed narration) points to the thematic importance of 'reconstructing identity in ecologically appropriate ways' with a particular emphasis on identification with place, where place is defined in terms of 'the entire planet as the only natural autonomous bioregion'. Deudney calls this reconstructed identity 'Earth nationalism', and argues that it could pose a challenge to standard conceptions of nationhood, and offer a 'fresh way to conceptualize environmental protection as national security'. At the heart of these speculations is 'a 'green' sensibility [that] can make a strong claim to being the master metaphor for an emerging post-industrial civilization'.[12] The desirability of a master metaphor is refuted by postmodernists who prefer to let a thousand flowers bloom, each reflective of local circumstances. And yet, as just mentioned, no a priori requirement militates against a metanarrative that could overarch and lend coherence to local renditions of it. It may be the case, in fact, that only a narrative with pretence to dominion could develop the breadth and power to take on so formidable an adversary as Western modernism, or the growth paradigm.

The ideational superstructure

Though Marx's body of work is complex and nuanced, certain somewhat simplistic conclusions derived from a Marxist point of view are nonetheless widely held. One such conclusion is that the social can be 'read off' the economic: the structure of the polity, its culture and its most salient public ideas, are secondary to if not entirely derivative of economic conditions. The mode and relations of production, on this view, are the backbone of society, providing it with form and stability. Workers are compelled to submit to managerial authority in a socio-economic context alternatives to which are beyond their perception or contemplation. 'By education, tradition, and habit', writes Marx, '[the working class] looks upon the conditions of [the capitalist mode of production] as a self-evident law of nature'. It is not necessary under these circumstances to forcibly coerce workers who have no choice other than to sell their labour to live. Social stability is maintained by little more than 'the dull compulsion of economic relations'.[13]

Marx's reductive emphasis on the economy and his positivist methodology led him to posit law-like propositions expressing causal connections between the economy and other social phenomena, and to a firm belief in the inevitable collapse of capitalism under the weight of its own inherent contradictions. That this collapse did not in fact occur prompted a reaction against economic reductionism (or economism) by Antonio Gramsci, among many others, which challenged the positivist science of Marxian analyses and emphasized instead the importance of human subjectivity and agency. The effect of this challenge was to shift the debate about capitalism from its material aspect to its socially constructed characteristics; to shift emphasis, in other words, from the base to the superstructure as an alternative explanation for the durability of capitalist systems. This new line of inquiry allowed the possibility that the superstructure was independent of, though not entirely divorced from, the economy – which led directly to the proposition that, if capitalism did not collapse because of its inherent economic tensions, then it may somehow be stabilized by its relatively autonomous superstructure. This proposition came to be known as the dominant ideology thesis according to which 'the coherence of industrial society is to be explained primarily by the *ideological* incorporation of the labour force'.[14] The ruling class, on this view, can supervise the construction of beliefs that are more coherent, and ultimately more cogent, than those of subordinate classes, and this dominant ideology functions to incorporate the lower strata of society into a socio-economic whole even though that structure may work against the material interests of workers.

This proposition substantively revises Marxian doctrine which argued for an ideology that is of secondary importance only. Marx plainly asserted in *The German Ideology* that 'The ideas of the ruling class are in every epoch the ruling ideas',[15] but that fact, for Marx, was little more than an unintended consequence: the class that controls the means of material production coincidentally controls the means by which ideas are generated and propagated through society. Ideas are promulgated in the public domain by a dominant elite as an expression of their particular economic interests, not as a means to capture and control workers' belief systems. Such an intent is unnecessary in light of the coercive nature of capitalist social relations.

The nature and status of this putative ideational superstructure, its genesis and causal implications, are contested issues as this brief synopsis indicates. Moreover, calling upon the *longue durée* of the modern age as a temporal frame, and identifying within it a single ideational theme, represents a significant extension of the neo-Gramscian approach to international relations. Such analyses are more commonly applied to shorter historical episodes, such as the Pax Americana, or they focus on events of the more recent past, such as the emergence of neoliberalism and the discourse of globalization since the economic crises of the 1970s. In contrast, the neo-Gramscian approach applied here aims (among other things) to discover evidence for the existence of a core ideology which has remained consistent over a much longer period of time, beginning approximately at the transition in Europe from medievalism to the modern age. To begin the process of illuminating this hypothesized superstructure, I discuss in the following section the advantages gained by adopting a wide historical perspective.

Temporal frames

The now-common phrase 'economic growth' was not added to the political lexicon until after the Second World War, but the commitment to growth – or to material progress, as it was previously known – has much deeper roots. A full assessment of the entrenched nature of this commitment, then, requires a wide historical lens. I have referred earlier to Braudel's contributions to historical studies through the French *Annales* school, and in particular to his suggestion that temporal frames constitute a useful way of conceptualizing political events. These frames are of three types that correspond approximately to short-, medium- and long-term intervals. I have argued that the growth paradigm represents a single period of epochal time, and that its history, as well as its political and ecological implications, are most clearly apprehended in the context of, and with tools appropriate to, the *longue durée*.

Temporal frames are analytically valuable for three reasons. First, they fit well with Gramsci's perception that social groups, as they move through history, form a succession of (ultimately unstable) configurations. Periodization is therefore a key aspect of Gramscian analysis, where the notion of periods refers to those times during which 'organic' historical movements penetrate deeply into society, and are relatively long-lasting. I characterize the growth paradigm as one such period. Second, each frame brings into focus different sorts of events which tend to dominate particular intervals.[16] For example one might see (short-term) trades on the New York Stock Exchange occurring within a (medium-term) context of American hegemony which, in turn, is a single episode among many instances of state hegemony within the (long-term) modern age. This approach suggests that immediate events (*l'histoire événementielle*) 'can be recorded, but they do not explain themselves. To be explained, they must be understood within their context in time and space'.[17] Braudel's frames (or Gramsci's periods) thus sensitize the analyst to the major features of particular temporal landscapes, and to the need for cross-referencing among them for purposes of explanation. This is of particular importance with respect to the explanation of systemic structural change which involves necessarily the interaction of events at all three levels. Individual action (in most instances, an important contributor to any such change) is perforce constrained to the here and now, but it can affect medium-term events (such as regime changes, or polarity shifts) which cumulatively alter features of the *longue durée*, just as longer epochs will constrain the evolution of micro-events within them. The third advantage is that longer temporal frames help illuminate the ideational dimension of social life. John Ruggie refers to the prevailing configuration of this dimension as a social episteme – a socially constructed entity that is a collective representation of collectively perceived reality; it is, in other words, a 'dimension of social structure'.[18] Applying this observation to one of the very few available examples of systemic transformation, Ruggie notes that 'the demise of the medieval system of rule and the rise of the modern resulted in part from [the fact that] the mental equipment that people drew upon in imagining and symbolizing forms of political community itself underwent fundamental change'.[19] More specifically, Ruggie linked the emergence of the sovereign territorial state (a form of spatial differentiation) to a new image of the natural world (derived from Newtonian mechanics) that portrayed people and things as atomistic units functioning in a field of forces. 'Every civilization', writes Ruggie, 'tends to have its own particular perspective',[20] a social episteme which constitutes the ideational foundation of social practice.

This direction of enquiry has been more recently pursued by Robert Cox, who offers an interpretation of contemporary global pluralism based on the notion of multiple civilizations instead of states. Cox, like Ruggie, emphasizes the importance of belief systems to the character of civilizations. In the past, those beliefs were often expressions of religious doctrine (Judeo-Christian, Islamic or Confucian for example) that 'enabled people encompassed within a civilization to develop a shared consciousness and symbols through which they could communicate meaningfully with one another'.[21] It is significant, however, that neither Ruggie nor Cox emphasized this ideational superstructure at the expense of diminishing the role played by the natural environment. As much as by myth, language and religion, civilizations have been shaped, Cox argues, by the physical foundations of their technologies (stone, copper, bronze, iron, steel, silicon), and by their economic relationship with the land (nomadic, subsistence, urban). Cox joins these two factors in his definition of civilization as 'a fit or correspondence between material conditions of existence and intersubjective meanings'.[22] And similarly at the medieval/modern juncture, Ruggie points to a variety of material factors that contributed significantly to the transformation of European society and the evolution of a new dominant episteme. These included such things as a favourable climate in the early Middle Ages which induced a population spurt, the cultivation of new land, a trend to urbanization, and new technologies of force such as the crossbow, or the feudal castle.

In sum, the benefits of temporal frames, and of the *longue durée* in particular, are threefold: they bring historical context to the foreground, they bring to sharper relief the major ontological features and events typical of the period in question, and they illuminate the ideational superstructure which gives meaning to and defines the prevalent social relationship with those features and events. Gramsci used the term 'historic bloc' (*blocco historico*) to denote distinct eras the features of which penetrated deeply ('organically') into society, and which were long-lasting. Drawing on Braudel as well as Gramsci, Cox similarly refers to 'historical structures', such as the Pax Britannica or the Pax Americana, in his analyses of political change over time. In terms of the present study, however, the relevant historical context is wider still – a single epoch, commonly referred to as modernity, which is congruent with the growth paradigm. Its dominant ideational feature, or social episteme, is a belief in progress and the shared expectation of continuous improvement in material standards of living. This episteme finds its political voice today in the common call for increases in economic growth, nationally and across the world polity as a whole. The following sections trace the historical evolution of the ideational superstructure of the growth paradigm, indicate various points of contention regarding its political import and, most importantly, show how the superstructure came to be disarticulated from its social and material foundations.

Historical evolution of the ideational superstructure, part I

Pre-capitalist and early modern history

'The Enlightenment was a magnificent revolution', said Gramsci. '[I]t gave all Europe a bourgeois spiritual International in the form of a unified consciousness ... In Italy, France and Germany, the same topics, the same institutions and same principles were being discussed'.[23] Among other events, it was this 'magnificent revolution' that separated the feudal and modern eras, and that gave birth to the seminal idea of progress. This word is defined by historian Ronald Wright as 'the assumption that a pattern of change exists in the history of mankind ... [and] that it consists of irreversible changes in one direction only, and that this direction is toward improvement'.[24] This is not to say that human history before the Enlightenment was devoid of achievement. Gothic cathedrals, for example, were significant accomplishments of architecture and engineering; and lesser inventions such as the compass, gunpowder and printing press, among many other things, were also important products of human ingenuity. But, as Ernest Tuveson puts it:

> [N]one [of these various products] was thought of as 'progress' – simply as ingenious contrivances of persons, mostly anonymous, to meet immediate needs.... Lacking was the *idea* of progress; namely, the idea that purposive, concentrated effort ... guided by increasing knowledge of nature, could achieve defined goals of improving 'man's estate' in objectively measurable ways – and that such effort is of great moral, and indeed spiritual value. This idea, along with [democracy] has been the most enduringly influential force in the modern world.[25]

Dissenting voices were heard, but were not compelling enough to derail the forward motion of progress. The Romantic movement in Europe, for example, rejected the emerging universalism of Enlightenment thinking in favour of a preference for subjectivity and uniqueness – and, in some instances, in favour of a return to a mythical Golden Age that preceded industrialization.[26] And Romantics objected as well to a new conceptualization of the world that saw European civilization as 'dynamic, an active agent inspired by the doctrines of Progress', whereas '[n]on-European civilizations were thought of as passive and fixed'.[27] A second strand of reaction against Enlightenment thinking was developed later by Karl Marx in response to the uneven development imposed on society by the burgeoning forces of capitalism – but neither Marx nor the Romantic movement truly rejected progress outright: the latter embraced the benefits of material progress, but lamented the corruption of values that universalism seemed to entail; and Marx objected to the lack of distributive justice, not to progress as such. Notwithstanding these various objections, faith in progress, asserts Wright, soon 'hardened into an ideology – a secular religion'.[28]

There is no easy or definitive way to explain the transformation in public thinking that pushed the notion of material progress to the forefront three centuries ago. Explanations vary according to which among a confluence of historical factors are deemed more important. For example, the Italian Renaissance envisioned the possibility of continuous progress, though mostly with respect to knowledge; the European Enlightenment engendered the pursuit of rational and scientific enquiry, introducing an era of material improvement; the rise of capitalism and the Protestant ethic in the context of a competitive market system spurred the process of capital formation and accumulation, even as new wealth poured into Europe from colonial empires; the Industrial Revolution boosted material productivity with machines and new sources of energy; and the emergence of the state system, with its emphasis on the accumulation of national wealth and power, provided a political context in which the foregoing were given free rein. Collectively, these changes spanned that time in history when medieval feudalism gave way to modernity and a newly emergent market society. Historian A. W. Arndt has remarked that, unlike the feudal economy it displaced, market society called on the everyday habits of individual self-interest to shape the contours of economic life, and looked for the first time to the lure of material progress to impel society forward. '[T]here is no doubt', writes Arndt, 'that it increasingly differentiated Western European society from anything that had gone before [or had] existed elsewhere'.[29] This new role for people in the market was matched by a similar change for governments of the day too. Prior to the transformation to modernity, the abiding tasks of government were, much as they are now, the protection of vital interests against other political systems, the maintenance of order, and the provision of an acceptable standard of welfare defined in the context of contemporary cultural norms. But with respect to this latter task, early rulers were assessed not according to future expectations, but against norms

> drawn from the memory of golden eras of the past when the frontiers were quiet, crops ample, taxes modest, state granaries full [and] the roads free of bandits … the expectation for the society as a whole was that, although it might suffer good times or bad at the whim of harvests, the vicissitudes of war, or the quality of rule, there would not be overall progress.[30]

The emergence of the idea of material progress and its embodiment in a new market society signalled a historic change from this way of thinking.

In medieval society, economics were not a dominant aspect of life. The ultimate authority was the Roman Catholic Church, which taught that economic motives are 'powerful appetites' and that 'like other strong passions, what they need … is not a clear field, but repression'.[31] The Church made it clear that the pursuit of profit for its own sake provoked guilt and endangered the soul, especially regarding usury (lending money at interest), which was declared to be a mortal sin. This opposition to usurious profit did not reflect an esoteric religious belief; it was, instead, a pragmatic response to economic gouging which took place in medieval times during periods of famine or war-caused shortages of staples. Medieval economic organization, with its religious overlay, was conceived as a means to stabilize social relations, to reproduce the material well-being of the past, not to enhance it. Its objective was 'perpetuation, not progress'.[32]

The Great Divide, as sociologists call it, separated feudalism from early capitalism. The traditional forces of myth, religious values and natural law gave way at that time to industrialization, urbanization, secularism and the rationalism of reciprocal exchange in the marketplace. Bureaucratization and the fragmentation of pre-capitalist culture ensued. 'As the world became more rationally intelligible', write Abercrombie et al., 'so it became less meaningful from a moral and religious point of view'.[33] This is not to say, however, that religion lost its import or relevance to the nascent capitalist system, as Weber made abundantly clear in *The Protestant Ethic and the Spirit of Capitalism*.[34] The opposite, in fact, was true. The overarching Catholic worldview dominant during feudalism was challenged by new, powerful contender religions that argued for much more autonomy and responsibility for individuals. The resultant shift in emphasis from society to people did not obliterate religiosity, but rather made it more conducive to the capitalist spirit of economic competition, thereby ensuring a continuing and important role for religion as the ideological backdrop of early capitalism.

The attack on the Catholic Church initiated in the sixteenth century by Protestant reformers Martin Luther and John Calvin shone a new and liberating light on the individual. Protestantism voiced a concern for 'the progressive sanctification of the individual by means of moral improvement [that] created a moral climate of individualistic religiosity and self-improvement which was congruent with [emerging] secular values'.[35] Calvin in particular legitimated the approbation associated with material success. His doctrine of predestination asserted that the salvation or damnation of each human soul was predetermined, and that nothing could be done in this world to change that. Individuals' natural concern about their status in the afterlife led them to look for signs of godly favour on Earth, and this evidence seemed to be clearly provided by relative degrees of material prosperity.[36] It followed that the likelihood of salvation, now linked to the accumulation of wealth, could be improved by a life of rectitude, severity and diligence; that worthiness could be identified with work; that more success meant more worthiness; that wealth was to be put to good use, not squandered; and that investment could be an instrument of piety as well as profit. 'In place of the old ideal of social and economic stability … [the Reformation] brought respectability to an ideal of struggle, of material improvement, of economic growth'.[37]

As previously mentioned, the term 'economic growth' did not come into popular usage until the twentieth century. Prior to that, improvements in individual welfare, public living standards or national wealth were referred to (by classical economists at least) in terms of material progress. But even notions of material progress do not much pre-date the beginning of the eighteenth century. Only by the middle of the eighteenth century had progress become a public expectation, most markedly in England, which led the way in industrial development. Cumulative changes began to become visible in ever shorter periods of time such that improvements in living standards eventually became discernible within the lifetime of an individual. Significantly, this marked the point at which the idea of material progress, now brought within the perceptual horizons of ordinary people, could be regarded as desirable, and realizable. By the latter part of the eighteenth century, Adam Smith had articulated a widening consensus reflective of the hope that 'the progress of England towards opulence and improvement [would be] universal, continual, and uninterrupted'.[38]

England was at the forefront of these epochal changes for a variety of reasons. It was, at the time, the richest nation in the world and it was less polarized socio-economically than other European nations. A large upper-middle stratum of commercial bourgeoisie formed the nucleus of what would become a mass consumer market for the new goods and services generated by the Industrial Revolution. Feudal power had been broken earlier and more effectively than elsewhere by a strong monarchy, which also provided encouragement to mercantilist classes and to a new generation of scientists, engineers and scholars. Of equal importance, the enclosure movement, by which common land was taken over by manorial lords for the production of cash crops instead of feudal subsistence, released an army of dispossessed peasantry into the urban maelstrom of industrial labour.[39]

Though England led the way, similar processes were at work throughout Europe, and all such processes were occurring under the dominion of Enlightenment thinking. This optimistic era 'was animated by the desire to demystify and secularize, to subject natural forces to rational explanation and control, as well as by the expectation that doing so would promote social welfare, moral progress, and human happiness'.[40] The newly emerging market economy embodied all these characteristics. Even if still partially constrained by socio-political controls based in tradition and in state power to command, it was dynamic and expansionist. Geographical expansion was impelled by a persistent quest for less expensive labour and resources, by efficiencies of scale and by growth of demand. Improvements in transportation technologies made it that much easier to bring the non-market periphery inside the expanding market mechanism, and the new ethos of individual competitiveness released and channelled the revolutionary elixir of capitalism: private ownership of the means of production, the drive to accumulate capital, mobile waged labour and the impulse to maximize personal welfare among consumers.

The effects of market society on the ideational superstructure

The evolution of the ideational superstructure of the growth paradigm, and its gradual disarticulation from its material base, began with the emergence of modernity. The modern age, at least in terms of its main philosophical themes, is often said to have originated with René Descartes and his radical bisection of the world into a mind/matter duality in which mental subjects confront material objects. This division established a conducive context for the Newtonian portrayal of the physical world as separate from subjective experience, and as mechanical in nature, the workings of which were accessible by a combination of experimental manipulation and reason. The disenchantment of nature – the rejection of myth, magic and holism in favour of analytical reason and control – was the seminal event in the process of abstraction of ideas from the socio-natural world. Protestantism reinforced that process, and added a moral justification to it by encouraging the liberation of individuals from their social context. No longer beholden to the spiritual supervision of the Roman Catholic Church, many people now saw that '[their] relation to God [could be] conceived as immediate and decisive. This led to a claim to personal autonomy in both secular and religious affairs and restrictions on government interference'.[41] The notion of competitive individualism in a socially permissive context led ultimately to the portrayal of the individual as the rational, utility-maximizing agent of neoclassical economic theory, some two centuries later.

The historic confrontation at the Great Divide between feudal traditionalism and capitalist rationality accentuated the growing gap between economic activity and political and religious oversight. The newly emerging belief propounded by Adam Smith that the economy could be largely self-regulating raised the possibility that public responsibility for social welfare could, and perhaps should be, withdrawn: a belief in the quasi-automatic provision of welfare by an abstract process of market activity was beginning to gain credence. But this new proposal raised a hard question: how could the social stratification that separated rich from poor now be justified? Traditionalism had formerly legitimated the status quo by reference to natural law: the landed aristocracy was naturally privileged with respect to their power, wealth, and property rights, but by the same token was obliged to provide welfare for the poor through (in England) the Poor Laws.[42] How could society move beyond political and religious supervision of the economy, in effect withdraw public responsibility for social welfare, yet still justify and render legitimate the unequal distribution of power and wealth?

Thomas Malthus was among the first to forward an ostensibly scientific basis for the denial of social obligation and the ascendance of individual responsibility by calling upon Darwinian laws of nature. Poverty, he argued, was a consequence of scarcity, scarcity was caused by overpopulation, and overpopulation was the result of a failure among the peasantry to practise sexual abstinence. The Poor Laws removed the incentive to change this pattern of behaviour; their repeal would bring public policy in line with modern laws which science had just begun to reveal.[43] And Malthusian doctrine fit well with new theories of utilitarianism, especially Jeremy Bentham's expostulations regarding the importance of egoism and the individualistic pursuit of self-interest, which emphasized especially the right of limitless appropriation of utility. The primary function of government, on the utilitarian view, was to reconcile divergent interests in society with the general requirement of optimal social utility, expressed in terms of the greatest good for the greatest number, rather than to provide welfare as such.

The philosophical separation of subject from object, and the new preeminence of individual over society, represented revolutionary change in Europe but another more mundane and more deeply pervasive change – the monetization of economic life – also helped to usher in the market society, and to contribute to the evolution and abstraction of the ideational superstructure. For buying and selling to exist in a market society, every task (with notable exceptions such as slave and household labour) must generate monetary reward: everyone must have cash. Some 60 to 70 percent of the working population in medieval times laboured without monetary payment,[44] but increasing trade and commercialization brought about the necessary changes. In particular, the rapid development of town life and a new merchant class spurred the process of monetization of economic transactions, a process that tended to spread outward from cities in concentric circles, gradually encompassing more and more of rural society. 'By the 16th and 17th centuries', writes Heilbroner, 'cash and transactions were already beginning to provide the very molecular force of social cohesion'.[45] The monetization of social relations contributed to the disembedding of economy from society because it allowed the separation of use value (value derived from the actual use of real goods and services) from the abstract symbology of exchange value, measured by money, and it opened the door to the theoretical possibility of unlimited accumulation of wealth. Monetization set the stage for a new way of thinking about wealth which, until then, had been limited by natural tendencies to spoil or decay. Money is merely symbolic, and abstract, and that which is abstract need not be constrained by natural limits; it can be summed indefinitely.[46]

Karl Polanyi clearly identified the historical point in time at which money and markets came to dominate the gestalt of social relations: it occurred with the commodification of land, labour and capital. He emphasized that, with this change, the market had come to depend on a contrivance – an abstraction – because land, labour and capital, their commodification notwithstanding, 'are obviously *not* commodities; the postulate that anything that is bought and sold must have been produced for sale is emphatically untrue in regard to them'.[47] Labour, Polanyi argued, cannot be separated from the lives and living conditions of individual people, and land is just another name for the natural environment. Capital is a broad term that includes money as well as productive plant such as warehouses and factories; but more generally still, capital may be construed as the set of durable artifacts of society which collectively form the patrimonial heritage bequeathed to future generations. This broader definition includes both the built and the natural environments. Like productive plant, however, this patrimony is also vulnerable to shortages and surfeits of investment flows, and may not survive the vicissitudes of business. Polanyi objected vigorously to all this. 'Undoubtedly', he writes,

> labor, land and money *are* essential to a market economy, but no society could stand the effects of such a system of crude fictions ... unless its human and natural substance as well as its business organization was protected against the ravages of this satanic mill.[48]

For Polanyi, the commodification of labour was particularly egregious because 'labor is only another word for the forms of life of the common people', and therefore the development of the market system was accompanied by 'a change in the organization of society itself. All along the line, human society had become an accessory of the economic system'.[49] Monetization obliged people to follow their own economic self-interest and '[t]hus the pattern of economic maximization was generalized throughout society and given an inherent urgency which made it a powerful force for shaping human behaviour'.[50] Transactions became universal activities; the upkeep and well-being of people came to depend on the price at which bargains were concluded. Nature, work and patrimony had been commercialized into land, labour and capital, anthropomorphized into landlords, labourers and capitalists, and finally abstracted into the symbolic ephemera of rents, wages and profits. The evolution of the growth paradigm and its continuing disengagement from material realities were continuing apace.

The effects of economic science on the ideational superstructure

The emergence of a market society in Europe was not the work of professional planners, nor was it shaped predominantly by economic theory. The transition from medievalism to the modern age was the result of a complex convergence of events, some fortuitous, such as the Industrial Revolution, others contrived, such as the forcible dislocation of landed peasantry from their agricultural heritage. But these profound changes did attract the sustained attention of economic scholars of the time. Classical economists of the eighteenth and nineteenth centuries were drawn to their fields of inquiry by the obvious and profound changes through which their generations were passing. Economies were growing rapidly and, without exception, the desirability of material progress was taken by them as given. Their focus, therefore, was not on why growth occurred; instead they sought to understand how it occurred, and to determine whether or not any constraints might surface which would modify, hinder or stop the processes of growth.

For Adam Smith, growth was sustained by population increase and the territorial expansion of the British Empire, both of which stimulated demand and therefore production. A larger market, Smith argued, was conducive to the division of labour, which promoted specialization, leading in turn to the enhancement of skills and the invention of new tools and procedures. Resultant improvements in productivity allowed for the accumulation of capital and the reinvestment of that capital in new plant, more workers, and ultimately a still-larger market. As Thomas Malthus had argued, however, and as Smith was aware, a growing population pressing upon a fixed supply of land could be problematic. Apart from relying on territorial expansion, Smith did not pursue this issue much beyond the observation that a nation is best off and most progressive when there is still a gap between population and the maximum number that land can support. David Ricardo sharpened the sense of conflict between population and resources by developing his theory of diminishing returns in the use of land. It is not necessary to rehearse the formalities of his argument here, except to note that a growing population, forced onto increasingly marginal land, would eventually squeeze industrial profits to zero.[51] To avoid this outcome, Ricardo identified and emphasized two other sources of growth: technical innovation, and international trade. He is best known for his contribution to the latter; his theory of comparative advantage in trade between nations is a staple of contemporary economic thinking.

Smith wrote on the eve of the Industrial Revolution; John Stuart Mill wrote 75 years later and brought the era of the classical economists to a close. All of them were interested in the new and dynamic growth which enveloped Europe, and each sought to look ahead to what might be the end of growth. Malthus was particularly (and in many respects falsely) pessimistic about the prospects of indefinite expansion. Smith and Ricardo tried to forestall an end to growth by identifying conditions that could sustain it. Marx argued that growth could only continue if the contradictions of capitalism could be resolved through a proletariat insurgency. Only Mill embraced the likelihood of a post-growth stationary state, arguing that less frenetic forward motion in society would open the possibility of improvements in institutions, public education and human affairs generally.

Mill's *Principles of Political Economy* brought together the work that preceded him, and offered the definitive (classical) statement regarding growth. He formalized and elaborated the argument that increases in production depended upon the properties of land, labour and capital; that these elements could be quantitatively increased, or qualitatively improved such that the contribution of each was enhanced. But he also argued that there is an inherent tendency for growth to cease as factors of production meet diminishing returns. 'It must always have been seen', he wrote, 'that the increase in wealth is not boundless: that at the end of … the progressive state lies the stationary state, that all progress in wealth is but a postponement of this, and that each step in advance is an approach to it'.[52] Uniquely, Mill was not fearful of the stationary state, arguing that it would open the way to intellectual, social and moral improvement.

After Mill, the question of how growth occurred slipped off the agenda of most political economists. This was so simply because growth was proceeding apace, and unproblematically, in Britain, in continental Europe, and in the United States. As Abramovitz puts it, '[e]ven the dismal science learned to smile; it absorbed the century's wider faith in unbounded progress'.[53] Economists could ignore growth because it had become a fixed part of the intellectual landscape. It was normal, therefore uninteresting, so they focused instead on, for example, the sources of periodic fluctuations in economies, the causes of and remedies for unemployment, and problems of resource and wealth distribution. Growth did not reappear as an item of scholarly and political interest until the 1930s. The world's centre of political gravity had by then shifted from Europe to the United States, but the American economy had slipped into the Great Depression. Under the circumstances, proactive economic initiatives were clearly required to stimulate the processes of growth. Shortly thereafter, the onset of the Second World War impelled increased industrial production for military hardware, which added to the revived interest in growth. I elaborate on these more recent political themes in the next section of this chapter.

During the long hiatus from, approximately, Mill to the Second World War, the discipline of economics itself underwent a radical transformation, from the classical to a neoclassical phase. The change to the neoclassical mode was the result of an explicit decision to raise economics to the status of the physical sciences. '[T]he pioneers of the new economics in the late 19th century', writes one economic historian, 'adopted the then dominant view of the harder sciences, which saw the world as a smoothly functioning machine'.[54] Apart from simple calculations, classical economists had not referred to or relied on mathematics to generate and test hypotheses, but as another writer notes '[t]he decision to follow physics was the decision to mathematize. Mathematics can work only with what can be formalized. In economics, this has meant, in practice, what can be measured'.[55] The new objective of neoclassical economics was neither to explain growth nor to rectify social issues such as unemployment, but to resolve analytically and in quantifiable terms the issue of how to achieve the best possible utilization of given resources; its focus, in other words, was on allocative effectiveness and efficiency. This shift in thinking was called the marginal revolution.

Neoclassical economics was originally called marginalism because it emphasized incremental changes to economic variables, especially the effect of price changes on quantities of goods demanded by consumers and supplied by producers. The role of the price system in allocating goods to their highest value uses became the most important concept of neoclassical economics; prices were pushed to the top of the hierarchy of variables. Adopting this new approach to the quantification of economic behaviour, earlier conjectures from the classical era were reconstructed within a positivist framework. For example, Smith's hypothesis that free markets, in which everyone followed his or her own self-interest, would lead to outcomes beneficial to all, was translated into mathematical formulas. His conclusions were verified and given the imprimatur of science. The apparent explanatory and even predictive utility of marginal economics was quickly recognized as a formidable intellectual achievement. Its model of competitive general equilibrium,[56] and its appeal to a harmony of interests and balanced forces, were consonant with the Newtonian spirit of the time. It demonstrated mathematically the allocative efficiency of a (pure) market system, which provided the warrant for minimal government regulation and lower taxes, and which suited as well the Victorian philosophy of self-help and self-reliance. It set the theoretical stage, in short, for the arrival much later of neoliberal capitalism.

The transition from classical to neoclassical economics added impetus to the process of abstraction of economic activity from social community and socio-natural interdependencies. That process included, as previously discussed, the monetization of market relations and the commodification of factors of production, but it took firm hold with the pivotal decision to make the discipline of economics deductively rigorous and timelessly mathematical, instead of contingent and socio-historical. Several consequences followed from this, not least of which was a tendency to shift issues of economic management from policy-makers to an elite stratum of economic specialists whose technical analyses were now beyond the comprehension of non-experts.

More specifically, however, modernized economics – characteristically materialistic in its orientation to possession and consumption – paradoxically became more idealistic, especially in its treatment of land as a factor of production. Cartesian dualism had already provided a philosophical distinction between subject (humans) and object (everything else) and on that basis, on the classical view, land had been objectified – it was seen as passive, unproductive and without economic value until acted upon by people's labour. John Locke's conclusion that value is a function of expended labour was further developed by Ricardo, and was later radically reinterpreted by Marx as the proper foundation and most important characteristic of Communist society; but neoclassical economists rejected the labour theory of value, and repudiated Marxism. Its quest for formal explanations for economic behaviour supported the more abstract conclusion that subjective individual preferences could be aggregated through market transactions, and that prices for goods and services, which reflected their true market value, could be established automatically and independently of labour.

Neoclassical economics idealized Locke's observation that land was nothing more than a passive factor of production but, although Locke's opinion was dominant at the time, his was not the only one. Indeed, earlier and richer interpretations of land understood it to be the physical basis for human existence. The term land was merely a convenient identifier during the classical era for the broader reality of nature which also included the oceans, atmosphere, solar radiation, and all forms of non-human life. Land was the preferred shorthand simply because of the predominance of agriculture in European economies of that era. Both Adam Smith and John Stuart Mill, as well as the French physiocrats, took the more commodious view that land was neither passive nor inert, that it was productive in its own right, and that it embodied powers (such as water in motion) which could substitute for human labour. As indicated, however, neoclassical theory followed mathematics, not society: it disengaged itself from the alternate stream of thought that attached value and productive importance to (what today would be referred to as) natural capital.

The conception of land as nothing more than the part of nature that has economic significance – that has value to people – entailed a redefinition of land as property, but as such it became only one form of capital among others. If capital is defined as a good that endures and yields an income, then land is a form of capital and a theory that includes a treatment of capital is sufficient, and no separate consideration of land is necessary. Indeed, as Daly and Cobb note,

> [neoclassical] economists want as far as possible to abstract from the physically differentiated character of the commodities they treat. The preferred idea has been that, while fertility of the soil varies and mines vary in the richness of their ores, all [capital] is potentially useful, given the right technology.[57]

The forces of nature as such have disappeared from this theory so that '[t]he goal of increasing capital can proceed without attention to what is physically happening to the land'.[58]

Now floating free from material constraint, neoclassical theory did not impose any numerical upper limit on national economic growth,[59] or by extension on gross world product, and present-day annual growth projections offered by the World Bank and the OECD, among other organizations concerned with macroeconomic management and long-term trends, rely upon this theoretical licence. GNP, in fact, is unique among economic variables in its capacity to grow forever. Herman Daly calls on the differences between micro- and macroeconomic theory to explain this curious anomaly.[60] GNP is a macroeconomic indicator that conflates costs and benefits into a single category of economic activity, Daly points out. In contrast, microeconomic calculations (at the level of the firm, for example) are based on a clear division of costs from benefits. The point at which increasing marginal cost (MC) equals declining marginal benefit (MB) defines the optimal scale of microeconomic activity beyond which growth (of a firm's output) would be uneconomic. Daly notes that '[q]uite aptly, the MB=MC condition is sometimes called the "when to stop rule"'.[61] No such rule obtains at the aggregate level of national or global economic activity, however, because

> microeconomics deals with the part, and expansion of a part is limited by the opportunity cost inflicted on the rest of the whole. In a finite whole, growth of one part encroaches on other parts, imposing an opportunity cost. Macroeconomics deals with the whole, and the growth of the whole does not inflict an opportunity cost, because it does not encroach on anything – there is no 'rest of the whole' to suffer the cost.[62]

Modern-day ecological economists counter this abstraction by pointing out that there is in fact a larger whole on which global economic activity impinges, namely, Earth's ecosystem, and that, therefore, opportunity costs are indeed imposed, the measurement of which would be improved by a clearer distinction between costs and benefits in macroeconomic calculations. Conflating both under a generic category of economic activity uncritically assumes that activity is beneficial when, given considerations of negative environmental impact, it may not be. As with microeconomic calculations, there is no a priori reason why benefits must exceed costs in macroeconomics either. If the latter dominate even as GNP rises, then the resultant condition is one of uneconomic growth.

Neoclassical theory, however, was not originally intended to account for the causes or processes of economic growth, and this shortcoming was not attended to until the 1950s. At its inception (that is, straddling the turn of the century) and under the guidance of theoreticians such as Alfred Marshall, Léon Walras, William Jevons and Carl Menger (Walras and Jevons both originally trained as physicists), the theory reflected the intellectual posture of the time, taking growth for granted and not inquiring into its social, political, demographic or technical roots. In effect, social structure, institutions, population changes and technological innovation were all treated by neoclassical theory as exogenous variables, or

> autonomous data [that formed] the constraints and conditions to which prices and resource allocation adjusted. But the causes of their changes were not subjects for economists to investigate, and their implications were mainly neglected. Neoclassical theory ... imposed boundaries on economics ... it left growth outside its borders.[63]

The underlying assumption regarding growth was that it varied with enlargement of the labour force, and with greater output by labour due to the more widespread use of capital such as industrial machinery. This latter supposition, however, was tested in the mid-1950s by Robert Solow, who discovered that only a small percentage of new growth could be attributed to the increased use of capital. He surmised that the unaccounted remainder – around 80 per cent, it was subsequently referred to as the 'Solow residual' – was caused by streamlined production processes and technological improvements to machinery, that is, by qualitative rather than quantitative changes.[64] This in turn raised the question of whether and to what extent innovative ideas, embodied in those new processes and technologies, might be construed as an independent factor of production supporting economic growth. This novel hypothesis, if true, could help explain a puzzle first encountered by the classical economists, namely, why long-run growth increased so persistently over time despite the well-known problem of diminishing returns to factors of production.

As indicated above, neoclassical models did not explain growth, and they assumed that the long-run rate of growth is determined exogenously. 'New growth theory', developed primarily in the United States during the 1980s and 1990s, took the contrary view that innovative ideas can arise from within economies, and can subsequently be applied to existing processes and technologies in order to improve their productivity. Because this approach sought to bring the causes of growth within the parameters of its economic model, it is often referred to as 'endogenous growth theory'. It links growth to a faster pace of innovation and more investment in human capital, and it affords a central role to knowledge as a critical motive force in a growing economy.

In a detailed examination of the tensions that persist between conventional neoclassical growth and endogenous growth theories, Thomas Homer-Dixon notes[65] that the former seeks to subsume the role played by ideas under the broader category of human capital, which can be improved through investment in, among other things, education and training. Drawing on work by Stanford economist Paul Romer, however, Homer-Dixon observes that, while human capital and ideas are mutually reinforcing, they are also distinct in important ways. For example, ideas are non-rival – their use by one person does not reduce their availability for use by others – whereas the availability of individual people is limited by their physical capacity to participate in events. Relatedly, ideas are more durable than human capital because people expire, but ideas live on in the form of, perhaps, principles of engineering, patented designs or codes of conduct. While some of those ideas may be excludable in the sense that their use is constrained by intellectual property rights, many others spill into the public domain where they can be retrieved by other economic actors, which increases their ability to innovate. This virtuous circle of improved growth from within the economy evidently supports the notion that 'ideas are a factor of production unlike labor and capital, because they actually exhibit *increasing* returns; in other words, the economic benefits derived from investment in the production of useful ideas do not decline over time'.[66] This helps explain why, given constant labour and capital, there are not necessarily declining returns on capital investment.

If this analysis by endogenous growth theorists is correct, then, as Homer-Dixon points out, '[i]deas, in and of themselves … have the power to produce economic growth'.[67] From the classical reduction of land to a commodified property-relation, and from the neoclassical insistence on the substitutability of various forms of capital (including human for natural capital), endogenous growth theory pushes the abstraction of economy from society, and from its socio-natural foundations, further still. But Homer-Dixon's broader analysis of the role of ideas (or 'ingenuity' in his more nuanced terminology) in society and economy shows clearly that technical innovation, which is most pertinent to economic growth, is contingent on the prior exercise of social ingenuity, by which economic and political institutions and processes are constructed: these are the infrastructural elements without which the potential for technical progress would be severely constrained. And, moreover, the full range of publicly provided market supports, from education systems to judicial institutions, would not be available without government involvement in socio-economic affairs, yet government is ignored in the neoclassical/endogenous models as an important determinant of growth. 'If economic institutions are key, then so is government', writes Homer-Dixon, 'and if government is key, then so are all the political and social forces that shape how government works'. The 'neat, clean, and quantifiable analyses of the roles of capital and labor in economic growth' must be abandoned for the 'murky and analytically intractable world of government and politics'.[68] I endorse this conclusion, which serves notice that economic reasoning must break out of the narrow mathematical confines of neoclassical/endogenous theory, and move instead to the domain of socio-political relations where issues of economic development properly reside. His conclusions also support the position that the abstraction of ideas from their social foundations, like the abstraction of the economy itself from its socio-natural foundations, will inevitably encounter contradictions that imply the need for a rearticulation, and reharmonization of the ideational and material components of human society.

The remorseless logic of mathematics had been intended to rescue economics from the often complex and dense prose of the classical economists, and Adam Smith's work, perhaps, suffered more than others' by this transformation. It is well known that Smith offered a cogent analysis of the social benefits of enlightened self-interest, but he also argued that self-interest was most effectively pursued when a shared understanding of what constitutes reasonable behaviour provided a context for it. He did not neglect the role of the state, or the need for instruments of social justice, including means to improve the quality of life of the labouring poor through the provision of, for example, educational services; nor did he disavow the need for public policy to deal with, for example, monopoly power. Though given new credence by neoclassical theory, the richness and complexity of Smith's original work was lost. The importance of the institutional framework and set of moral values within which markets operate was denied, and explorations into reasons why some nations were rich and others poor (the original objective of Smith's work) were forgotten.

Smith's better-known *The Wealth of Nations* (1776) was preceded by his *The Theory of Moral Sentiments* (1759). He argued consistently through both works that people were naturally inclined toward society and that a desire to obtain approval, and to be worthy of that approval, engendered self-control and restraint. Smith's economics are remembered insofar as they call upon individual self-interest but his moral framework has been lost in the arcane mathematics of neoclassical economic theory. Notwithstanding these concerns, however, the continuing appeal of neoclassical formalism derives from the fact that Western market economies are, evidently, the most successful form of economic organization yet invented. Neoliberal capitalism delivers the goods, at least in the short term, and holds out the promise of benefiting those who remain poor or disadvantaged. It is this performance, and this promise of a better future, that sustains the intellectual dominance of the model.

Historical evolution of the ideational superstructure, part II

Modern political history

As indicated in the previous section, neoclassical economics helped open the door to, but did not itself promote, growth. The modern interest in growth, after 70 years of neglect by theoreticians and policy-makers, came from a renewed sensitivity in international relations about the need to support national security through wealth creation, and from the heightened need for political answers to a host of other problems which followed in the wake of the Second World War. In the international context the outbreak of the Korean War gave early impetus to military industrial production, but it was the Soviet challenge in a Cold War setting that pushed growth forward as a security objective. In a 1953 *Foreign Affairs* article, P. D. Wiles wrote, 'in a long cold war the rate of growth is the most important thing, for in the end the country that grows most gets biggest'.[69] And in 1956, Khrushchev boasted that '[our] high rate of development of social production [will] enable us ... to catch up and surpass the most developed capitalist countries in per capita output'.[70] The condensed history of economic growth in the post-the Second World War era which follows draws primarily on an especially lucid account by H. W. Arndt.[71]

In 1957, the successful launch of Sputnik shocked the American administration. Soviet accomplishments were immediately connected with their exceptionally high growth rates which, at the time, were twice as high as the American GNP increases.[72] The same event prompted Britain, whose relative power was being surpassed by France and Germany, to look at growth in strategic terms. Because of this international rivalry, 'In the 1950s momentous political importance came increasingly to be attached to ... comparisons of growth rates', and nowhere was this more apparent than in the 'great GNP race' between the United States and the Soviet Union.[73] Abramovitz sums this up succinctly: 'The rivalry between the U.S.S.R. and the United States made each country anxious to prove that its system was capable of producing ever higher material conditions and was therefore worthy of emulation, friendship or even alliance'. And, in the larger international context, '[m]ore than ever before, nations viewed their security and power as resting on an economic base. To ensure their independence, they concluded they must grow; if ahead, stay ahead; if behind, catch up'.[74]

A long list of new challenges also faced many countries after the Second World War, including starting national reconstruction projects in Western Europe, avoiding economic depression in the United States and elsewhere, as had happened after the First World War, minimizing involuntary unemployment, dealing with economic stagnation in the Third World, and coping with the radically altered landscape of international relations. Indeed, after the Second World War,

> [Americans and others] began to meld a variety of endeavours – concerns with material well-being, economic stability, reducing inequity within and between nations, and even world peace – into a single fixation. To some extent, economic growth [intersected] each of these separate concerns, hence its binding nature.[75]

In keeping with neoclassical economics, explaining and enhancing the processes of growth required in the first instance a numerical indicator to measure its forward motion. GNP was that newly developed indicator. The American Commerce Department first began reporting national product statistics in 1934, as part of a larger political commitment to understand and repair the damage done by the Great Depression. National accounts were further shaped and revised during the Second World War, in response to the need to know by how much defence production could be increased, and how that would affect the economy as a whole.

Productivity had not been encouraged during the depressed 1930s because increased output per unit of labour would exacerbate unemployment, but in the 1940s and 1950s, productivity became the new watchword of economic policy. The newly established Organization for European Economic Cooperation (OEEC) created a European Productivity Agency, which began to publish a *Productivity Measurement Review* in 1955 in which the emphasis was on increased output; but even so a shift toward growth in absolute terms and independently of productivity gains had begun to occur. In part, this change had been stimulated by the UN Economic Commission for Europe which published its first *Economic Survey of Europe* in 1949. This survey noted that rapid recoveries in Japan and Germany were threatening to induce an international struggle for new markets and that, under conditions of stagnation, this threat could be serious. Under conditions of sustained growth in world production and trade, on the other hand, competition could be good for all. This invocation of classical arguments (developed by Ricardo in particular) signalled a shift in thinking which was picked up by economists, but not yet by policy-makers. Indeed, the UN *Survey* also deplored 'a certain tendency in Western Europe to regard present economic programs as a non-recurrent and exceptional effort, rather than as an initial and integral part of a continued economic growth over a longer period'. This problem was contrasted with other regions where 'rapid economic growth is expected. In the Soviet Union, for example, the aim is to treble output within about twenty years'.[76]

In the United States, Nelson and Laurence Rockefeller commissioned, in 1958, a panel of eminent citizens to prepare a report on 'The Challenge of the Future'. What the panel produced was called *The Key Importance of Growth to Achieve National Goals*, in which economic growth began to emerge as a remedy for the continuous pressure of competing claims on national income. More rapid growth seemed to be the only way to meet the demands of defence spending, constructing public infrastructure and utilities, and increasing social expenditures on education and health care. In addition, growth seemed to provide an answer for all major ailments of Western economies, including balance-of-payments problems, dollar shortages, unemployment, poverty at home and underdevelopment abroad. As a US Congressional committee noted at the time,

> [t]he critical need for economic growth is found in the tasks placed upon the nation, both foreign and domestic … [a] high rate of economic growth is essential if … public responsibilities are to be discharged without limiting the advance in living standards effected though individual efforts.[77]

This latter caveat had been presaged in 1952 by British economist R. F. Harrod, who had optimistically opined that '[w]e should think in terms of raising the real standard of living by … 50 or 100 percent in a generation'.[78] Notably, however, this new attention to living standards only took root after the more immediate and urgent economic consequences of the Second World War had been overcome. It was a residual objective of economic policy, to be attended as circumstances allowed.

New public responsibilities – new 'tasks placed upon the nation' – were of course not exclusive to the United States. C. A. R. Crosland, economist and British cabinet minister, observed in 1956 that economic growth had begun to occupy 'an exalted position in the hierarchy of goals of government policy, both in the United States and abroad, both in advanced and in less developed countries, both in centrally controlled and decentralized economies'.[79] He went on to note that states as diverse as the United States and the United Kingdom, the Soviet Union, Yugoslavia, India, Sweden, France and Japan had all established targeted growth rates for the 1960s which, he surmised, indicated dissatisfaction with past performance, and a political expectation that more was required.

In order to meet the rising expectations of claimants to national wealth the United States, in 1961, joined 19 other OECD countries in an agreement to aim at '50 percent growth of collective real GNP during the decade of the 1960s'.[80] Economic growth had figured heavily in the 1960 Kennedy/Nixon election campaign, and the agreement just mentioned fit well with Kennedy's 'New Frontier' platform, and with the newly invigorated American tradition of expansion. In 1960, however, unemployment had also resurfaced as an issue in the United States and Western Europe, with populations rising, more women entering the workforce, and new technologies streamlining industrial production. A UN *World Economic Survey for 1960* observed that

> [w]hat is required is not merely to maintain a high level of output but to sustain a steady rate of growth that is adequate to absorb each year's new entrants into the labour force as well as the manpower released by advancing technology and rising productivity.[81]

It seemed clear at the time that long-term planning and a more active role by government would engender the rationality and continuity sought by business, industry and investors. In the prevalent climate of the 1960s, most European countries moved toward a more purposeful control of economic growth. This temper was also shared by the OEEC which, in December 1960, changed its name to the Organization for Economic Cooperation and Development (OECD). This change signalled its shift from, essentially, an organization for the administration of Marshall Plan aid to an influential policy forum for developed market economies. The focus on economic development, reflected in its new name, identified the OECD not only as a policy forum but also as a club of donor countries who believed that planned growth would benefit less developed countries (LDCs) by ensuring the continuous expansion of world trade. In order to better finance this expansionary agenda, the newly constituted organization pledged, as mentioned above, to achieve a 50 per cent increase in real GNP for its 20 member countries, from 1960 to 1970.

This penchant for planning and shaping the world's economy, however, was soon to meet its nemesis. Under the tutelage of Milton Friedman, the Chicago

School of Economics developed (during the post-war period) the new intellectual and ideological foundations for a neoliberal ethos that stressed the virtues of a free market, unhindered by government intervention.[82] By the late 1970s and early 1980s, the British Conservative government of Margaret Thatcher and the American Republican administration of Ronald Reagan had both embraced this ethos, which entailed a new agenda that marked the end of the Keynesian era. Deregulating business activity, reducing public expenditures on social programmes, privatizing public assets and adopting monetarist economic targets (by which money supply was manipulated in accordance with growth indicators) were all characteristics of a new ideological regime which holds sway to the present time. I will return to an examination of the neoliberal era in a more explicitly neo-Gramscian context in Chapter 4. For the present I note that, in the foregoing discussion of modern political history, the shared commitment to growth was largely keyed to practical matters, without an explicit recourse by policy-makers to the notion of a dominant ideology; without recourse, in other words, to the ideational domain. In contrast, I have contended that the role played by the ideational superstructure is of central importance. I advance this theme below.

Discovering the superstructure in history

Sociologists Abercrombie, Hill and Turner, like many political scientists, are interested in better understanding what makes societies stable. In particular, they want to know why, given the centrifugal forces inherent to capitalist societies, the latter have remained relatively robust and well integrated through many generations. To answer this question they have undertaken historical research to determine whether capitalist stability could be attributed to an ideological superstructure, or, if not, then what stabilizing influences might be at work. Their survey encompasses the feudal era, as well as early capitalism, 1780–1880 CE; and late capitalism, post-the Second World War, but exclusive of the neoliberal revolution dating from the Thatcher-Reagan era in Anglo-American politics, which occurred after their publication date. Their conclusion is bluntly stated: the ideological incorporation of subordinate classes is a thesis that is 'empirically false and theoretically unwarranted'.[83] Available evidence does not support the existence of superstructural influence in any of the three eras examined, and, moreover, tangible economic and political factors together suffice to explain the stable evolution of capitalism without recourse to the domain of ideas. Their argument is briefly summarized in the following paragraphs.

The dominant ideology of pre-capitalist Europe was Christianity. Religious institutions and beliefs controlled the ideational landscape but, according to Abercrombie et al., lords were separated from peasants by language, culture, and morality, and the apparatus of transmission for public ideas was weak. Catholicism integrated and unified the dominant class, but the peasantry existed outside of cultured circles. Domination over them was secured not by ideology, but by economic and political exploitation by landowners. Firm control over legal titles to land, over conditions of tenancy, over all the means of production (such as water systems and mills) and ultimately over military force ensured social stability, Christianity notwithstanding.

A prominent ideology of the subsequent era, early capitalism, was called philosophic radicalism,[84] which was grounded in the reformed interpretation of individual responsibility and the newly expressed precepts of utilitarianism. It supported the entrenched rights and privileges of the landed aristocracy, and of the new entrepreneurs who shared many of their interests; and it encouraged among the lower classes a workable compromise between individual improvement, on one hand, and a deference to authority, respect for hierarchy and an attitude of submissiveness (all characteristics of Protestantism) on the other. As with Catholicism, however, the impact of philosophic radicalism beyond the ruling classes was limited by the lack of institutions for mass education, by the absence of mass media, by minimal adult literacy and by low rates of social interaction between bourgeoisie and proletariat beyond the workplace. Rather than the widespread normative acceptance of (or ideological indoctrination by) a dominant belief system, Abercrombie et al. point to 'a realistic appreciation of the strength of the existing order',[85] as the feature of early capitalism that built and maintained social stability. Coercion, not ideology, was the bedrock of stability in the early capitalist era too.

By late (post the Second World War) capitalism, the private, family-centred economy had been displaced by the concentration of industrial and commercial ownership in the hands of large corporations, pension funds, insurance companies and the state. In this era, the transmission apparatus for the dissemination of a potentially dominant ideology was at last in place – but the previous, more or less coherent, ideology of philosophic radicalism no longer existed: it had been fractured into a number of separate components, each of which attracted support from a distinct social sector. A widespread public belief in liberal democratic rights of citizenship, in equality, and in the need to prevent the emergence of a dominant class, for example, stood opposed to state activity that promoted the process of capital accumulation, which benefited groups that represent capital. And, different fractions of capital responded differently to different elements of dominant belief systems: large corporations tended to support the post-the Second World War welfare compromise, for example, because it socialized the costs of providing a high-quality labour force, but small business was less inclined to support state intervention, or public policies that encouraged the concentration of capital, the strengthening of unions or that otherwise increased the costs of doing business. Nor were workers 'incorporated' by any coherent belief system despite easy and widespread access to the mass media, and other mechanisms of information dissemination. As discussed in Chapter 2, the increase in the sum total of wealth and consequent improved standards of living, plus the limited success of piecemeal reform under democracy regarding workers' rights, do not necessarily add up to a normative acceptance of capitalism. Consent or acquiescence among workers is more likely the result of an asymmetric power relationship between a subordinate class and an overwhelming adversary. It is, once again, Marx's 'dull compulsion of economic relations' that structures and stabilizes society, on this view, not an ideological superstructure.

The strengths and tactical advantages exercised by the capitalist order, from feudalism through to the modern age, and the pragmatic acquiescence in that order by workers, are foreground conditions which clearly help to explain social stability – but unexamined background features of society also contribute significantly to that stability. As Abercrombie et al. suggest, the taken-for-granted imperatives of daily life impose a 'massive and constraining quality [that] resists change or challenge', and they attribute the 'coercive quality of everyday life and of the routines that sustain it'[86] to functional or instrumental conditions which apply irrespective of whether or not common values are shared among participants in the economic system. Gramscian analysis, however, illuminates the ethical underpinnings of society and the normative conditions that serve to legitimate the coercive aspects of socio-economic relations emphasized by Abercrombie et al. Though capitalism as such may not be willingly embraced, the compulsion imposed by the deeper cultural norm of progress – to which citizens willingly consent – is equally important from the neo-Gramscian point of view as the coercion exercised by instrumental routine, or by the formal institutions of the economy. The commonly held belief in and expectation of improved living standards, profoundly embedded in the routines of daily life, give it meaning and a sense of direction, and therefore ideational stability.

These authors arrived at the conclusion that no coherent ideology dominates the socio-political landscape of the modern age, and yet they record that 'we assume that all forms of capitalist economy have beliefs which justify accumulation'.[87] Elaborating, they go on to say that

> the dominant groups whose voices are transmitted through [various institutions], and perhaps through all governments regardless of their political persuasion, are indeed concerned with profit and the reproduction of capital … there is certainly an ideology of accumulation which permeates all the institutions of modern capitalist society [though] its content differs from that of early capitalism.[88]

The beliefs and the 'ideology of accumulation' mentioned above are not recognized by these analysts, however, as the implicit influence of the ideational superstructure of the growth paradigm which impinges on 'all governments regardless of their political persuasion'. By emphasizing the functional, operational or instrumental character of capitalist societies, Abercrombie et al. have undervalued what constructivists call the constitutive nature of intersubjectively held beliefs and expectations; they have identified the coercive aspects of society but have missed the background condition – the consensual commitment to growth – which remains constant throughout their historical survey.

As a critical theorist whose work overlaps significantly with the neo-Gramscian school, Robert Cox is more sympathetic than Abercrombie et al. to the role played by ideas in the formation and stabilization of social structures, but by adopting temporal frames of too-short duration, he too misses the ideational backdrop of the growth paradigm. I review his work briefly in order to clarify his conception of historical structures, and to show how those structures, though apparently quite different historical formations, can as readily be understood as fundamentally similar, medium-term manifestations of the growth paradigm.

Cox developed from Gramsci[89] the notion that, in large measure, world orders are social constructions which reflect collectively held beliefs that legitimize and normalize relations within and between states, and that changing ideas could as readily transform world orders as could changing material capabilities. Adopting this approach, Cox focused his attention on what he termed historical structures, several of which are discernible over the span of the last three centuries. Each structure is understood to be an international framework for action that 'constitute(s) the context of habits, expectations and constraints within which [social forces act]'.[90] Similar to the Gramscian conception of the historic bloc (*blocco historico*) which shaped domestic Italian politics, these structures represent certain historically specific configurations of forces represented by a confluence of ideologies, institutions and material conditions. When there is coherence among the elements of these three categories of forces, one may speak of hegemonic historical structures. As long as they persist, structures are maintained through the twin Gramscian devices of coercion and consent. The latter is derived from the common ideational commitments of the era; the former is exercised through institutions which instantiate those commitments, and through the material capabilities generated by economic production. As previously discussed, neither Gramsci nor Cox take the mode of economic production to be deterministic of the ideational element of historic structures; modes of production merely establish the terrain on which social forces act out their relations of power, and define the horizon of possibilities for those actions.

Cox has identified three examples of historical structure which illustrate variations over time, as one structure supersedes its predecessor. The first instance (1789–1873) is the period of liberal international economy dominated by Britain. During this period, the main ideational theme was expressed in terms of 'economic doctrines [that were] consistent with British supremacy but universal in form – comparative advantage, free trade, and the gold standard – [and that] spread gradually outward from Britain. Coercive strength underwrote this order'.[91] The next period (1873–1945) is described by Cox as non-hegemonic. The balance of power in Europe had been destabilized, leading to two world wars; free trade was displaced by protectionism, and the world's economy was fragmented into economic blocs. From 1945 to the present, a new hegemony has emerged as Pax Americana. Similar in structure to the Pax Britannica, it endorses an open trading world and 'confidence in economic growth and ever-rising productivity as the basis for moderating and controlling conflict'.[92] Doctrines have been adjusted to a more complex world economy, and new international institutions provide the surveillance and compliance mechanisms through which ideological commitments are maintained.

The shortcoming of this analysis, as with the survey by Abercrombie et al., is that Cox does not contemplate that which remains constant through the succession of changes just mentioned. During all eras of both hegemonic and non-hegemonic world orders, a commitment to growth persisted, though the particular set of ideas and institutions in which this commitment was embodied varied over time. For example, the commitment was not explicit as a policy objective during the Pax Britannica because economic growth during that time was not in any way problematic or needful of public scrutiny. This was so because growth under the impetus of the Industrial Revolution was proceeding apace: it was simply assumed as present and good, an integral part of an ineluctable process of material progress. The pursuit of growth, though under a different set of international political parameters, continued through the non-hegemonic era to 1945, then was picked up again post-Second World War as an explicit policy objective, and finally it was turbo-charged under the neoliberal agenda paramount today.

Cox barely reflects upon this consistent underlying feature of world orders, and he does not question the underlying premise of growth which links hegemonic orders through history. The dynamic of expansion is taken as given, and his speculations about the possibilities for post-neoliberal counter-hegemonies are all scenarios compatible with the precepts of the growth paradigm. His most recent work focuses on the set of ills commonly linked to globalization (including environmental damage), but the solution to these problems is not a rejection of growth as such, but simply reimposed social control over predatory capitalism. In short, Coxian historical structures are amenable to interpretation, from my vantage, as sets of particular contingencies riding on a deeper dynamic which does not change substantively over time. The neo-Gramscian analysis developed in this study highlights a paradigmatic era that is broader than the medium-term events encompassed by Coxian historical structures.

That Cox did not illuminate an ideational superstructure which overarched his survey may be attributable to his firm grounding in, and propensity for, the empirical realities of conflicting social forces. Mapping production systems and historical structures is, for him, a strictly inductive process. His *Production, Power and World Order* is replete with detailed analyses of myriad 'social forces in the making of history' (the book's subtitle); and yet neo-Gramscian analysis does not direct attention exclusively to those forces. I recall that historic blocs (or the historical structures which Cox accentuated) are created by a particular constellation of social forces, but that each constellation is a coherent ensemble of material capabilities, institutions and ideas. Empirical research more easily tends to the former two elements, but 'the real inspiration of this adaptation of Gramsci lies in the exhortation to consider global structural change and world order in terms of … their ethical and ideological as well as their material dimensions'.[93] Cox emphasized that these various elements are in fact mutually implicating – relations among them are reciprocal – and that none is ultimately determinate of the historical structure produced: the precise mix of their respective influences is a question that must be answered through a close examination of the relevant historical periods. Cox has undertaken this project, but perhaps with too great a predilection for the material means and social forces through which ideas are expressed, and with too little attention to the ideas themselves.

To put this somewhat differently, it may be that Cox tries too hard to sustain a balanced approach between the various factors that shape social relations. In trying to find a middle way between the extremes of Marxist economism and Hegelian idealism, Cox's work, as one writer put it, 'shifts back and forth from social force to ideology to institutions to system',[94] leaving the reader uncertain which if any of the elements involved is the most influential or definitive one. The result, according to a Marxian critic of neo-Gramscianism,

> offers little more than a version of Weberian pluralism oriented to the study of international order.... Variables which comprise a social order – the economy, the polity, the civil society – are given no overall structure. However laudable in theory, the true consequence of [this factor approach] is to produce a pluralist empiricism which lacks the power to explain the systemic connection between values, social relations and institutions'.[95]

It is important, in my view, to recover this systemic connection: it is in fact a key point of the present study that a wider temporal frame than that used by Cox brings to focus the *longue durée* of the growth paradigm, revealing that its ontology is dominated by a hegemonic idea, and that this idea serves as a unifying theme. Conceived in neo-Gramscian terms, the growth paradigm is a world order in which the role played by ideas has taken precedence over the role played by either material capabilities or institutions, both of which can be conceived as expressions of, or at least as compatible with, the dominant ideational feature of the era, as originally expressed in the Enlightenment conception of progress.

Conclusion

Neo-Gramscian analysis stipulates that ideational and material factors function together as an organic whole. It was his insight into this reciprocal relation that allowed Gramsci to differentiate his understanding of hegemony from that of Karl Marx, his intellectual predecessor, who had granted preeminent status to material economic processes structured by the ownership of capital, from which the ideological and cultural superstructures of capitalist societies were derived. For Gramsci, and for neo-Gramscians working in the international arena, base and superstructure are mutually implicating: the ideational element of hegemony denotes the domain of intersubjectively held beliefs and morality; the materialist premise functions as a limiting horizon that constrains discourse, preventing its mystification by linking it to the natural world. If one aspect is evidently dominant and apparently unsynchronized with the other, then that dominance and disharmony may be understood to be not only historically contingent and therefore temporary, but in fact indicative of incipient structural tensions.

The growth era is such a period of time when one aspect clearly dominates the other; indeed, the growth paradigm inverts completely the Marxian conception of base-superstructure by having pushed to the forefront the ideological commitment to growth which now shapes the socio-economic relations, not to mention the material foundations, of that growth. I have used various terminologies in this chapter to identify the ideational component of the growth paradigm, such as a collectively held belief system; an ideology; a social episteme; a secular religion; an abstraction; and, in keeping with neo-Gramscian critical theory, an ideational superstructure. Each is intended to emphasize a particular facet of the concept at play, but each ultimately refers to the same thing: a belief in progress that, over the course of the last three centuries, has evolved into a ubiquitous and exclusionary political commitment to economic growth which now forms the non-negotiable core of the contemporary international political economy. The ideational superstructure of the growth paradigm is a hegemonic belief system that dominates the socio-political and material landscape of the world, and that imposes a forward-moving and expansionary dynamic on that landscape.

With regard to the issue of the dominance of the growth paradigm, several explanatory possibilities have by now been mooted. Reasons grounded in main-stream IPE theory, and reasons illuminated by a levels-of-analysis approach, were presented in Chapter 2. These included, most significantly, the relative importance of functional explanations. In contrast, the present chapter has emphasized the ideational component of the paradigm as a source of explanatory potential. Here one finds a set of beliefs holding that growth, effectively disen-gaged from its material foundations, is not limited; that growth is conducive to personal and societal freedom; and that growth is a virtually universal political expedient: and on that basis has become an immanent feature of world culture whose normative foundations recommend and purportedly facilitate a better, safer and more prosperous future for all.

It was J. K. Galbraith who pointed most clearly to economic growth as the pre-ferred remedy for the tensions associated with inequality and competing claims on limited resources. In the 1950s, such claims were coming from public and private interests, from capital and labour, from the rich and the poor, and it was in this climate that he began to turn his attention to such issues, especially in *The Affluent Society*. He observed how 'increased production [had become] an alternative to redistribution'; that it was 'the great solvent of the tensions associated with ine-quality'; and that 'it is the increase in output … not the redistribution of income, which has brought the great material increase, the well-being of the average man'.[96] And it was Galbraith who observed that economic growth was the one solution to which everyone could agree because it penalized no one. All contend-ing parties, public or private, employer or employee, rich or poor, could agree on economic growth as a policy objective simply because it held the promise of bene-fiting them all. For this reason above all others, Galbraith concludes that

> No other social goal is more strongly avowed than economic growth. No other test of social success has such nearly unanimous acceptance as the

> annual increase in the Gross National Product. And this is true of all countries developed or undeveloped; communist, socialist or capitalist.[97]

Cultural factors in Western Europe and the United States also promoted economic growth as a political objective. Reflecting the Protestant values of thrift, efficiency, hard work and good management, growth came to be seen as a reward for personal initiative, achievement and, more generally, the advancement of knowledge. The value of growth, in other words, was not limited to its material dimension. Adam Smith had remarked that the progressive state is a cheerful and happy state; a society, he said, is not necessarily enamoured of material goods as such, but is instead most content when it moves forward, moving past and beyond the morbidity of stagnation. Growth, moreover, could not only engender the impetus to improve, it could also make possible greater control over the material world,[98] and therefore over the direction of forward motion. Rising material standards by themselves may or may not make people happier, but they had clearly increased the individual's range of choice. Growth had, in this sense, come to be associated with freedom: personal freedom to choose among products in the marketplace, economic freedom from political restraint, and political freedom to steer the engines of industrial development into the future. The overarching belief in growth as the ultimate political expedient had finally been joined with a normative justification of universal significance.

The process of abstraction outlined in this chapter disembedded the global economy from its social and natural setting, and allowed the evolution of an ideational superstructure which guides the movement of the growth paradigm through time. This disarticulation, however, indicates that the ideational and material components of neo-Gramscian hegemony are not in harmony, and I will argue on that basis that the abstraction of the superstructure points directly to the ethically compromised core of the growth paradigm, a topic I take up in Chapters 4 and 5. There I will argue that an idea divorced from its socio-natural context is also distanced from political control, which implies greater reliance on the quasi-automatic redistributive functions of the invisible hand, a concept very much at play in neoliberal capitalist ideology. This reliance, I will show, is misled. In Adam Smith's time, market forces were constrained within a robust societal ethos that gave direction and purpose to the mechanical operations of the economy. Absent that constraint, unfettered ideas about freedom may be, as Niebuhr would suggest, ill-considered expressions of the amorality of large groups.

Ideas provide the interpretive framework by which the world is apprehended, but their abstract quality makes them susceptible to manipulation by those who have the means and interest to do so. Whatever their status, however, ideas can subsist only in the minds of living people in real historical circumstances. In keeping with the Gramscian injunction to maintain a constant connection between the ideational and the material world, I turn in the next chapter to an examination of the social forces that have propagated the idea of growth through time.

4 The class structure and normative foundations of the paradigm

Introduction

The ideational superstructure of the growth paradigm is an abstraction distanced from the socio-natural world by processes identified in the last chapter, but the idea of growth necessarily arises from that world and ultimately must be reconciled with it, or dispatched. More to the point in this chapter, however, is the fact that ideas are carried forward by real social actors living in real historical times, and for particular reasons which help explain the dominance of the growth paradigm. I examine this below, with reference to class as a unique form of social actor.

Neo-Gramscian analysis of the growth paradigm directs attention to its placement in history, its ideational/material construction and to the social forces that propagate it through time. The simplest representation of those forces is provided by the two-class dichotomy characteristic of Marxist socio-economic analysis, which roughly divides the human population into two categories – the rulers and the ruled – which in turn may be construed as constituting the most fundamental structural aspect of the growth paradigm in its power dimension. These two strata have evolved over time and are identifiable today as a transnational managerial class composed primarily of economic and political leaders, and, subordinate to it, transnational civil society, broadly described as the social sector that inhabits the political space between the individual and the state, and that crosses state boundaries.

Complementing this Marxist dichotomy, Theodore J. Lowi has offered a rationale for a sustained focus on elite rule which is apposite. He has noticed that, in the social sciences, one may discern cycles of criticism which are, basically, periodic attempts to locate and attribute responsibility for commonly endorsed but otherwise questionable beliefs or social practices. Locating that responsibility exactly, however, can be problematic, especially in a pluralist polity which has no permanent leadership stratum. As Lowi observes,

> In a self-contained, balanced, self-correcting universe – the pluralist political system – the whole notion of responsibility is expendable. The notion might be evoked, but it is not intrinsic; it is quite possible to elaborate on [the pluralist scheme] without using it at all.

In contrast, elite theory explicitly brings the critical faculty to bear. 'The elite point of view', Lowi writes, '...is part of the spirit of criticism. It is adopted as a point of view precisely because it allows for a more systematic form of treating political phenomena in a combined empirical and normative way'.[1] In other words, it allows for the attribution of responsibility, and for the criticism of those who bear it. Given the environmental considerations which underlie my analysis of the growth paradigm, this point of view is appropriate. I will focus in this chapter primarily on the evolution of the emerging stratum of rulers often referred to in critical theory literature as the transnational managerial class (TMC). In the latter part of the chapter, I will discuss the normative foundations of the growth paradigm with particular reference to the malformed idea of economic freedom adopted by the TMC in contemporary international relations.

Social forces in neo-Gramscian critical theory

Because historical materialism is attuned to the basic structure and processes of society at large, it illuminates a wide range of discrete groupings of people and the roles they play in society. Particular constellations of such groups or social forces are thought to form the deep foundations of political and economic power. As Robert Cox puts it, 'power is seen as *emerging* from social processes rather than taken as given in the form of accumulated material capabilities'.[2] Fordist capitalism, for example – as a new social process – brought organized industrial workers into existence as a new social force, whose incorporation into national societies impacted upon forms of state and state policies in many developed countries. In more recent times the internationalization of production has thrust transnational corporations to the fore as a powerful social force which has, arguably, helped to transmute the welfare state into the competitive state. Even hegemonic structures and world orders in international relations originate, persist and decay over time according to the mixture and interplay of groups within and across state boundaries, from the vantage of historical materialism.

Cox has noted[3] that it was the *Annales* school which widened the focus of historical studies to comprise not only those who held and exercised power, but also those who inhabited and gave form to subordinate sectors of society. The domain of civil society, as it has become known today, included the daily routines of people as well as the social groupings they formed. It was this level of agency that Braudel referred to as *l'histoire événementielle*, encompassing immediate or short-term events. The wider focus of the *Annales* school is also evident in contemporary historical materialism which tends not to be state-centric; it takes the state–society complex as its basic unit of analysis instead. A whole social entity is posited in which constituent parts are interactive and mutually implicating. Moreover, because modes and relations of production are often shared within wide regions, social formations tend to be transnational in scope. Critical political economy is more sensitive to the perception of social strata that share similar identities and interests, and that straddle state borders, than to classes or other social groupings that are contained within those borders. The analytical perspective at play, then, highlights both societal holism and transnationalism.

An important feature of transnational social forces is that they are arranged hierarchically. Cox has observed that the sovereign equality of states is merely a 'useful fiction [which] obscures the perception that the actual relationships among the constituent units [of the state system] are hierarchical or clusters of hierarchically arranged units'.[4] Hierarchy is the de facto reality which persists between social strata within states, between states and between social strata that join states together transnationally. Hierarchy, I would add, is the historical constant against which impulses to egalitarianism are perennially, but ineffectually, opposed. Patterns of domination and subordination among large groups which result from the intrinsic social tendency to hierarchy are represented by the term class.[5] Class analysis constitutes a major sub-field of sociology, and is of particular analytical interest to some strands of IPE as well. My usage of the term is briefly clarified below.

All complex societies are, to various degrees, stratified, which means that 'the total stock of valued resources is distributed unequally, with the most privileged individuals or [groups] enjoying a disproportionate amount of property, power, or prestige'.[6] These 'valued resources' are the touchstones for three types of class, namely, economic (unequal distribution of property), political (unequal distribution of power), and cultural (in which case prestige differentials result from the discriminatory treatment of cultural values). In turn, this tripartite typology can be further subdivided, almost indefinitely, into categories such as ethnicity, caste or gender, or with respect to other variables such as income, education, status and so forth.[7] Max Weber followed this path toward a multiplicity of class cleavages in his development of a pluralistic, multidimensional model of social stratification.

In contrast, Marxists and neo-Marxists often retain the traditional conception of class as a dichotomy between pairs of antagonistic groups, identified through specific historical epochs as master–slave, feudal lords and serfs, or capitalists and workers in the modern era. In this regard, I follow Marx, not Weber. Parsimony is one clear advantage gained by this, but another distinction is useful as well. Weber's pluralistic approach tends to regard classes, or strata, as aggregates of individuals distinguishable on the basis of particular characteristics such as income level or type of employment. Classes understood in the Marxian sense are more likely to be real social groups with a common shared bond, perhaps even a common consciousness. On this view, classes are more likely to be (empirical) social actors, not just (analytical) categories arranged along a stratification continuum. The latter do not generate outcomes that reflect the deliberate purposes of goal-oriented agents. That role is reserved for real actors who are guided by sets of principled beliefs and/or activist agendas.

Cox has said that '[t]o assert the centrality of production … leads directly to the matter of social classes'.[8] This is so not only because the organization of production divides employer from employee, but because production as such – beginning from the first cultivation of crops and domestication of animals – could and did generate a surplus of food over the needs of subsistence. This social surplus was used (among other things) to support specialists who functioned independently of the production process, such as chiefs, administrators, soldiers and priests, and who constituted the first ruling classes. It is commonly held that 'the origin of the division of society into rulers and ruled corresponds to the production of social surplus'.[9] I take as given, then, the premise that all settled societies are stratified, that strata are hierarchically arranged, and that dominant strata have access to coercive power (ideological or material) by which subordinate groups are ruled, with or without their consent.

Any empirical examination of this premise, however, will inevitably encounter myriad complexities, as adumbrated earlier with reference to Weber's pluralistic approach to the sociological study of classes. It is not clear even in the first instance whether elites rule because leaderless masses are incompetent, as Lenin has somewhat paradoxically argued,[10] or that people are rational and therefore have organized themselves into hierarchies because a social contract among unequals is necessary to get things done. This latter point of view is reflected in the writings of Adam Smith, among many others, and is consistent with the functionalist school of thought which sees social organization in terms of reciprocity and mutual benefit, rather than coercion.

Another problem with class analysis is that the membership parameters of particular groups (such as shared identity) may be hard to ascertain because of internally inconsistent interests and objectives; or, the status of groups relative to others may not be clear because groups dominant with respect to those below may be subordinate to those above. This latter problem reveals the context-dependency of roles played by collective actors in a fashion reminiscent of the agent–structure debate in IR, which identifies groups as either reified structures or as autonomous agents depending upon which level of analysis has been deployed. Compounding these complexities is the fact that the perpetual and active interplay among social groups can only be meaningfully understood as a dynamic and historically contingent process. Classes and other social forces change in composition, size and relative importance in the social hierarchy; some disappear and others take their place in the constant flux of social evolution. Thick volumes have been dedicated to tracing through time the various collective components of state–society complexes, their inception and demise, and their socio-political import. I noted in Chapter 3 that Cox followed this empirically oriented, inductive approach to his study of the evolution of social forces in history.

Valuable as the pluralistic approach has been, I do not follow it here, preferring instead to stay with the Marxist predilection for dualism, with a focus on the broader but still tangible (and historically constant) dichotomy of two classes in tension: the rulers and the ruled. These form, in effect, the generic overlay beneath which shifting relations between historically transient groups are conducted. This division occurs within all domestic polities and, arguably, it occurs in international relations as well. Classical Marxist theorists and, in the 1960s and 1970s, dependency theorists, were among those who drew attention to what they perceived to be an evolving class structure in the international domain.[11] More recently, Nicholas Onuf, approaching the same problematic from a constructivist point of view, concluded that contemporary political society comprises two classes: a cosmopolitan ruling class whose 'organizational ties permit, even require, historically separate skills to be joined such that world politics and the world economy are now inextricable'; and a second class comprising, in effect, everyone excluded from the first group.[12] For my purposes the two classes in question are, with respect to contemporary human society as a whole, the transnational managerial class and transnational civil society, both of which are implicated in the construction and forward motion of the growth paradigm.

This bisection, however, brings to sharper relief the question of whether these classes are merely analytical strata, useful only for heuristic purposes, or are real empirical social groups, as Onuf would argue, with shared identities, interests, values and goals. My contention is that they are both, because they are analytically perceptible as being in the process of emerging from history but have not yet been fully formed empirically. An evolutionary trend is moving human society as a whole toward a bifurcated condition in which class divisions are becoming more real, and more politically relevant. The increasingly wide division between rich and poor, for example, both between and within states,[13] is suggestive of this trend. Before discussing the development, composition and characteristics of the transnational managerial class, and transnational civil society, I clarify the relationship between the rulers and the ruled with reference to the neo-Gramscian conception of hegemony.

Neo-Gramscian hegemony

As understood by Gramsci, hegemony is not just about the exercise of preponderant power by a dominant class; it puts emphasis instead on leadership, a term that highlights the consensual nature of hierarchical social arrangements without neglecting the importance of coercive force which may be required from time to time to actively support or reproduce the social consensus. Stuart Hall – an especially lucid interpreter of Gramsci's *Prison Notebooks* – has remarked that hegemony requires 'the installation of a profound measure of social and moral authority',[14] anchored by the state but including strata of subaltern[15] and dominated groups or classes who have been won over by concession and compromise, a process Gramsci refers to as *trasformismo*. Hegemony is not simply a reflection of the interests of a particular class occupying a dominant position in the mode of economic production; ordinary people are in alliance too. As Hall puts it,

> the raising of popular thought is part and parcel of the process by which a collective will is constructed, and requires … extensive cultural and ideological struggle to bring about or effect the intellectual and ethical unity which is essential to the forging of hegemony … a struggle first in the ethical field and then in that of politics proper.[16]

The end result of this struggle was a historic bloc, for Gramsci, but in the present context it is the growth paradigm. Both structures include a horizontal dimension of class solidarity, and a vertical (ideological) dimension which links ruling and subordinate strata together. Walter Adamson describes this vertical dimension as 'a relatively stable (organic) relationship between structure and superstructure, between the productive, economic life of a society and its political and cultural awareness, between its being and its consciousness'.[17] I emphasize here that, on the neo-Gramscian view, the foundations of the growth paradigm are not just economic: they are political, cultural, intellectual and ethical.

Given the dynamic and transformative nature of social evolution over the longer term, however, it follows that hegemony is a historically specific and ultimately temporary moment in the life of a society – a specific constellation of social forces which is not permanent. These forces have to be 'actively constructed and positively maintained'[18] in the short term, but tectonic shifts over the longer term are inevitable. Transformative change is most likely to emerge from civil society because that stratum is less ideologically coherent than the proportionately smaller managerial class, and because democracy, where it exists, promotes the articulation of those differences. Tensions between opposed ideas are inherent to hegemonic structures. This constant pressure for change suggests that systemic tensions or irresolvable contradictions within extant hegemonic formations may indicate incipient breaking points at which paradigm shifts could occur. That discussion will be pursued later, in my concluding chapter.

Class evolution

The transnational managerial class

The Gramscian approach historicizes and renders dynamic the unproblematic conception of class associated with fundamentalist Marxism. Classes may share certain common conditions of existence, but are otherwise 'crosscut by conflicting interests, historically segmented and fragmented in their actual course of historical formation'.[19] Class unity is not assumed: it must be produced, constructed or otherwise created by specific economic, political and ideological practices.

The social construction of class as a unified social force entails an evolutionary process of self-identification, and the development of a class consciousness, which implies that different levels of consciousness will obtain at different historical phases (or 'moments') of evolution. Gramsci speaks of three stages of class development which were conceived to occur within domestic polities, but which I adapt to the wider domain of international politics and to the longer temporal frame of the modern age. The first and most elementary of these stages is the *economic-corporate* moment, characterized by an uncoordinated sharing of basic common interests: for example, tradesmen will associate with and support each other, and manufacturers will do the same, but there is no bond between these two sectors. That link is achieved at the second, or *class-corporate* moment, when 'consciousness is reached of the solidarity of interests among all the members of the [wider] social group – but still in the purely economic field'.[20] Here, shared economic interests are made explicit and are coordinated to join groups together. At the third *ethico-political* moment, class is finally transformed to a common culture which transcends purely economic solidarity. Gramsci describes this as follows:

> [O]ne becomes aware that one's own interests ... transcend the limits of the merely economic group, and can and must become the interests of other subordinate groups. This is the most purely political phase, and marks the decisive passage from the structure to the sphere of the complex superstructures ... [it is the phase that brings about] intellectual and moral unity ... thus creating the hegemony of a fundamental social group over a series of subordinate groups ... the dominant group is coordinated concretely with the general interests of the subordinate groups.[21]

As Stuart Hall notes, this moment 'begins to propagate itself through society, bringing about intellectual and moral as well as economic and political unity.... It is this process of coordination ... that constitutes the 'hegemony' of a particular historical bloc'.[22] Importantly, this unity, coordination and hegemony consolidate social forces and their objectives around a single theme, which offers a clear focal point around which opposition may gather. Dissident movements will rise, on the Gramscian view, from those sectors of civil society that most clearly perceive and experience the tensions and contradictions which inevitably underlie hegemonic structures.

The evolution of classes and hegemony within states leads Gramsci to identify national structures which he called historic blocs. An extrapolation of this approach to the broader domain of the growth paradigm requires two steps from the original Gramscian position. First, the analysis must be adapted to include similar structures which arise in the context of international relations. Robert Cox has accomplished this adaptation in his examination of the evolution of discrete historical structures, such as the Pax Britannica and the Pax Americana. But Cox's work, as previously discussed, is empirically extensive and inclusive of a plethora of social forces – trade unions, professional associations, bureaucratic, state and international agencies, states themselves, and classes, among many others – which generates a historical tapestry of too much complexity for present purposes. The second step, then, is to extract from Cox's analyses only those social forces and trends that might serve to indicate the evolution of international or transnational classes. This step entails, in effect, a reinterpretation of his empirical work such that certain broader, underlying – and overarching – trends might be made evident. Specifically, this process will reveal the evolution of a transnational managerial class, a related evolutionary trajectory for transnational civil society, and an overarching episteme or ideational superstructure which provides direction and legitimacy to these evolutionary processes.

As mentioned, classes can be seen to evolve over three discernible phases. I will show that, in the international domain and with reference to the growth paradigm, the first, most rudimentary (economic-corporate) phase occurred at the time of the ascendancy of the mercantilist state, when similar but uncoordinated actors pursued common interests – the acquisition of wealth and power – competitively. The second (class-corporate) phase is apparent at the time of the emergence of the liberal state, and the liberal world order, which joined all states and major economic actors together in common cause, but only in the economic domain. The third (ethico-political) phase occurred after the Second World War when civil society was at last incorporated into the sphere of interests of the dominant actors; it was at that point that the hegemony of the growth paradigm, including its ethical orientation to freedom, was finally attained. This history is developed in the following pages, drawing on and reinterpreting Coxian analysis, primarily, with a view to illuminating processes inherent to but not specifically revealed by his original work.

Phase I

The emergence of the state system in Europe, usually dated from the conclusion of the Thirty Years' War and the Treaty of Westphalia of 1648, brought into existence the foundational concept of *raison d'état*. The political logic of this new idea gave expression to the internal and external dimensions (order and autonomy, respectively) of state sovereignty by which states were rendered distinct, and by which 'the specific interests of particular states superseded universalist notions of natural and divine law as the ultimate criterion of action'.[23] The external tools of *raison d'état* – military might, and techniques of statecraft and diplomacy – were developed originally by Italian regional powers, then were taken on by fledgling states in the wider European arena as the means by which to regulate the new balance of power among centralized territorial units. This early stage in the development of the state system, characterized by the relative enhancement of state power in a context no longer unified by medieval universalist propensities, is known retrospectively as the mercantilist era.

Republican, aristocratic and monarchic states existed side by side but, apart from their immersion in the new era of Enlightenment thinking, no general ideas concerning the proper constitution or behaviour of states prevailed, or could be imposed. 'The only test of their status in the system', writes Cox, 'was their power to compel recognition on the part of other states ... [and] the solitary goal of a state was its own conservation and aggrandizement'.[24] The need to have access to a reliable income stream to pay the costs of conservation and aggrandizement solidified the relationship between centralized state political power and merchant wealth, the latter of which also served to finance overseas exploration and colonization. This new partnership between capitalist (bourgeois) managers and the traditional holders of public power – monarchs and aristocratic landowners, now state leaders – marked the beginning of the coalescence of a new social force, a new class of international actor.

Cox's historical analysis reveals the complex arrangements linking mercantile interests with land-based wealth in England, France, the Netherlands and Spain, among others, and illuminates their shared interest in the growth of the world economy – and their rivalry for dominance of it. In contrast, the agrarian/peasant sector, in various forms and in various states, served as tax base and market for manufactured goods, but otherwise did not share in the power, wealth or aspirations to dominance which were characteristic of the ruling classes. Nothing bound this sector in common cause, or common consciousness, so no indication of an emerging civil society as class is evident at the mercantilist era. Put differently, a civil society enlivened by the common purpose of improved national and individual welfare did not emerge immediately from the transitional era in Europe. Material progress remained for the most part an advantage available only to those who controlled political and/or economic power. This era, 'not fully emancipated from the past, not fully entrant upon the future',[25] as Heilbroner puts it, was devoted to building up national economic strength by predatory trade, and by subsidy to rising manufacturers. Mercantilism as pre-capitalism was not intended to benefit the people; on the contrary, frugality was encouraged, and consumption of anything that could be exported was discouraged.[26]

It would be some time, in fact, before an expanding total social output might benefit a wider spectrum of classes; and it would be some time before wealth came to be expected from a system of continuously increasing production. In antiquity, '[w]ealth was still a surplus to be seized by conquest or squeezed from the underlying agricultural population'.[27] The original surplus which fed capitalist investment was not derived from savings generated by innovation or efficiency; it came from colonial plunder, and from the forcible transfer of subsistence labour from traditional agricultural pursuits to the new arena of waged industrial production. Economic growth became an integral and self-sustaining part of daily life only when the lure of profits encouraged new investment, but at its origin the growth paradigm depended on 'a commanding authority which ordered the new pattern into being'.[28] The growth paradigm, in other words, was originated by elite power for the benefit of the few, not the many.

In keeping with the historical materialist focus on contradictions and tensions within and between social forces, several important instances were identified by Cox that would presage the demise of the mercantilist state and would lead, in the wake of the French Revolution, to new forms of state and to a new liberal world order. Listed briefly these include, first, a continuing tension between feudal traditionalism and nascent merchant capitalism. Through mercantile policies, states assisted in the accumulation of wealth but remained opposed to dismantling feudal structures such as control over land and peasantry by the nobility, which blocked capital accumulation. Second, state power rested on an increasingly resistant peasant class. The internal logic of sovereignty, which stressed the need to maintain control and stability, and which had figured importantly in the formative stages of European states, was neglected, and the acquiescence of domestic populations in the pursuits of ruling classes was eroded.

And third, notions of particular and fragmented states functioning in a balance-of-power setting came to be 'challenged in the realm of ideas by a new secular universalism that conceived of a rational state-supported world order governed by rules ... an organization of perpetual peace was the political condition for a wealth-of-nations vision of world economy'.[29] Immanuel Kant, Adam Smith, G. W. F. Hegel and René Descartes, among others, were all instrumental in launching an ideational or superstructural challenge to the particularism of the mercantile era. This challenge marked the formal beginnings of the ideational superstructure of the growth paradigm, as discussed in Chapter 3.

For Cox, the tensions listed above anticipated the evolution of new national historic blocs, and the incipient emergence of an international historical structure – a liberal world order dominated by Britain. From the longer point of view adopted here, the end of the mercantilist era marked the end of the first evolutionary phase of the transnational managerial class. The fragmented and uncoordinated pursuit of similar interests, typical of the economic-corporate moment, was soon to give way to the liberal state, the liberal world order known as Pax Britannica, and the second phase of class evolution characterized by a shared consciousness of common goals.

Phase II

Disregard for the welfare of peasantry and working classes, exacerbated by the forced maximization of exports and limitation of imports typical of mercantile practice, led ultimately to popular insurgencies in Europe and America, coming to a head in the former with the French Revolution of 1789. A groundswell of demands for inclusionary rights for the people was eventually calmed by the post-Napoleonic settlement of the Congress of Vienna in 1815, which attempted to 're-introduce universalist principles of public law into a state system that before the Revolution had been activated solely by the pursuit of individual state interests'.[30] Europe was now perceived not merely as a set of fragmented territories, but as a social order in which the internal dimension of sovereignty – the relationship of government to the people – was recognized anew. A system of conferences among the Great Powers of the day was established to forge a consensual and politically legitimate basis for the management of interstate relations.

The Grand Alliance of major European powers, however, had 'ceased to be an effective instrument of European collective will'[31] by 1822 because of widespread and tumultuous changes which affected many national polities, but the Congress of Vienna had nonetheless reintroduced notions of political legitimacy, responsibility and social order into the European arena, which collectively served as a prelude to the development of the liberal state, and a new liberal world order. These ideas joined states in a common belief in the efficacy of economic expansionism, and in a newly perceived need to perpetuate the economic system as prior to and distinct from the preservation of particular state actors in that system.

The new liberal order was anchored by British hegemony in the world economy. Because that hegemony was unchallenged, foreign policy cabinet minister Castlereagh 'sought openness for all countries, not special advantages [for Britain in commercial matters]. In this, Britain left behind eighteenth-century mercantilism for nineteenth-century free-trade conceptions'.[32] Doctrines of *laissez-faire* were espoused by the aristocratic managers of foreign policy, and by the industrial and financial operators of the day in a political environment stabilized by a continental balance of power, and by British hegemony. The role of the state, and the state system, was 'to ensure the conditions for this open world economy while refraining from interfering with the operations of economic agents'.[33] In Britain, the political domain remained in the hands of the aristocracy, but control of economic affairs fell to the ascendant bourgeoisie.

> Aristocratic managers understood that the limits within which they must manage were fixed by the conditions necessary for bourgeois economic expansion. This shared understanding, and the aristocratic-bourgeois division of labour, constituted the bourgeois hegemony in Britain, the basis in turn for British hegemony in the world economy.[34]

Regime changes in Europe in the mid-nineteenth century generally favoured the installation of liberal states, but the need to mobilize public and parliamentary support for national and foreign policies was not yet fully embraced. Indeed, despite the new sensitivity to the demands and welfare of the peasantry and working classes 'democracy remained anathema to established authorities, a threat to both property and power, to both economy and polity'.[35] The incorporation of civil society into a Gramscian hegemonic structure had not yet occurred at this historical moment, but the second phase of class formation, in which all major socio-economic actors of the ruling classes are joined in the common consciousness of shared interests and expectations, had begun.

In his discussion of the emergence of the liberal form of state, Cox acknowledges that the process of liberalization (that is, the widening acceptance of principles of *laissez-faire*) can be effectively analyzed from a functionalist perspective which illuminates tasks the state was expected to perform to enable the maximization of wealth. One such task was to continue dismantling obstructions to economic freedom inherited from feudal traditionalism and mercantilist practices. Laws of succession, for example, inhibited the commodification of land and various labour statutes still regulated the recruitment of labour and predetermined the wages which must be paid. In a similar vein, the repeal of the Poor Laws in Britain in 1834 helped to dissolve the paternalism of pre-capitalist Europe which forced the peasantry away from the security of feudal relationships, to become instead a mobile, nationwide labour market. The liberal European state also provided the sanction of coercive force which was necessary to allow the market mechanism to work without disturbance. State power was centralized to protect special interests, and to ensure stability for the system as a whole. And, finally, the liberal state functioned to mobilize capital, directly through public expenditures in roads, harbours, railroads, and postal, educational and judicial services; and indirectly through the establishment of limited liability corporations which encouraged private capital formation.

In contrast to the foregoing state-centric perspective, Cox's historical work is more attuned to the perception of struggle and conflict among groups, so for the most part he focuses on the roles played by opposed social forces in the construction of (national) historic blocs and (international) historical structures. The social forces perspective, though complex in its Weberian pluralism, reveals readily discernible trends, the most significant of which for present purposes was the continuing polarization of classes in European society. Liberal reforms in Britain helped to bring a new middle class into existence, and assisted its participation in the state – but that class tended to align itself and its interests with the bourgeois/aristocratic ruling class, while most workers and peasants continued to be excluded, sharing neither in the political process (through suffrage or representation) nor in the economic benefits generated thereby. Underclasses in Europe and elsewhere were to remain external to the dominant social order of the day until the evolution of the welfare state after the Second World War, at which time the third phase of Gramscian hegemony comes into view.

Much of the preceding discussion has centred on changes that occurred in nineteenth-century Britain, but similar processes of liberalization and social polarization were underway in continental Europe and in the United States as well. A period of steady expansion in the world economy from the 1840s to the 1870s consolidated the liberal world order, as the more advanced states enjoyed growing prosperity and increasingly profitable opportunities in manufacture and trade. 'The liberal world order', Cox writes, 'was the creation of an expansionist society, British in the first instance and European in the following instances – *les bourgeois conquérants*'.[36] Overseas territories controlled by European powers in Latin America, Africa and Asia conformed readily, with various degrees of self-government, to the requirements of the liberal world order: from India to Guatemala, a 'single expansionist movement of global reach'[37] permeated the global stage. In countries penetrated by European powers, political and economic leaders were in the main glad to have access to investment capital and new technologies. Coercion was not often required to ensure compliance with liberal principles, or with the expectation of increasing prosperity.

Apart from the hegemonic influence of Britain during the Pax Britannica, the stability of the liberal world order during the nineteenth century can be attributed, according to Cox, to the newfound harmony of economic interests shared by the bourgeoisie/aristocratic ruling class in Europe; to the *haute finance* managers of the world economy, who ensured a steady flow of new capital which helped offset the adverse effects of rapid change, in Europe and in the penetrated countries; to the economic boom that sustained governments and undermined revolutionary impulses; and to the fact that civil society did not yet have the means to mount a coherent challenge to ruling forces. A critical theoretical focus on tensions inherent to the new world order, however, also reveals that the self-regulating market was corroding social systems (as Karl Polanyi has documented), leaving people vulnerable to unemployment and other hardships. And inequalities were becoming more extreme, and more widespread, casting doubt on the optimistic expectations of classical economic theory which anticipated harmonious state–society relations. Moreover, the impulse to protectionism, particularly in the United States, was only submerged, not obliterated. The end of Pax Britannica, and a new era of rival imperialisms, was about to occur.

The period from the 1870s to the 1890s saw the gradual dissolution of the liberal world order and a breakdown of British hegemony. A long economic depression, from 1873 to 1896, exacerbated persistent class antagonisms which required, for many European states, a new inward focus on bridging those chasms and consolidating the national order. Coincidentally, the European balance of power became more fluid and less stable,[38] especially in the midst of a wider shift from a Eurocentric to a world system of competing states which now included the United States and Japan. The spread of industrialization determined military-political potential to a significant degree, so competition for power required states to promote and protect their own industrial infrastructure. Together these factors tended to cause a revival of protectionism, and a renewed expansionary thrust for markets and colonies. '[T]he incentive to expand was irresistible', writes Cox. 'It was rationalized and publicized by ideological forces – Christian proselytizing, *la mission civilisatrice*, and racial supremacy doctrines',[39] and while those ideological forces were real and vital, they were also a cover for an expansionary impulse motivated by a commitment to growth which was characteristic of the era. All major world powers had joined in the fray by the end of the nineteenth century, and their rivalries pushed them into Africa, Asia and the Pacific region. A growing gulf between industrialized and non-industrialized sectors of the world provoked the perception that available frontiers of exploitation were rapidly closing, and that pre-emptive action was required to capture new resources, and new markets, for the benefit of national interests.

Cox's analysis led him to identify three major periods of time, and three corresponding socio-political structures, stretching from the medieval/modern juncture to the emergence of neoliberalism in the 1970s. The first of these is the Pax Britannica, anchored by British hegemony; the second period is one of rival imperialisms, just described above, which is non-hegemonic in structure; the third period is the Pax Americana, imposed by American hegemony after the Second World War, during which time the Keynesian welfare state flourished before giving way to the neoliberal ideology which still dominates the politico-economic landscape today. The perspective developed here, however, urges a different interpretation; specifically, Gramscian blocs and Coxian historical structures are local configurations of the wider and more continuous architecture of the growth paradigm. To put this in Braudelian terms, Gramsci and Cox illuminate conjunctural, or medium-term temporal frames, as opposed to the *longue durée* of the paradigm. Cox's discussion of a non-hegemonic interval between the Pax Britannica and the Pax American follows naturally from his analysis of the social forces that impel historical structures, but the dissolution of the liberal world order in favour of protectionist policies (which dominated from the latter part of the eighteenth century to the end of the Second World War) merely indicates a change in tactics, not a retreat from nor a decisive rupture with the fundamental commitment among all major political and economic actors to continuous economic growth.

The continuing evolution of the ruling class, and concurrently the gradual approach of Gramscian hegemony, are also evident during phase II in light of the slow emergence of civil society as a political actor. Even as merchant and political elites were managing protectionist growth during Cox's period of rival imperialisms, civil societies were gaining strength and prominence as a prelude to their ultimate incorporation into the emerging structure of the growth paradigm. For example, the widespread movement of civilian populations from rural to urban settings, and new techniques of mass production, were causing people to be 'brought into durable, compact groups in the factories, and in the urban areas where workers lived political action became more feasible and more threatening to the liberal order'.[40] The spread of literacy, the popular press, mass-based political parties of socialist allegiance, and an explicit set of social grievances all contributed to what was beginning to be perceived by political and economic elites as 'the labour problem'. But, as Cox notes, civil society was not yet positioned to present a coherent threat to the management class. The growing concentration of capital in factories, and the increasing application of new technologies to industrial production tended to fragment workers into a skilled, educated and permanently employed fraction, and a less skilled fraction that did not have the resources to organize trade unions, cooperatives or political parties. Given this fragmentation, the state could selectively respond to unionized workers by subsidizing or recognizing the legitimacy of their organizations. This tactic of co-option of a fraction of labour, which left the proportionately much larger fraction of unskilled labour outside looking in, served the protectionist purposes of rival states by promoting nationalism (that is, by including the upper echelons of labour in national planning), by helping to bridge class antagonisms, and by responding at least in part to demands from civil society for improved welfare.

Top–down co-optation, called *trasformismo* by Gramsci, fitted well with protectionist and nationalist proclivities but, past the turn of the century, pressure for welfare continued to well up from below. The First World War temporarily reconciled those pressures by requiring national unity behind state goals. The First World War enabled governments to rechannel popular unrest, and to mobilize all social forces behind national goals in what can be seen retrospectively as the germ of the welfare state. This process of consolidation led, through the need for national economic planning, to tripartite social structures that linked the state with major employers and unions, and to a reinforced appreciation among the elite for the need to enhance social welfare. This latter consideration, however, still only encompassed large-scale, unionized industry. The majority of workers in small-scale enterprise, family firms, retail shops, households, agriculture and so forth were still non-union, and were still excluded from the welfare provisions of the state and big business. After the First World War, desultory efforts to restore a liberal world order were undertaken through, for example, the initiative to organize the League of Nations, the International Labour Organization and the International Chamber of Commerce. These and other such efforts were not successful, or only partially so, with the result that protectionism remained entrenched, and the liberal world order weakened.

The evolution of a transnational managerial class has proceeded thus far in fits and starts. It began at the elitist origins of modernity with the consolidation of aristocratic and bourgeois interests into an economic-corporate alliance (phase I). It continued through the development of various forms of state in Europe, and through the era of the Pax Britannica, at which time dominant strata were joined ideologically in a common commitment to a liberal world order (phase II). Civil societies played no significant role in this evolutionary process except as tax base and suppliers of labour and other resources. The protectionist era that followed the dissolution of British hegemony signalled a breakdown in liberal internationalism, but not in the shared underlying ideological commitment to economic growth and expansionism. Subsequently, assertions of nationalist power led to the First World War, at which point the continuing pressure from lower social strata for improved living conditions was co-opted into the shared pursuit of national interests, the most compelling of which was self-preservation. This momentary consolidation of interests between elite and mass sectors set the stage for the welfare state which would finally emerge in the wake of the Great Depression, and after the Second World War. The more permanent incorporation of civil society into socio-political systems after the Second World War marked the next phase of the evolution of the managerial class – from domination to leadership – and the final phase of the evolution of the growth paradigm.

Phase III

The centre of gravity of international relations had shifted from Europe to the United States by the end of the Second World War but there were, at that time, conflicting tendencies in America. One tendency was to continue with the national planning techniques and processes developed since the First World War by which deliberate state policies were implemented in conjunction with the major economic actors of the day in finance and industry, and with the unionized echelons of big labour. The other was to return to a liberal world order, and an open world economy. 'The history of international economic institution building after World War II', writes Cox, 'traces the victory of the liberal internationalists over the proponents of state capitalism'.[41] American hegemony and the global expansion of US-based corporations drove the rapid growth of the world economy, and encouraged the emergence of new forms of state which were more responsive to systemic requirements. The new liberal state was similar to the pre-war welfare-nationalist state, but was more outwardly oriented. Cox elaborates:

> The central premise of the hegemonic order was that the world economy is a positive-sum game in which some businesses and some national economies may benefit more than the others but in which all have the opportunity to gain.... [T]he highest interest of all countries [is] to facilitate the expansion of the world economy and to avoid restrictive national measures of economic policy that would be in contradiction in the long run with world-level expansion.[42]

This new orientation did not, however, preclude state policies that served the welfare needs of national populations, nor did it indicate a move away from perceived obligations to civil society. On the contrary, a new form of welfare state, the organizing principle of which came to be known as embedded liberalism,[43] explicitly recognized the desirability of incorporating the needs and expectations of civil society into policy processes and programmes. It had in fact by that time become clear that the market-sustaining functions of the liberal state had to be broadened to compensate for the shortcomings and negative externalities of the market. Unemployment, injury, sickness and, in the larger picture, resource depletion, were now perceived to be, in important ways, the result of or exacerbated by impersonal economic forces and as such required the active intervention of the state. This new perception reflected an abandonment of early liberal predilections, previously discussed, to attribute social distress to personal failings. That 'impersonal economic forces' were now recognized to be at play in the world economy can also be taken as an indication of the growing separation between state and market, and indeed of the autonomous power of the ideological commitment to market principles which were, by then, profoundly abstracted from their roots in economic service to a social community.

When the interests and practices of the ruling class were extended to embrace civil society in a consensual whole, and when concessions were offered by the former to facilitate that wider embrace, then the transnational managerial class had evolved from a position of domination to one of leadership, in which the broader spectrum of social interests was acknowledged and taken into account by economic and political leaders alike. At that point, one may begin to speak of Gramscian hegemony, which was extended beyond the merely economic to include civil society in an explicitly normative formation. This phase was made manifest in several distinctive ways, such as Fordism, Keynesianism and Franklin Roosevelt's New Deal, and it came to be known under several different names, such as social democracy, the social market economy, the welfare state or, in its international manifestation, embedded liberalism. It represented a compromise between the ruling and ruled classes, a grand bargain that rested on the shared expectation of increasing benefits generated by an opening world market, and the expectation that those benefits would be shared reasonably among deserving or needy sectors of national societies.

Fordism was one of the earliest instances of this new compromise. A term coined by Gramsci in the 1930s as shorthand for Henry Ford's writings and industrial processes in the United States, it comprised two main features: the first was production-line specialization[44] which linked the routinized labour of semi-skilled workers to a process controlled and paced by machines. The second feature of Fordism was its advocacy of higher wages, which served to reward the exercise of discipline (and compensate for the loss of individual craftsmanship) in a rationally organized firm, and to put purchasing power in the hands of those workers who, as consumers, could then absorb the steady stream of goods mass-produced by a rapidly industrializing society. Fordism was perhaps the prototypical expression of Gramscian hegemony in the industrial sector. It was holistic and inclusive, purposely constructed to allow generalized access to mass private consumption, and thereby to improved material standards of living; it was in that sense constructed on consensual foundations. As one writer summed it, '[T]he working class was invited to benefit from its own submission to management authority within the firm',[45] a process Gramsci called micro-corporation. And, characteristically of Gramscian hegemony, this submission to authority also indicated that Fordism was hierarchically organized by private managers who recognized the coercive nature of mass production. The fragmentation of workers' jobs and their subservience to production machinery served to strengthen management's power over labour, even as labour itself agreed to the terms of the new arrangement.

Another major indicator of the onset of Gramscian hegemony was Franklin Roosevelt's New Deal – essentially, a set of policy measures enacted by the American Democratic Party between 1933 and 1940 in reaction to the mass unemployment and social dislocation caused by the Great Depression – which thoroughly embedded state-provided welfare in the United States. The New Deal comprised a social security system and retirement benefits, an unemployment insurance programme, and financial aid to the poor. It endorsed state control of prices and production in agriculture, the promotion of trade unions, and massive public works in transportation, power generation and communications systems. Its measures were overwhelmingly popular, despite the fact that the New Deal was also vulnerable to criticism from the right as excessive interference in the marketplace.

Fordism and the New Deal both took their theoretical bearings from British economist John Maynard Keynes, whose seminal *General Theory of Unemployment, Interest and Money* (1936) focused attention on the need for the institutional management of market activity. Consistently high levels of investment and aggregate demand were required, he argued, for full employment. These could be accomplished through direct investment in public works by the state, and by the transfer of wealth from rich to poor. This latter provision improved the lives of those less well-off, and also stimulated economic growth by putting money in the hands of the people most likely to spend it. Keynesian management techniques required state intervention, and state planning. And, moreover, because planning entailed some degree of control over external economic contingencies, it prompted at the same time a concern for expansionism that could bring supplier countries within the orbit of national aims and expectations. As Cox puts this point, 'The promotion of social welfare, which is the legitimating function served by economic planning, became implicated in economic nationalism and imperial expansionism'.[46] More fundamentally, the welfare state was premised on an assumption of growth, and was intended to revive and sustain growth in a market-led economy. This premise is apparent in that, in times of recession or stagnation when social services are most urgently called upon, the welfare system will be drained of resources even as public revenues are diminished; it was a system not sustainable in anything other than a growing economy.

Keynesianism validated the state in promoting material welfare and growth, and in regulating the social and economic affairs of civil society, and this was most clearly apparent in the United States with Fordism and the New Deal; but Western Europe was also implicated in the transformation of capitalist society which, in its broader aspect, I interpret as the spread of Gramscian hegemony. The Marshall Plan was the most immediate instrument through which the ideals of state interventionism were exported from the United States to Europe after the Second World War, but more generally this hegemony was institutionalized in the Bretton Woods system of international financial management, of which Keynes was a principal architect. The International Monetary Fund, the World Bank and the GATT were all indicative of a new international realignment of the capitalist order under a dominant American influence. The internationalization of the New Deal, the rebuilding of liberal democracy in Europe, increased support for the political centre, class compromise and corporatism, Keynesian forms of macroeconomic management and the widening application of Fordist production, were all component parts of the Pax Americana, of Gramscian hegemony, and of the post-war growth paradigm.

This is not to say that Gramscian hegemony after the Second World War was only capitalist, though it was predominantly so. Redistributive regimes in the Soviet Union and China were fundamentally different. Forced collectivization was anathema to market capitalism but, from a Gramscian perspective, it did embody both coercive and consensual elements which shaped a socialized whole according to the tenets of an ideational superstructure. Coercion was manifested as central control over civil society, and consensus was evident with regard to proletarian and peasant ascendancy in a communally oriented ideological setting. And both elements were implicated in the larger growth paradigm because, in the Soviet Union in particular, sustaining the Bolshevik Revolution required the Soviet state to modernize and industrialize as rapidly as possible in order to match the military capabilities of the advanced capitalist states. As Cox puts this point, the evolution of Soviet and Chinese regimes was 'dictated by the desire to achieve the most rapid increase in productive forces so as to enhance the regime's survival capacity in a conflictual world'.[47] In this sense, redistributive states were as much caught up in the growth paradigm as capitalist – and indeed, for similar reasons: social stability and the pursuit of material prosperity for all.

The class compromise between the rulers and the ruled, which encompassed both capitalist and redistributive forms of state in the twentieth-century global polity, marked that point in time when Gramscian hegemony was most clearly evident, but transformative changes were imminent. Consensus-based leadership appeared to be giving way to the dominating effects of a newly globalizing world economy, and the welfare state was being transmuted into the competitive state. As I suggest below, however, only the form and not the substance of Gramscian hegemony and the growth paradigm was affected.

A series of abrupt and profound changes radically altered the world's politico-economic landscape in the 1970s, and these changes collectively marked the time of transition from post-Second World War Keynesian social democracy to the new neoliberal framework which advocated the minimization of state intervention in the rapidly globalizing international marketplace. Among the more significant events of the time were these: In the United States, declining productivity growth and competitiveness prompted then-President Richard Nixon to suspend, in 1971, the convertibility of the dollar into gold, and to impose import surcharges on Japan, Europe and the Third World, prompting a new round of protectionism among major economic rivals; the rise of OPEC and, subsequently, two global recessions (1974–1975 and 1980–1982), induced high rates of inflation, low growth, low rates of investment and substantial surplus production capacity; large quantities of petro-dollars were recycled into industrialization projects in Arab, Latin American and East Asian states – but recessions undermined export commodity prices and drove up interest rates, which abetted Third World demands for a New International Economic Order; and, the United States lost the war in Vietnam, having been forced out of the country in 1975. These and other tectonic shifts which occurred over a period of some 15 years eroded public confidence in the social bargain which had been struck after the Second World War.

In a revealing analysis of the impact of these changes on American social values, Michael Adams[48] argues that a popular rejection of state activism, which had reached its high-watermark with Lyndon Johnson's Great Society, (or, perhaps, Pierre Trudeau's Just Society in Canada) centred on what Adams identifies as the socialism, hedonism and idealism of the post-war world. Socialism had been allowed a foothold in America by FDR's New Deal, but it also prompted a reaction from the right. The Keynesian economic theory which underwrote state interventionism was now under attack from a new school of economic thinkers that advocated monetarism instead of demand management as a way to encourage sound economic reasoning in the marketplace. Hedonism in America and abroad, exemplified by the cultural excesses of the 1960s, had been the apparent result of too-generous social programmes. And idealism, expressed in the political conviction that Communism had to be stopped, and that America must do it, had been harshly discouraged by the military debacle of Vietnam. The response to these shifts in values, under the tutelage of Ronald Reagan, was to attack state paternalism and to reinvigorate the values of competitive individualism. The need for a strong America, in the wake of the various crises of the 1970s summed briefly above, was sufficient to vindicate, so Reagan argued, tax cuts, the deregulation of banking and industry, an attack on union power and the many other facets of an emergent neoliberal ideology which were beginning to surface in the United States, and in Britain under Margaret Thatcher.

In short, profound and far-reaching changes in the global polity ushered in a new version of capitalism – neoliberalism – and a new era of economic globalization. According to some analysts,[49] this shift also signalled the erosion of social consensus, and the dissolution of Gramscian hegemony in favour of dominance, coercion and competition. Stephen Gill in particular argues that neoliberalism is oligopolistic, a 'politics of supremacy rather than a politics of justice or hegemony'.[50] In this regard there is no doubt that institutional change was widespread and univocal. Corporatist agencies and social programmes associated with post-war Keynesianism were marginalized, first in the United States and Britain, then throughout much of the capitalist world. And these changes did arguably reflect a rejection of the grand bargain that characterized the earlier era of Gramscian hegemony, as I have identified it, which extended from the Fordist industrial revolution through to, approximately, the mid-1970s. But this was not in fact a consequential change. The shift to neoliberalism, like the shift from the Pax Britannica to the era of rival imperialisms which Cox identified, can more plausibly be understood as a conjunctural episode – an event drawn from the medium-term temporal frame – within the larger architecture of the growth paradigm, and within a longer period of Gramscian hegemony.

The renewed emphasis on competitive individualism notwithstanding, the social consensus in favour of economic growth was not broken, and in fact was strengthened considerably. Two factors may be cited to support this contention. First, Reagan's economic programmes of fiscal stimulus (through military spending, primarily) and supply-side tax cuts helped to generate a post-1982 boom which seemed to justify and vindicate the socio-economic changes he initiated as part of his 'new morning for America'; and resurgent economic growth catalyzed the return to individualism which had long been intrinsic to the American psyche. The 'preternaturally likeable Ronald Reagan',[51] as Michael Adams calls him, charismatically and effectively bridged the transition from state paternalism to competitive/possessive individualism without compromising the underlying shared commitment to growth, and in fact popular faith in that commitment, and in the new neoliberal approach to it, was strengthened by what appeared to be Reagan's successful economic performance.

The second factor in support of the contention that Gramscian hegemony was changed but not broken stems from earlier observations documented by sociologists Abercrombie et al., as discussed in Chapter 3. I recall that those analysts, in their historical examination of the dominant ideology thesis, argued against the existence of such an ideology in the post-Second World War world political economy – an argument I have rejected – though they did concede that the transmission mechanisms for dissemination, such as systems of mass education and communication, were firmly in place by that time. It is this latter point that is of particular importance with respect to the growth paradigm. Despite the collapse of the welfare state, individuals, now freed to fend for themselves, were immersed in the culture of consumerism generated by mass media,[52] which had by then penetrated into virtually all corners of the globe, and which served to bind consumers ever more closely to corporate expectations of continuous growth, and to state policies which endorsed and encouraged those expectations.[53]

The transnational managerial class: redux

At the third phase of class evolution, the interests of the dominant class merge with those of all subordinate groups to form a whole entity, as described above – but the precise nature of that dominant class has been to some extent submerged in the foregoing discussion. Here, then, I identify more clearly the particular actors of which the ruling class is composed, and sketch its current status in the global polity.

Cox writes that 'World hegemony can be described as a social structure, an economic structure, and a political structure; and it cannot be simply one of these things but must be all three'.[54] On this view, the growth paradigm, conceived as world hegemony, or as a dominant form of governance, comprises a global economy with a dominant mode of production; a political system of states which finds the hegemonic order conducive to national interests; and a web of international social relationships which connect super- and subordinate classes of different countries. Leadership of world hegemony is attributed to a transnational managerial class (TMC) that includes key economic actors (central bankers, CEOs of MNCs, heads of international financial institutions and so forth), and political actors (primarily state leaders) who play a supportive and enabling role. It is the function of political actors to generate market-compatible regulatory regimes, and to provide and maintain the international organizations through which the universal norms of world hegemony are expressed. Economic and political actors derive their legitimacy from the common culture that enfolds them and civil society in a unified social formation, at that point in time when Gramscian hegemony is attained.

It is not uncommon for contemporary critical IPE literature to make reference to a transnational managerial class, which is uniformly described as comprising political leaders and an economic elite, both groups having joined forces such that, as Onuf said earlier, world politics and the world economy are now inextricable. The work of Kees van der Pijl[55] of the Amsterdam School of neo-Gramscian analysis offers a prominent example: his detailed examination of the social evolution of transnational capitalism focuses on particular individuals and organizations (including Freemasons, prominent families such as the Barings and Rothschilds, key newspapers and influential behind-the-scenes venues such as the Bilderberg Conferences, the Trilateral Commission and the World Economic Forum) which, he argues, are now collectively recognizable as a social class. In contrast and from a sociological perspective, Leslie Sklair[56] theorizes transnational relations by looking to particular economic practices (such as industrial production, the provision of laws conducive to economic growth, and consumer behaviour) the origin of which can be traced back to specific social strata. He identifies an economic stratum dominated by transnational corporations, commodity exchanges and surveillance institutions such as the World Bank and IMF; a political stratum that constructs a regulatory environment conducive to liberalized trade; and a cultural-ideological stratum dominated by transnational mass media which 'produce values and attitudes that create and sustain the need for [goods and services]'.[57]

Notwithstanding these observations and analyses, however, it is not immediately apparent that this collective formation of political and economic leaders self-identify[58] as a management class. It seems more likely that state leaders would regard themselves as sovereign policy-makers who collude or compete as circumstances require, and that the economic elite would emphasize competition as much as common cause. These differences and crosscurrents have led Cox at least among critical theorists to treat the concept of class as applied to international politics with some circumspection; indeed, his more recent work does not refer to a transnational managerial class at all, but to what he now evocatively calls a *nébuleuse*[59] comprised of state, corporate and intellectual representatives who work together – through official and unofficial, international and transnational networks – toward the formulation and maintenance of a policy consensus for globalized market capitalism. State power and corporate power are 'integrated in a comprehensive authority structure',[60] he observes, which includes a wide range of powerful institutions and organizations including the WTO, World Bank, IMF and OECD; G8 preparatory meetings and summits; regular meetings of central bankers; and the Trilateral Commission and annual meeting of the World Economic Forum in Davos, Switzerland. Though it may be premature to posit the existence of a fully formed managerial class, the *nébuleuse* certainly foreshadows the possibility: the integration of state and corporate power, the internationalization of production and concomitant divisions of labour, and the growing divide between rich and poor within and between nations, are all portentous in this regard.

That a TMC already exists in nascent form is evident from the foregoing and for two additional reasons. First, if production leads inevitably to class formation, as historical materialism asserts, then one may anticipate that globalized production would generate a globalized class structure stemming from the international division of labour. And second, there is a substantial new subset of contemporary IR literature which now focuses on the emergence, characteristics and activities of transnational civil society, but this terminology can only have meaning in a context that includes a counterpart to it, namely, a stratum of rulers with a collective presence in the international arena as opposed to which an emergent transnational civil society can be defined. On balance, I support a less tentative interpretation of the TMC than offered by Cox. I do not see the *nébuleuse* as a recent political phenomenon which arose *ex nihilo* during the post-Keynesian era of neoliberal globalization. The temporal frame employed here reveals the leadership stratum as having evolved from a continuous history of elite rule. There have always been leaders, and the inchoate TMC is the modern transnational manifestation of that fact. Further, and more importantly for this discussion, despite the differences and divisions which fragment the leadership stratum, it is nonetheless uniformly bound by the common commitment to economic growth as a policy priority. I have emphasized consistently that the growth paradigm is an instance of ideational hegemony. Above all else it is the belief in the efficacy of growth that unifies the TMC, and that, at the Gramscian hegemonic moment, embraces civil society too.

I have traced to this point the evolution of a ruling class which emerged at the medieval/modern juncture; which developed through three phases, culminating in the Gramscian hegemony after the Second World War; and which was over time increasingly oriented toward material progress, capital accumulation and economic growth irrespective of culture, level of development or regime type, according to the dictates of the ideational superstructure of the growth paradigm. In Chapter 5 I will attend to the evolution and current status of transnational civil society, especially with regard to the potential of that social stratum to instigate radical change, but before doing so I discuss more explicitly in the concluding section of this chapter the reasons why the commitment to growth came to be such a dominant force. The neo-Gramscian point of view makes clear that those reasons did not arise from civil society. The growth paradigm was an elitist project at its inception. National civil societies were only gradually incorporated into it, and transnational civil society was not folded into the paradigm until well into the twentieth century. Those who are ruled lend political legitimacy and cultural support to hegemonic structures such as the growth paradigm, and civil society is the most likely source from which change may originate, but the dominance of the paradigm must ultimately be explained with reference to political leadership. I indicate in the following section that several reasons have combined to explain the orthodoxy and exclusivity of the commitment to growth, but that a normative argument is particularly apposite.

The normative foundations of the paradigm

I discussed in Chapter 2 various contributions to the paradigm which were associated with the three levels of analysis: structural, functional and psychological contributions were derived from the systemic, state and individual levels respectively. Each was found to offer unique insights into particular characteristics of the paradigm, but none was identified as being determinant. Taken together as an explanatory matrix, on the other hand, those characteristics reveal a host of compelling reasons why the growth paradigm has achieved its currently dominant status in international relations. These reasons, nevertheless, fall short of an understanding of the normative foundations of the paradigm; they do not reveal why the pursuit of economic growth is perceived to be the right thing to do. I address this issue next, with particular emphasis on the notion of freedom.

An underlying tension was found to inhabit relations among all three levels of analysis examined in Chapter 2 – a tension derived from the free agency which is implicit in the agent–structure configuration that links the levels together. For example, the systemic constraints imposed by mobile capital are evident, but can as easily be construed as consequences of state behaviour which could, if necessary, be regulated by domestic or international policy. Systemic forces, in other words, are significant but ultimately avoidable if states choose to exercise their autonomous agency. The argument that the dominance of the growth paradigm can be explained with reference to functional reasons at the state level of analysis also draws on the notion of freedom because, as above, the sovereign right to national self-determination releases states, in theory at least, from the disembodied influence of systemic forces; and also because the functional approach posits a set of desirable ends which are willingly pursued as a matter of free choice. I have already identified those functional reasons, beginning from the mercantilist pursuit of material wealth and extending through to J. K. Galbraith's description of economic growth as a social lubricant which meets virtually all the needs of contemporary state policies. Similarly, individuals in the neoliberal world order claim the right to personal freedom from undue interference by the state, so the state cannot categorically determine individual behaviour. And, at the same time, genetic or psychological propensities to accumulate wealth on a competitive basis could, presumably, be contained or redirected by the free exercise of individual will. Thus neither structural, nor functional, nor psychological contributions to understanding the growth paradigm can be determinative if the notion of free agency is allowed any play.

With Theodore J. Lowi, I note that rulers have two main types of responsibility: moral and material.[61] The latter is, in effect, the pragmatic responsibility to get things done. Lowi puts it this way:

> Because the material well-being of the populace depends on economic growth, social services, and social protection, the rulers who organize and direct their provision should be given the necessary powers to make things work and should be rewarded for their efforts.[62]

The former (moral) responsibility is described as follows:

> [I]f there must be rules, there must be rule inventors; if there must be guidance, there must be guidance givers. Thus do leaders provide a moral framework for society, a framework increasingly critical as society grows in complexity and scale. Those who provide this framework merit the powers and privileges they enjoy.[63]

On this view, which I endorse, rulers are responsible for the moral integration of society and for the rules which provide guidance toward collectively agreed objectives. It is this aspect of leadership which I pursue here. The normative argument propounded below and in the next chapter is both explanatory and evaluative. The explanatory argument posits that the dominance of the growth paradigm can be attributed in large part to decisions taken by rulers for moral reasons that favour economic growth over alternative policy priorities; the evaluative argument posits that the morality supporting those decisions, and the commitment to growth itself, are questionable.

The growth paradigm, in its orientation to betterment, has always had an intrinsically moral dimension but this in itself does not support the conclusion that rulers drew on that feature to rationalize or justify decisions made. The

Enlightenment, and the bringing into being of the growth paradigm, were, arguably, exercises in moral improvement, but it would be incorrect to conclude that material progress was pursued by governments during all of the previous three centuries to improve the lot of the masses, or that individual gain was pursued in order that the exercise of private vice would be transmuted by Smithian doctrine into public virtue. Even though the Enlightenment commitment to reason, to betterment and to freedom has remained consistent throughout the modern age, interpretations of state and individual behaviour which call on the self-interested pursuit of wealth and power, at least during the earlier phases of this age, seem much more pertinent.

The explanatory argument which pertains to the dominance of the growth paradigm, and which draws on its normative dimension, did not become relevant until the beginning of the twentieth century – not by coincidence, as Gramscian hegemony began to mature – at which point a new set of international issues began to emerge in relation to which state leaders adopted a specifically moral posture. International relations have often raised ethical challenges, but Reinhold Niebuhr alerts the analyst to the possibility that such issues may become more prominent (and less tractable) as human society becomes larger and more complex, which means that new issues in which ethics play an important role are likely to emerge at later stages of social evolution. Such is the case with respect to the growth paradigm: its normative dimension has only become salient (and problematic) in relatively recent history. I illustrate this argument with reference to episodes during which ideas about alternatives to unfettered growth threatened to gain a foothold in the public domain. Two such instances have occurred in recent history, and both gave voice to normative reservations about the processes and objectives of economic growth. Neither instance has been successful in reorienting the international political economy. I construe the defeat of those threats as indicative of the normative preeminence of the growth paradigm, and I argue in particular that the paradigm's normative power derives from its embrace and defence of a particular conception of freedom, so that an attack on growth is tantamount to an attack on freedom. I introduce the relationship between growth and freedom below.

The concept of freedom is contested in social philosophy and in political practice, but I take as given that it is generally seen in a positive light, by rulers and ruled alike, and I assume that the origin of modern conceptions of freedom can reasonably be traced to the European-wide rejection of the universalistic shackles of Empire and Papacy at the feudal/modern juncture. For present purposes, in other words, I understand freedom in terms of the individualism, rationality and pursuit of new opportunities which are characteristic of the modern era. Somewhat more formally,[64] I define freedom in terms of the traditional distinction between its negative (freedom from) and positive (freedom to) modes. The former is expressed as freedom from constraint or coercion that blocks self-realization; the latter is the freedom to realize one's own conception of well-being. The two are linked as follows: A is free from B to do C, where A is the agent, B is the constraint that blocks self-realization, and C is the desirable end to be attained.

The relationship between freedom and growth was initially forged in the Reformist thrust to individualism, and in the disembedding of economy from society, both of which lessened collective constraints on economic behaviour (that is, increased freedom) and encouraged production and accumulation (that is, increased growth). Concurrently with those changes, the newly emerging state system, and *raison d'état*, provided a larger context within which the linkage between growth and freedom could flourish. That system and the political logic by which it was constituted were premised on a shared commitment to freedom from interference and freedom to pursue self-determination, expressed respectively in terms of autonomous foreign policies and inviolable domestic control. The exercise of those freedoms created the permissive condition of anarchy under which the untrammelled pursuit of wealth and power (viz. growth) ensued. And, during this same era of change and expansionism, capitalism arose to join growth to freedom of (consumer) choice, and freedom of (entrepreneurial) opportunity. In sum, while I acknowledge the complex provenance of the relationship between economic growth and freedoms variously defined, I accept as relatively unproblematic the conclusion that the normative dimension of the growth paradigm is evident not only in its orientation to material progress, but in its linkage to freedom as well.

I alluded above to two historical episodes when ideas about alternatives to unfettered growth threatened to gain a foothold in the public domain. The first, which was expressed as a set of normative reservations about the processes and objectives of growth, pertained not to growth as such but to its management and its apparent effects on social organization; issues were raised, that is, about how growth should be controlled, and by whom. These objections found expression in a political reaction from the left opposed to capitalist accumulation, culminating in the construction of redistributive regimes in, predominantly, the Soviet Union and China. The second episode was characterized by a set of reservations that emanated from a historically entrenched substrate of resistance to progress/growth, ranging from the Romantic movement to Meadows' *The Limits to Growth*, and into contemporary discourses of environmental governance. Here the issue has been less about control over the process of growth, and more about its intrinsic desirability, and its biophysical limits. This point of view drew on a variety of perceived problems with the open-endedness of Enlightenment thinking, and eventually crystallized around the key concern that a cornucopian image of a boundless planet might be misleading. Both instances raised challenges to growth, and to freedom, which have been effectively defeated. I discuss these in turn.

Robert Cox has argued that there are really only two modes of socio-economic development, namely capitalist and redistributive.[65] 'Both accumulate in order to grow',[66] he notes, and in that respect they are the same. Where they differ is that, for the former (capitalist) mode, 'an unconscious process of welfare promotion purported to lie in the market'[67] is given relatively free rein, and is divorced as much as possible from political intervention. For the latter, social goals are, at least in theory, politically determined after conscious (rational-ethical) deliberation. The challenge to the growth paradigm which emanated from the tension between these two ideal-types was not expressed in terms of whether growth should occur, but how the process of growth should be controlled and optimized for the best interests of society.

This tension regarding the degree to which government should supervise economic activity has always been inherent to the growth paradigm but in Adam Smith's time, when the liberal state and the liberal world order were just emerging, it was not a fundamental concern because market forces then were still constrained within a robust set of social relations which tended to give direction and purpose to the mechanical operations of the economy. At that time, as Polanyi would say, the economy had not yet been disembedded from its social context; or, in terms of this study, the ideational component of the growth paradigm had not yet been fully disengaged from its socio-natural setting. As capitalism gained momentum, however, its effects on society began to be more pronounced: in particular, Marx began to take note of its tendency to develop unevenly, and to polarize societies. The reaction from the political left was to promote and incite an anti-capitalist revolution from below which would shift control over production processes from the bourgeoisie to the proletariat, and which would leave as its legacy a classless society and an ordered economy which would reward ability, compensate need and eliminate radical economic disparities. History now shows, however, that proletarian revolutions are rarely successful and that, in general, communism has been less durable than capitalism. The issue of control over the process and objectives of growth was decisively resolved in 1989 in favour of the capitalist, not the redistributive, mode of development.

The end of the Cold War can be understood as the triumph of democracy over totalitarianism. On the face of it that outcome is true, as it may also be true that a popular thirst for political freedom in the Soviet republics and in Eastern Europe pushed back the Iron Curtain and pushed down the Berlin Wall. But I argue instead that the growth paradigm dictated the outcome of the Cold War, and that economic freedom was the key underlying issue, not political freedom. Capitalist economies have, in the main, consistently out-produced centrally-controlled systems,[68] and the proximate cause of the end of the war was economic, not ideological: a larger GNP was the battering ram that forced the first cracks in Soviet totalitarianism. The American administration under Reagan was able to exploit an economic boom to support large expenditures on a renewed arms race, focused on the Strategic Defense Initiative in particular. The attempt by the Soviet Union to keep up led to near-bankruptcy, and the consequent unravelling of the state and its managed economy.

The spread of democracy is a positive outcome of the end of the War, but that outcome was secondary to the more important objective of removing debilitating constraints on economic, not political, freedom. This is not to say that the ideological dimension of the bipolar conflict was unimportant; indeed, that dimension was the most significant feature of East–West tensions in the early post-Second World War era. But the growth paradigm is, as I have indicated, both a structure of normalcy and a widening, forward-moving process which can overtake other priorities, including support for democracy. Most recently (just prior to the end of the Cold War), that forward motion was exemplified by Reagan's endorsement and promulgation of neoliberal capitalist ideology and practice, which shifted the global polity closer to the 'minimal intervention' ideal-type of economic development. In doing so, it intensified faith in the automatic and effective redistribution of wealth on the basis of comparative productivity advantages, as exercised by states, corporations and individuals alike, and simultaneously discredited governmental oversight of redistribution. And, it reinforced reliance on economic growth: if market-induced equalization were not to reduce living standards already enjoyed, increased wealth for the relatively poor would necessarily have to be drawn from an ever-larger economic pie. Moreover, democracy itself was rendered more vulnerable by the victory of capitalism. Cohen and Rogers have already shown (as previously discussed) that the materialistic orientation and short-term thinking encouraged by capitalistic behaviour are deleterious to the proper functioning of democratic institutions. Now, with the defeat of redistributive regimes, democracy is obliged more than ever to rely on the market to prevent the polarization of societies into rich and poor sectors. If the successful exercise of democracy, in other words, is in any way dependent on the absence of radical economic disparities, or the absence of pronounced social polarization, then it is now also dependent on the market's purported ability to prevent or mitigate those disparities.

The first set of reservations with respect to unfettered economic growth took the form of a preference for deep governmental intervention into the marketplace, with the objective of evening out significant differences within states. Given the ever-widening counter-preference for minimal intervention, however, the Cold War became less a conflict between democracy and totalitarianism, and more a normative conflict revolving around the core concept of economic freedom, which had come to be seen as the fountainhead of social improvement. The normative explanation for the dominance of the growth paradigm, then, calls first on the notion of negative freedom – freedom from political constraint, coercion or regulatory intervention in economic affairs. The moral power of the paradigm is in this sense warranted by the historically substantiated and apparently sound belief in the rectitude of untrammelled economic freedom, as demonstrated by the outcome of the Cold War.

Complementary to the foregoing, the second set of reservations respecting the growth paradigm brings to light the notion of positive freedom (defined in terms of the objectives to which self-determination is oriented) as it pertains to the dominance of the commitment to growth. These reservations did not target the issue of control over the process of growth, but its intrinsic desirability and biophysical impact. In their modern instantiation they have crystallized around the key concerns that a globalized and growing economic system might be implicated in the erosion of social support systems, and in planetary ecological degradation; but these concerns have not deterred growth in either capitalist or communist systems. They too have been defeated by the moral preeminence of the growth paradigm.

I recall that the linkage between negative and positive freedom is such that agent A is free from B to do C. The question addressed now is, precisely what are the objectives to which human society as a whole is oriented, given the positive freedom of self-determination, and are those goals being achieved? I have identified the growth paradigm as the dominant form of global governance to which human society accedes. Global governance, in turn, implies the intentional pursuit of a set of particular objectives – necessarily broad in nature, but of fundamental importance nonetheless. These include equity, prosperity, betterment of the human condition and, not least, ecological safety and the continuity of social systems through time. The TMC, though its collective vision of the future of human life on Earth has never been clearly articulated beyond a platitudinous endorsement of the foregoing, affirms that these goals can and will eventually be met. Various reservations expressed about growth, however, have suggested that they will not. How does this tension, currently resolved in favour of the TMC, illuminate the positive freedom inherent to the growth paradigm?

In order to illustrate that the growth paradigm embodies a normative commitment to positive freedom, that this commitment rests on a moral approbation of economic growth, and that this approbation has defeated ethical concerns about growth, I examine three particular examples of normative goals which exemplify the more generic objectives of global governance listed above. These goals are reducing North–South economic polarization, ensuring intergenerational equity, and protecting biodiversity on Earth. I will discuss these in turn, but first I note that reaching goals – exercising positive freedom – requires proactive agency. Freeing oneself from constraint – attaining negative freedom – may also require agency, but such action is enabling, not productive. For global governance to be productive, it must be proactive with respect to the exercise of management and steering capabilities.

I have shown above that, with reference to the Cold War and the communist–capitalist ideological confrontation, economic growth overpowered the perceived need for governmental intervention to achieve a reasonable measure of socioeconomic equity. The distributive ethic itself was not damaged in that confrontation. The emphasis shifted from equality of outcome to equality of opportunity, but a norm of fairness was evident on both sides of the debate and, arguably, continues to inform the practices of world institutions which have taken on responsibility for the prevention of unjust economic behaviour in the post-Cold War setting. Growth had simply come to be seen as an effective surrogate for redistribution, and constraints imposed on the process of growth had come to be seen as constraints on freedom.

In the wake of the success of capitalism, the notion of growth as surrogate for redistribution has been applied to the North–South problem too, in that a globalized economy conducted on neoliberal market principles is expected to reduce world poverty, just as intrastate poverty will be reduced on the strength of those same principles. On that view, amelioration of the North–South problem would follow naturally from the defeat of communism and the spread of neoliberal capitalism; its resolution would simply provide another example of the benefits of economic freedom from political constraint. No compelling evidence, however, is yet available that would indicate an imminent correction of the problem. North–South divisions are not being resolved or ameliorated and in fact, many would argue, are worsening and will be further exacerbated by rapid population growth in the South. This tectonic division in human society seems immune to neoliberal prescriptions, and evidently speaks to the need for a clarification of the normative objectives to which human society should aspire – and to the need for proactive intervention. The North–South problem is distinguishable from intrastate polarization by its scale (the number of people living in poverty), by its severity (the discrepancy between living standards of rich and poor), and by the sense of humane urgency which might reasonably correspond to those features. Taken together, they suggest that dynamic political intervention to achieve the desired objective is morally justifiable; an intervention, that is, which goes significantly beyond present practices of encouraging economic growth within developing nations, corporate investment in Third World economies, or official development assistance of various kinds. And yet, contrary to the stipulation that positive freedom requires the exercise of proactive agency, no such intervention is now being contemplated.

The absence of political leadership in morally vexed world affairs is also evident with respect to the issue of intergenerational equity. Here, its purpose would be to make economic development sustainable – 'to ensure that it meets the needs of the present without compromising the ability of future generations to meet their own needs', according to the familiar definition offered more than 20 years ago by the Brundtland Commission.[69] Sustainable development is a multifaceted objective which raises complex questions about the long-term viability of renewable resources (such as arable land or the marine fishery), and non-renewable resources (such as oil or fresh water); and it brings into sharp focus the most significant challenge that overarches multiple generations, namely climate change. It is hard to foresee a stable, economically prosperous and ecologically benign future if the planetary climate itself is pushed into a new and unpredictable regime. The scale and critical nature of these sustainability issues present reasonable grounds for political management of capital assets; and, moreover, they raise thorny ethical questions about the respective rights of present versus future generations of people: all of which suggests that rational-ethical deliberation, responsible oversight and proactive management might be propitious. But, once again, no such management is in view.

The problem of reduced biodiversity is clearly a significant part of the larger gestalt of that which we bequeath to the future, because species lost are lost forever and cannot be replaced by other forms of natural or constructed capital. As with other resource issues, complex questions are raised here about the roles played by flora and fauna in Earth's ecosystem, and about the impact of species loss on the viability of human society. But the instrumental point of view, which is essentially anthropocentric, does not capture the key normative characteristic of this problem: species loss raises unanswered questions about the intrinsic value of non-human life, and in doing so broadens the domain of concern beyond instrumentalism and anthropocentrism. For so long as those questions remain unresolved, it is ethically dubious to countenance the extirpation or extinction of irreplaceable life forms. The precipitous and ongoing decline of biodiversity on Earth[70] is not compatible with what might be called the normative dimension of the precautionary principle, but here too no evidence indicates the existence of collective and effective political management of human activity that is causally linked to species loss.[71]

Each of these three problems is debilitating in the present, dangerous in its extrapolation to the future, and morally questionable. Each is also susceptible to political management. It is not unreasonable to suppose that effective political agency could achieve the goals of poverty reduction, intergenerational equity, and the protection of biological diversity. Why has this agency not been exercised? One explanation is simply defensive of the neoliberal position; it supports the belief that insufficient time has elapsed for the market to produce predicted outcomes, or that there is still too much market distortion in the form of subsidies, tariffs, public ownership, excessive regulation and so forth, and that when these are finally removed or resolved, poverty reduction will ensue, resources will be efficiently managed and, given the commodious attitude that may accompany prosperity, non-human species will also be allowed their own form of self-realization. A second possible explanation for hands-off policies draws on the realist tradition. From that vantage, growth is pursued by elites not to reduce North–South disparities, to improve human society, or to preserve nature, but to maintain stability among competing interests in order that wealth and power could continue to be accumulated without disruption from below. A third explanation is organizational, not ideological. Lack of progress on these issues may simply be a reflection of the intractability of collective action problems of world-scale proportion, and of the formidable challenges of international institution-building.

A neo-Gramscian explanation, on the other hand, does not look to neoliberal prognostications, to realist tenets, or to the challenges associated with institution-building, but to the paradigmatic belief that economic growth will produce efficacious solutions without public intervention. On this view, the benefits of growth are overtly and, as it were, sincerely proselytized in the public domain by the TMC; indeed, sharing the expectation of a better future is an integral part of the active and ongoing process of incorporation of civil society into the Gramscian hegemony of the growth paradigm. Solutions for the problems listed above are seen by the TMC as necessary, desirable and possible, and the pursuit of those solutions by the TMC constitutes the exercise of positive freedom on behalf of human society as a whole. The embedded caveat which delimits the terms of positive freedom, however, is that government intervention with regard to these normative problems must be focused on more economic growth alone, from which appropriate solutions will ostensibly flow.

The contours of the paradigmatic belief in the efficacy of growth and its relationship to positive freedom can be clarified by employing the device of counterfactual narrative.[72] If equity and ecological safety were the preferred objectives of the TMC, then the North–South problem would not be tolerated, future generations would not 'damn us for our spendthrift ways',[73] and non-human species would not be threatened with extinction. These issues are clear, present and morally egregious; they ought not to be tolerated and, under a form of governance more ethically sophisticated than the growth paradigm, would not be. Appropriate political controls exercised by authoritative inter- or supranational institutions, conducive tax regimes, long-term planning which draws on rational-ethical precepts – these tools and methodologies, though clearly challenging to construct and deploy, should be within the reach of responsible political leadership; and the challenge to construct and use them, moreover, is of small proportion relative to the issues they are meant to address. That these issues have not in fact been effectively resolved speaks to the conclusion that the objective sought by the TMC is not the good life as defined with reference to equity and ecological safety. If it were, its realization would be imminent, or perceptible, or at least not receding. If the TMC, in other words, were directly intent on the specific objectives of equity and ecological safety, then those objectives would now be in sight. They are not, because the desirable objective of positive freedom is defined with reference to a different goal, namely growth. Expressed more explicitly in terms of the relationship between growth and positive freedom, the growth paradigm dictates compliance with the requirement to be free to maximize growth. This requirement is different from but complementary to the negative requirement to be free from constraint to pursue growth; nor is this set of requirements a tautology, but a redundancy that self-reinforces – in effect, turbocharges – the growth paradigm. Stated baldly, the ethical foundations of the growth paradigm preclude constraints on growth in order to achieve the objective of maximized growth.

The TMC is cognizant of pressing social and environmental problems, but is collectively seized of the opinion that the pursuit of economic growth is both the most practical, and the most morally sound approach to their resolution. The belief in its practicality is derived from a particular interpretation of Smithian doctrine – that public goods can be delivered without public intervention – which has been given the imprimatur of modern economic science. The belief in its moral rectitude is derived from a particular notion of positive freedom that reduces political responsibility to market forces, which in turn offer an easily accessible and ultimately fungible alternative to political action without compromising the right-mindedness of the TMC. It is this moral component of the growth paradigm which permits the TMC to portray an attack on growth as an attack on freedom, which undermines the legitimacy of the second stream of reservations expressed about growth, and ensures its failure.

The growth paradigm facilitates the freedom to pursue an image of the future that is equitable, cornucopian and ecologically benign. Its progressive teleology and orientation to a better future for all affirm its credentials as the right way to improve the human condition; and the belief that its idealized image of the future can be achieved on a cost-free basis adds an element of political expedience which renders the paradigm universally attractive and powerful in practice. That economic science and growth-as-freedom, however, have not clearly assured the long-term security of human society – and in fact that their effects may be counterproductive with respect both to prosperity and ecological safety – opens the possibility that transnational civil society, complicit to date in the paradigm, may reconsider their approbation of it.

5 Tensions in the paradigm and prospects for change

Introduction

Transformational change to Gramscian hegemonic structures will occur only if three conditions are met. First, the hegemonic structure itself must be clearly defined, presenting a distinct and unmistakable target for change. Second, it must be riven by persistent anomalies which indicate that its belief system has been overextended, and that change might be possible, and perhaps imminent. Third, there must be among the population of civil society 'organic intellectuals' around whom counter-hegemonic social forces might be organized. This chapter will assess the prospects for transformational change (that is, a paradigm shift) by examining the evolution and current status of transnational civil society, and by uncovering tensions and contradictions inherent to the growth paradigm which may presage conflict between counter-hegemonic social forces and those who remain loyal to paradigmatic commitments.

The hegemonic growth paradigm which structures the domain of international relations by functioning as a dominant form of governance has not been clearly defined to date, and therefore has not presented a distinct target for dissident opinion. In this regard, I have intended throughout to bring to sharper relief the contours, the substance and the meaning of the paradigm so that its trajectory and ramifications can be more readily perceived, at least from a neo-Gramscian point of view, and so that the first condition for change will have been met. Subsequent sections of this chapter will address the second condition for change by exploring various anomalies which suggest that the paradigm may be becoming incoherent. This chapter begins, however, with a closer look at transnational civil society. The Gramscian perspective in general, and the neo-Gramscian approach to international relations in particular, indicate that organic intellectuals – an expression that refers to political activists who unite theory with social practice – are unlikely to emerge from the ruling class. That group is homogeneously committed to growth as a policy priority, and all major international institutions (as constructed by that class) are likewise deeply committed to the paradigm. Civil society, on the other hand, though an active participant in the culture of consumerism, is less homogeneous because of its sheer size and complexity, and because the democratic impulse actively encourages a plethora of competing ideas within it. Moreover, given that the social costs of neoliberal economic growth, such as pollution or eroded social services, tend to fall mainly on the civil population, change is more likely to emerge from among those who bear such costs.

Social forces opposed to hegemonic structures and processes are obliged, on the neo-Gramscian view, not merely to oppose but to actively construct alternative social systems. This implies that a compelling counternarrative (or perhaps multiple counternarratives) must be made available to form, in effect, the ideational component of a counter-hegemonic structure; and that an organizational project must be undertaken by elements of civil society such that a transition from one leadership cadre to another, and from one set of functional institutions to another, can be achieved. Gramsci distinguishes in this respect between 'wars of position' and 'wars of maneuver', terms derived from the military lexicon but intended by him to apply to two different types of political change.[1] War of position refers to the longer and more arduous process described above in which a counter-hegemonic structure – in effect, a parallel paradigm – is put in place, as far as that may be possible, prior to the transition so that social disruption is minimized. War of maneuver refers to a decapitation strike which usurps command, control and communication systems, such as occurred with the Bolshevik Revolution of 1917.

This latter type of transformation, though faster and more violent, is less likely to be successful if the civil society affected by it is intimately engaged with the state, and is complexly institutionalized. Cox has noted that a war of maneuver often produces 'a fragile victory likely to succumb to the entrenched forces of a recalcitrant civil society',[2] but this was not the case in twentieth-century Russia. A strong and well-formed state–society complex did not exist, so the Bolshevik victory was durable. Western Europe, on the other hand, presented a different and more challenging set of circumstances, as Gramsci perceived from the vantage of the Italian Communist Party. In Europe, the liberal democratic state was more closely united with civil society, and the latter played a much more active role than in Russia. Gramsci saw, in the interwar interval of the 1930s, that capitalism and fascism could not be so easily defeated by communist insurgency, that the Russian example could not be repeated, and that wars of position would have to undertaken instead. Similar circumstances obtain today with respect to the growth paradigm. Given its broad consensus and deep social engagement, a 'war of maneuver' – a decapitation strike against the paradigm – seems impossible to conceive. No single force, independently of transnational civil society, could significantly alter its material or ideational components, or its trajectory through time.

Transnational civil society

The term 'civil society' has a complex history which will be truncated and simplified for present purposes.[3] In the sixteenth century, Thomas Hobbes conceived of civil society in contrast to the unrestrained conflict endemic to nature. The state was the guarantor of law within an ordered realm and that order constituted the foundation of human civilization separated and protected from the violence of nature. Hobbes' stark delineation of order versus chaos was made more nuanced by John Locke, who argued that the state could constrain, even abuse, as well as protect freedom and that a formal separation of the state from other social organizations, such as the economy, was necessary. A separate social sphere inhabited by autonomous individuals was envisaged by Locke as the entity, constituted in law, that could limit state power to constrain freedom. Karl Marx, for his part, argued that a civil society constituted on Lockean principles could not be free anyway because of the structures of domination which were produced by capitalist economic relations – structures which had developed precisely because of the separation of political and economic spheres advocated by Lockean liberalism. Thus and so the notion of civil society was mooted throughout early modern history, without definitive resolution. The discussion gradually receded to the background, with the notable exception of Antonio Gramsci's contributions, until approximately the 1980s when civil society re-emerged in the guise of oppositional movements in Eastern Europe, which contributed massively to the dissolution of the Soviet Empire.

This new, activist version of civil society, evidently self-organizing, purposive and potentially transformative, is also transnational in scope because of shared interests and modern means of communication and travel; and it answers to neither corporate nor state interests. As Robert Cox notes, '[transnational] civil society is now usually understood to refer to ... autonomous group action distinct from both corporate power and the state ... [which occurs in the] political space between constituted authority and the people'.[4] Gramsci had conceived of the Communist Party as the builder of that political space and as leader within it, but today no political party has assumed a comparable role of coordinating popular movements toward a particular transformative objective. Instead, as Cox observes, a 'post-modern collective prince'[5] formed by popular movements themselves may be an emergent, self-organizing characteristic of an activist civil society. On today's world stage, however, it is manifestly unclear as to which coalition(s) will lead, which group(s) will willingly follow, exactly what destination(s) might be pursued, and what role organic intellectuals might play in this amorphous context.

Transnational civil society (TCS) in the modern world is an inchoate and complex pot-pourri of elements which easily eludes analytical definition. It is simultaneously, as one observer puts it, 'a project, a process, and a space, all in search of an unresolved sociological form'.[6] Though its recent impetus came from the collective effort in Eastern Europe to escape the confines of totalitarian oppression, it has now taken on the more general character of a social force opposed to exclusion and domination of all kinds, especially if that domination is linked to globalization, that is, to any of various forms of economic, political or cultural hegemony. But the TCS is not merely an oppositional force; it is also the democratic counterpart to globalization in which network-building, alliance formation and advocacy all contribute to the construction of alternative social structures. Ultimately, however, its complexity precludes the simple reduction of the TCS either to a collective opposition to market-driven capitalism, or to a new collective expression of global democratic citizenship. 'There is a dialectic inherent in civil society', writes Cox. '[It is] both shaper and shaped, an agent of stabilization and reproduction, and a potential agent of transformation'.[7]

Ronnie Lipschutz argues that the TCS is emerging at this point in history for three reasons, the first of which suggests that networks of knowledge and action constructed by decentred local actors are the logical counterweight to a transfer of state sovereignty to supranational institutions. As with many analysts of economic globalization, Lipschutz makes the point that institutions such as the WTO represent new forms of universalized hegemonic authority, and that the devolution of sovereignty to subnational organizations facilitates a challenge, from below, to that supranational authority. Provocatively, Lipschutz suggests that this process of bifurcation has happened before in history: the creation of the system of Westphalian states was itself, he argues, the result of a coup from below. International anarchy was invented by the political leaders of civil society in medieval Europe explicitly to replace the universal authority of Empire and Papacy. In a similar fashion, transnational anarchy is now being created by political activists of the TCS in order, in effect, to stage another coup from below directed against the emerging universal authority of supranational institutions infused with the ideology of neoliberal capitalism.[8] An important difference between these two historical occurrences, however, is that the goals of this modern insurgency are much less well defined than those of sixteenth century European elites; the meaning of transnational anarchy is not clear, and its ultimate structure is unknown.

The second reason for the emergence of the TCS at the present time is that it embodies a functional response to the decreasing willingness and ability of state agencies to produce public goods and to deliver the necessities of social welfare. In this respect, myriad organizations have sprung up to address common concerns about environmental and development issues, human rights, threats to livelihood, threats to public health (such as AIDS), the rights of indigenous peoples, and so forth. In general terms the activism of the TCS, on this view, can be attributed to the erosion of the welfare state under neoliberalism. The third reason identified by Lipschutz is that the emergence of the TCS represents a 'large scale resistance to the Gramscian hegemony of the current international system',[9] by which he means the globalizing culture of consumerism. This argument is not well developed, however. Consumerism is assumed to be a necessary adjunct to neoliberal capitalism and is therefore not problematized; and the 'Gramscian hegemony' alluded to but not explained reflects the common but simplistic usage of the term as a synonym for the dominance of a particular (Western) cultural type.

In keeping with the analysis offered by Lipschutz, the development of the World Social Forum (WSF) also suggests that transnational civil society evolved on a track parallel to the one followed by neoliberalism, from the 1980s to the present. I have argued in Chapter 4 that economic growth in the West, accelerated by neoliberal ideology, was instrumental in the demise of the Soviet Union and in that respect the earliest indications of transnational public mobilization were indeed linked to changes in the global economy. Since then, mass demonstrations against various aspects of globalization have been orchestrated from within the TCS: the OECD-sponsored Multilateral Agreement on Investment (MAI) was effectively derailed in 1998 by popular resistance; meetings of the WTO were disrupted in Seattle in 1999, in Davos in 2000, and in Quebec City and Genoa in 2001. But these confrontations provoked the reaction from political and economic leaders that obstructive social forces were not offering a viable alternative to existing processes and objectives, and it was this reaction that generated the impetus for the formation of the WSF. As one analyst writes, 'Stung by the repeated criticisms that activists had no alternatives and nothing to offer but criticism, the anti-corporate globalization movement moved on to new terrain, creating their own global venue, the World Social Forum'.[10] The WSF first met in Porto Alegre, Brazil, in January 2001 at the same time, not by coincidence, as the World Economic Forum convened in Davos, Switzerland. Its objective was to establish a dialectical tension between a 'neoliberal utopia' and the notion of a 'critical utopia' based on the premise that 'another world is possible'.[11] Since 2001, annual meetings have attracted steadily increasing attendance.

Like the TCS, the World Social Forum is itself an elusive political phenomenon that may be an event, or process, or space, though its Charter of Principles[12] opts for the latter conception. Principle #1 describes the annual gatherings as an 'open meeting space [for] groups and movements of civil society that are opposed to neoliberalism and domination of the world by capital and any form of imperialism'. Its objective is to experiment in 'building a new world in solidarity' (Principle #14) by helping to energize a kind of de-territorialized democracy. The WSF is explicitly intended to be horizontally structured, and to generate a sense of pluralism and dynamism. It formally rejects the idea, however, of participatory democracy with, as Peter Smith puts it, 'its paraphernalia of electoral and party politics and concept of a non-political neutral, rational public bureaucracy administering on behalf of the winning party or coalition'. What is called for instead is 'direct, participatory democracy that is moving into society on a variety of levels'.[13]

Notwithstanding its self-conception as a free political space or a critical utopia, all but the smallest and most intimate of social organizations will evolve into a de facto hierarchy, and the WSF is no exception. Smith's analysis makes clear that it simply could not function without a lead organization which has power, and which makes binding decisions. In this case it is the International Council, an association of 150 non-elected networks, which decides where meetings will take place, and who will be allowed to speak. Not surprisingly, such decision-making has been contentious and problems about the use and effects of organizational and agenda-setting power (often pertaining to gender issues) are becoming common. And, in response to the fact that the WSF does not, at its meetings, establish common objectives, new organizations within the WSF are rising, whose intention it is to take independent action on a variety of fronts, with or without formal approval. More divisive still is the emergence of at least one counter-forum to the WSF (which is itself a counter-forum). The Mumbai Resistance, for example, revolutionary and Maoist in tone, has denounced the WSF as a reformist talk-shop and seeks instead to overthrow imperialist and capitalist systems by any means possible.

The image of transnational civil society as activist, self-organizing and purposive is, perhaps, most common, but other images are appropriate too. Cox has undertaken a broad survey of the world's civil societies,[14] and has identified at least five distinct categories, all independent of the activist or emancipatory stream described above. Briefly listed, these include the complexly structured civilian populations that participate in the highly evolved capitalism of Europe and America; the more culturally and historically embedded civil societies of Asia, of which Japan is emblematic; citizens cast adrift and victimized by state breakdown and predatory capitalism, such as has occurred in the former Soviet Union; and the peoples of Africa where, viewed broadly, civil society is at odds with oppressive state governments. The fifth category described by Cox reminds the reader that transnational civil society is also inhabited by less sanguine elements of 'the covert world', that is, terrorists, organized crime and drug cartels; and by other organized groups that encourage xenophobic populism, religious fanaticism or other such divisive or disruptive activities. The TCS, on this wider view, is even more layered and fragmented, and more difficult to discern analytically, than the social activist image might at first suggest.

Nonetheless I have chosen to portray transnational civil society in a simplified form, drawing on the Marxian predilection for a two-class dichotomy, and on the broader, historically constant notion of a division within all societies into those who rule, and those who are ruled. I have employed this parsimonious perspective in order to make the power dimension of the growth paradigm clearer, and to reflect the observation that human society, over the long term, may indeed be evolving into a more polarized social structure. With that in mind, I traced in Chapter 4 the evolution of a transnational managerial class from the medieval/modern juncture to the present. Along the way, I indicated that many national civil societies were gradually incorporated into state–society complexes bound by a common commitment to economic growth, and that similarly the TMC gradually incorporated the TCS into the coherent structure of the growth paradigm. The beginnings of Gramscian hegemony, I have argued, were evident by the time of the First World War, and were fully realized with the emergence of the welfare state, and embedded liberalism internationally, after the Second World War; and Gramscian hegemony has persisted beyond the demise of the welfare state into the era of neoliberal capitalism.

A number of features are binding the TCS into the two-class structure of the growth paradigm, not least of which is a pervasive and widening culture of consumerism with respect to which coercive forces and consensual compliance are clearly visible. Coercion is exercised by, among others, transnational corporations which propagate the culture of and push the need for consumerism through ubiquitous advertising. Aggressive campaigns to encourage the purchase of cars, pharmaceuticals, tobacco products, fast food and much more, attest to the persuasive power of producers of goods and services. By the same token, however, people consume because they want to; the attractiveness of material prosperity is strong because it springs from a deeply imbedded expectation for improved living standards. To track the status of this expectation, opinion polling regularly takes the pulse of 'consumer confidence' in the economy so that prognostications about future sales can be made. At the same time, mass media tout fast and consistent growth as good, healthy or promising, while slower or irregular growth is disappointing, worrisome or threatening, and it seems certain that these affective pronouncements will further sensitize consumers to the need to propel the economy forward. The culture of consumerism and the process of socialization shaped in part by the media nurture the notion that consumption is not just a right, but a duty to the well-being of the national economy.

The close ideological association of the rulers and the ruled, widening class divisions notwithstanding, is also evident in the proliferation of private–public partnerships (PPPs) as tools of governance. Comprising cooperative relationships between government, private for-profit firms and non-profit NGOs, these partnerships are oriented to 'the making and implementation of norms and rules for the provision of goods and services that are considered as binding by members ... of the international community'.[15] This new form of governance tool reinforces and substantiates the neoliberal argument that private actors are better suited to regulate their own affairs and coordinate their own activities 'because states and IOs alike lack the knowledge and expertise to solve increasingly complex problems in international governance'.[16] On this view, state failure in the provision of public goods is evidently more debilitating than market failure, and must therefore be minimized through the privatization and deregulation of formerly public services. A more benign interpretation of the rise of PPPs offered by Paul Wapner[17] suggests that the involvement of international NGOs in structures of governance is an indication of the maturation and responsible activism of transnational civil society, and that such involvement improves the democratic nature and accountability of international institutions. Whether PPPs are the result of a neoliberal attack on states' responsibilities, or they are the mature fruit of transnational participatory democracy – either way, the merging of state, corporate and civic affairs further enhances the holism of Gramscian hegemony as it evolves under the rubric of the ideational superstructure of the growth paradigm.

Governance undertaken by non-state actors is not restricted to the nuts and bolts of economic issues. There is a decidedly normative content to some of the programmes undertaken by public–private partnerships such as, for example, the Global Compact. An initiative of Kofi Annan which was first presented to the business community at Davos in 1999, it was formalized in July of 2000. Its objective is to identify good corporate practices based on universal principles, and to put those principles into effect through the cooperative efforts of the private sector and the UN, in partnership with international NGO networks and labour organizations.[18] Valuable as this initiative may be, it also blurs the nexus of public–private relations such that it is no longer clear where the burden of responsible governance ought to lie; and it signals a new willingness on the part of the UN Secretariat to harmonize its operations and expectations with market forces in such a way that the role of state governments, especially with regard to development issues, is diminished. The shift in emphasis to the private sector which is embodied in the Global Compact, moreover, has been further strengthened through the Millennium Declaration[19] of 2000, which committed the international community to reduce world poverty by half by 2015, and by the Monterrey Declaration,[20] which enshrined 'development for all' as the most important goal of the twenty-first century. The latter declaration makes clear that development should be enabled primarily by private funding, and that aid should be understood only as complementary to it; and that trade is the main engine of growth, from which development will follow.

This merging of public and private interests has been examined by Jean-Philippe Thérien of the University of Montreal. He has contrasted two worldviews regarding development issues, called the UN paradigm and the Bretton Woods paradigm, which had been fundamentally different but which are now closer together than ever. Their differences are embodied in the fact that

> [T]he Bretton Woods institutions speak more in terms of poverty, the UN more in terms of inequality. The former frame the problem of development as one of individuals who are not well adapted to the demands of the market; the latter define it primarily as a structural issue whose solution would require global redistribution measures.[21]

However, while the UN in general remains more interventionist than Bretton Woods institutions with respect to externalities or inequities related to economic globalization, Thérien notes that the Secretary-General and UNDP in particular have taken an ideological turn for economic pragmatism in their support for the need among developing countries to lower tariffs and other trade barriers, to facilitate the flow of imports, exports and international finance, and in general to open markets to the rest of the world. They have, in this respect, acquiesced in if not wholly endorsed the approach to development taken by the IMF, World Bank and the WTO. Globalization, he concludes, has not in fact generated a new compromise similar to the embedded liberalism of the post-Second World War. One paradigm has come clearly to dominate the other, reflecting a slant toward what he calls the centre-right of international politics. Public–private partnerships, I conclude from these analyses, are readily recognizable as the product of Gramscian hegemony in which the political priority attached to economic growth is at all times evident, and dominant.

Many prominent members of civil society have offered critiques of economic growth, from John Mill to Herman Daly, but no organized groups within transnational civil society have emerged with the specific agenda of opposing the political commitment to growth. The only significant exception to this occurs within what one analyst has called ecological resistance movements. Bron Raymond Taylor's survey of this stream within the TCS has revealed that threats to livelihood and health caused by environmental damage provide the most important motivation for these movements; but the second most important reason cited by groups surveyed in Europe and the Americas, in Asia and in Africa was the negative impact of economic growth and industrialization on the land. 'An important trend [within these groups]', writes Taylor, 'is to view growth and industrialization as illusions offered by elites to keep ordinary people from defending and promoting appropriate and sustainable alternatives'.[22] But, resistance to those 'illusions' is seldom revolutionary, and is instead intent on wresting concessions from the TMC. Ideologies of resistance are tempered with pragmatism in light of the widely held belief that 'concessions gained depend on the enforcement of the nations or states from which they were won'.[23] This approach is indicative of the *trasformismo* typical of Gramscian hegemony. The hierarchical structure of class relations precludes the possibility of radical change from below, the ideational superstructure of the growth paradigm preempts any serious attack on its core tenet, and ecological concerns are perforce reduced to issues about economic management, not economic growth as such. Though opposition to growth is apparent within this activist stream of the TCS, it is ultimately redirected into a generic opposition to the negative social and environmental effects of economic (neoliberal) globalization, which is likewise the only clear theme that the civil society organizations of the WSF share in common.

To date, opposition to economic growth has missed a distinct target – the idea of growth itself – and it has lacked organized representation within the ranks of transnational civil society. A neo-Gramscian interpretation of this situation suggests that a reason for this lack of action may be that the anomalies, tensions and contradictions which inevitably inhabit any hegemonic structure, and around which opposition might gather, have not been clearly identified. The next section focuses on this aspect of the hegemony of the growth paradigm in international relations.

Tensions in the paradigm

Temporal frames

The first tension is set up by a conflict between short- and long-term points of view which, in Braudelian terms, pits *l'histoire événementielle* against the *longue durée*. The former frame of reference has gained preeminence in modern human society. As Stephen Gill puts this point, there is 'a tendency for the collective historical memory to be supplanted by a consciousness preoccupied by the instantaneous and the evanescent'.[24] The compression of time, the postmodern sense of vertigo, and the need for continuous economic adjustments engendered by the rapid forward motion of human society into the future, have made the contemplation of history by political leaders difficult, if not irrelevant.[25] Moreover, a focus on the immediacy of the short term obscures perception of the growth paradigm as a single period of epochal time and, paradoxically, it obscures perception of the fact that the paradigm itself is a short-term event in the wider context of human evolution. The 300-year-old modern age (which is congruent with the era of the growth paradigm) includes an astonishing array of historical change and development but, simultaneously, it has occupied only the smallest and most recent segment of the much longer path followed by the evolutionary emergence of *Homo sapiens*. The trajectory of the paradigm/modern age can be depicted graphically as a spike, a dramatic surge in recent human activity preceded by a much longer period of time – several thousands of years – during which the human population and its aggregate impact on Earth were comparatively flatlined. This kind of graphical representation would look rather like a hockey stick with the long handle of history laid horizontally, and the blade pointing more or less straight up.[26] It would show clearly that the growth paradigm is a single historical episode, that it is unique in human history, and that it has developed very rapidly over a comparatively short period of time. In contrast to the leisurely pace of human development prior to it, the paradigm thus portrayed is a short, sudden and demonstrably anomalous change.

Many macro-trends native to recent human experience follow this same pattern of exponential take-off. Notable among them are population growth, total world economic output, total energy consumption worldwide, and carbon dioxide emissions to the atmosphere, all of which show the characteristic spike typical of human fecundity in the modern age. Of these trends, total world economic output and total energy consumption are particularly pertinent to the growth paradigm because of their direct embodiment of economic growth as such, and because of the intimate relationship between them. The discovery, capture and consumption of fossil-fuel energy was instrumental to the emergence of modernity and the powering up of the Industrial Revolution, and the rate and total volume of economic growth (as a quantitative process) in the modern age is directly proportional to the consumption of energy by human society. Furthermore and of more immediate relevance to the notion of temporal frames, the linkage of economic growth to the use of fossil fuels radically changed the public perception of time from what appeared to be a cyclical phenomenon to one which moved ever forward into the future. Enlightenment thinking had offered a rationale for the linear evolution of progress in society, but ready access to a massive stock of stored solar energy, accumulated over millions of years, provided the practical means of making continuous forward motion possible. It broke the link between human activity and cyclical flows of energy previously determined by the seasons, and by the limited capacity of the food chain to store and deliver energy from its ultimate source, the sun. Instead of seasonal access to the flow of incoming solar radiation, the discovery of fossil fuels allowed unrestricted access to a vast stock of stored and immediately available energy, which enabled a final escape from the constraints of cyclical time and a full embrace of time as non-repetitive and conducive to continuous betterment. The result was that human society could and did grow rapidly, indeed exponentially, simply by digging ever deeper into the energy well.

This fast and steep growth curve has also instigated a tension between its ecological implications, the nature of political decision-making which those implications entail, and the respective timeframes of these two processes. As John Ruggie has noted, 'The key epistemological problem for decision-making [about ecological issues] is the trade-off between potentially high risks and inadequate knowledge about them'.[26] A balanced trade-off between risk and knowledge is difficult to achieve because, given the complexity of ecosystems, the often indeterminate effects of human activity on them, and the short timeframe in which pertinent economic decisions must be made, reliable information may simply not be available. Ruggie warns that relevant information 'may be produced either too late or perhaps only as a by-product of the very outcomes that one is seeking to avoid'.[28] He calls for a 'bias shift' in decision-making, away from conventional problem-solving and toward risk avoidance, but he suggests that any such shift will be problematic because the costs of risk avoidance 'will be direct and visible whereas the benefits are likely to be diffuse and longer term'.[29] That costs are perceived to be direct but benefits diffuse and long term is a consequence of decision-making within an incremental temporal frame which foregrounds negotiation processes, treaty compliance and regime construction – and economic growth – without allowing due consideration for larger and ultimately more weighty challenges.

Taken together, these various tensions between short- and long-term points of view, and the manifest preeminence of the former, weaken the coherence of the growth paradigm. Additionally, the preoccupation with incremental time has effectively obscured the important issue of scale – that is, the issue of how big human society can ultimately grow in the long term relative to Earth's ecosystem – to which I will return later in this chapter.

Tension between the ideational and material components of the paradigm

The paradigm's history, as well as its political and ecological implications, are most clearly apprehended in the context of, and with tools appropriate to, the *longue durée*. The importance of this placement is that each temporal frame brings into focus a unique ontology. With regard to the growth paradigm, that ontology includes a dominant (ideational) social episteme and the (material) relationship between human society and Earth's ecosystem. The former might be called our social consciousness; the latter, our social being. For Gramsci, hegemonic structures occur when social consciousness (which includes a widely shared set of expectations) and social being (which includes the social relations of production as well as our linkages to the natural world) are commensurate or otherwise congruent. Such structures may be unstable or vulnerable to interrogation and attack, however, if contradictions inhabit either domain. The growth paradigm is not, however, currently threatened by an opposed set of expectations in the ideational domain; nor is it threatened by opposition from within the transnational managerial class or from within civil society which, evidently, still anticipates the salutary future promised by (perhaps a more socially responsible[30]) neoliberal capitalism. The prospect of imminent prosperity for both classes is key to the persistent and stable belief in economic growth. The paradigm is rendered vulnerable, on the other hand, by tensions *between* social being and social consciousness. The new prominence of large-scale environmental problems suggests that beliefs about the world are not congruent with the world as it is; that the ideational and material elements of the growth paradigm are not in fact harmonious. The collectively held belief in the efficacy of growth is an abstraction which has been disarticulated from its biophysical foundations. It overarches but is unaccountable to its material base. One sees this, for example, in comments such as that made by former US President Ronald Reagan. At an address to the University of South Carolina in 1983, he asserted that 'There are no such things as limits to growth because there are no limits on the human capacity for intelligence, imagination and wonder'.[31] The human capacities named by Reagan all inhabit the ideational domain, however. He has divorced them entirely from the natural foundations of which they are emergent properties, and to which economic growth is necessarily linked.

Cox has remarked on this disarticulation by contrasting the operation of the 'real economy', which takes time, effort and, necessarily, a reciprocal engagement of society with nature, with modern financial transactions which, comparatively, do not. The pursuit of short-term returns in the latter can 'undermine the social legitimacy of capital [and] the production process itself; for example, through predatory buy-outs and asset stripping'.[32] The distinction he draws is similar to that between use value and exchange value, which Daly and Cobb have emphasized by noting that the characteristics of money cannot be indiscriminately applied to the concrete use value of commodities themselves. '[I]f money can grow forever at compound interest', they say ironically, 'then so can pigs and cars and haircuts'.[33] Following Alfred North Whitehead, they call this the 'fallacy of misplaced concreteness'. Real wealth cannot grow exponentially, but money as a cultural symbol can, indefinitely. A lack of symmetry is apparent between what is measured (wealth) and the measuring rod (money). The problem at the core of the incongruent relationship between the ideational and material components of the growth paradigm is that the former, being abstract, is essentially unlimited (as Reagan ingenuously noted regarding 'intelligence, imagination and wonder') whereas the latter is not, at least until such time as the global economy might somehow be decoupled from Earth's ecosystem. The dominance of the ideational aspect of the paradigm facilitates the belief that states' GNPs, and aggregate world economic product, can increase forever even though the finitude of the planetary ecosystem and emerging environmental problems of global proportion suggest otherwise.

The task of re-establishing an appropriate balance between ideational and material factors has been taken up by various scholars of political science,[34] including Daniel Deudney, who are attempting to 'bring nature back in'. Deudney's approach to what he calls physiopolitics is functional-materialist; it rests on 'the simple assumption that the physical world is not completely or even primarily subject to effective human control, and that these material contexts impede or enable vital and recurring human goals'.[35] On this view, political responses to environmental issues are shaped by social, political and economic forces, but which responses actually work will be determined in important ways by objective material conditions. The effectiveness of the Kyoto Protocol and its successor agreements with respect to climate change, for example, will be determined not by the aptitude of policy-makers but by the climate itself. People choose, one may say, but Earth decides. The relationship between what we believe to be effective and true, and what is empirically palpable in terms of unfulfilled expectations and global ecological change, continues to be problematic and clearly indicates a significant tension inherent to the growth paradigm.

The unmet promise of material decoupling

Various efforts to reaffirm nature's role in the global economy run counter to the paradigmatic expectation that the impact of economic growth on Earth's environment can be reduced to harmless levels. Several approaches have been developed to test key tenets of neoclassical economic theory which bear on the issue of decoupling economic activity from environmental degradation. One such approach suggests that growth can induce an endogenous process (that is, a process inherent to growth itself) of decoupling such that environmental pressure will diminish as economic growth raises per capita income. According to this hypothesis, faster growth could be a solution to the environmental dilemma, not part of its cause.

On this view, environmental quality is characterized as a luxury good for which people will pay more only as they become richer. This is ostensibly so because a clean environment may be valuable to many people but, compared to the satisfaction of basic needs or the accumulation of desirable amenities, it is not a high priority. It follows from this that corporate-sponsored technological innovation will proceed more rapidly only when consumers are willing to pay a higher price for energy-efficient products; and environmentally responsible public policies will be enacted more expeditiously only when citizens are willing to pay a tax premium to subsidize their implementation. If this notion is correct, then higher per capita incomes will lead directly to overall improvements in environmental quality. Because this possibility is derived from the dominant economic theory which underwrites the growth paradigm (at least in its capitalist guise), and because an empirical evaluation of it has been undertaken by a variety of researchers, I pursue this issue below.

The theoretical link between economic growth and environmental protection was hypothesized as early as the 1970s[36] but empirical evaluation of the hypothesis was not possible until the 1990s when the UN-sponsored Global Environmental Monitoring System (GEMS) and other environmental data compendia began to make pertinent information available. Early indications suggested that the correlation may be supportable.[37] Specifically, the relationship between rising per capita income and environmental pressure in some instances followed the shape of an inverted-U, with income plotted on the horizontal axis and environmental impact on the vertical axis. The inverted-U curve indicated that the two variables increased together until a turning point was reached, after which rising income was correlated with declining environmental pressure. The relationship was first referred to as an environmental Kuznets curve or EKC[38] in 1993.[39]

Criticisms of the EKC hypothesis appeared quickly. S. M. de Bruyn's work entailed a comprehensive survey of this new EKC literature, and his review concluded that the hypothesis required substantial qualification. '[T]here is convincing empirical evidence', he writes, 'that economic growth does harm environmental quality, despite the decline in certain types of pollutants',[40] and that a more typical relationship between environmental pressure and growth is N-shaped, indicating that an initial period of de-linking is followed by a new phase of re-materialization, or re-linking of growth with environmental impact. 'One would expect this theoretically', as one commentator put it, 'as continued de-linking can go on only as long as the rates of reduction in environmental throughput or intensity per unit of income exceed production growth rates – and this is likely to come to an end and possibly even reverse'.[41]

Several weaknesses of the hypothesis have been made apparent by these critics. For example, environmental pressure is typically defined very narrowly in terms of a limited range of indicators, such as sulphur dioxide, oxides of nitrogen, suspended particulate matter, or changes in water quality. Inverted-U curves are most often found in the relationship between a short list of specific pollutants and income, but in many other cases pollution increases along all income levels, or N-shaped curves emerge. Importantly, these indicators relate mostly to emission rates, that is, to flows of contaminants, but environmental quality is affected by more than this. An EKC, even if it accurately reflects a downward turn in emission rates, says nothing about the accumulation of contaminants over time, the aggregated impact of pollutants on whole ecosystems, or the significance of irreversible damage. Moreover, EKCs seem to apply primarily to environmental problems that are easy to see, such as urban air and water pollution, and that are associated with a readily mobilizable political constituency, such as urban voters whose health has been compromised. Even in these cases, however, the turning points for these pollutants occur at income levels far beyond that which is foreseeable for the majority of the world's population. The EKC, in other words, is not immediately relevant to most developing countries.

Nor are the mechanisms clear that explain the decline in pollutants beyond certain income levels. Empirical studies offer only limited insight into the underlying driving forces because a variety of intervening variables such as technological innovation or composition of economic output are neglected in simple models which assume a direct correlation between income and environmental pressure. For example, material substitution may account for some emission reductions without accounting for the possibility of unknown environmental hazards from these new materials. Another possibility is that dirty industries have simply been relocated to developing states.

Finally, and perhaps most importantly, though higher income is in some instances correlated with reduced environmental pressure, it is also significantly correlated with stricter environmental policies.[42] This suggests that economic growth may be compatible with improvements in environmental quality only to the extent that environmental policy decisions are taken concurrently. If true, the inverted-U curve may be attributable to public policy, not growth. The postulate that economic growth will induce an endogenous process of decoupling of economic activity from environmental degradation, prior to the enactment of public policy, may in the final analysis apply only to a limited range of specific problems. As de Bruyn concluded, 'this effect [emission reductions] is small and does not outweigh the burden of economic growth due to a higher consumption of materials and energy'.[43]

A similar study[44] undertook an evaluation of the environmental impact of economic activity in OECD countries from 1960 to 1995. It highlights the key point that the EKC hypothesis does not clearly distinguish between relative de-linking, by which environmental damage diminishes per unit of GNP, and absolute de-linking, by which real reductions in environmental pressure are accomplished. Kågeson notes that, relative de-linking notwithstanding, '[C]arbon emissions per capita showed a clear tendency to increase with income'.[45] Moreover, carbon dioxide emissions to the atmosphere not only increased with income, they increased in absolute terms too, in lockstep with energy consumption.[46] This critical observation confirms the link between economic growth, energy consumption and emissions of carbon dioxide to the atmosphere. In fact, the second law of thermodynamics stipulates that economic growth as a physical phenomenon depends immutably on an ever-increasing throughput of matter and energy, both of which are drawn from and ultimately returned in modified form to the environment.[47] No evidence supports the possibility that this throughput can or will be reduced any time soon.

In sum, the EKC hypothesis offers no meaningful promise that economic growth can be de-linked from environmental impact as various countries move forward from current to future, higher levels of production and consumption. Also, because it does little to clarify the underlying mechanisms which purportedly link increasing personal wealth with environmental protection, the EKC hypothesis is not helpful in terms of orienting policy-makers to an environmentally benign set of political objectives, even though such objectives and the means to achieve them are of vital importance in terms of stabilizing the relationship between the human population and Earth's ecosystem. Unless and until goals specified by the growth paradigm are replaced, the ideational superstructure of the paradigm will remain in conflict with the global environment to which it is linked absolutely.

The conflicted goals of hegemonic leadership

Gramscian hegemony emphasizes the notion of leadership, a term that highlights the consensual nature of hierarchical social arrangements[48] characterized by a common orientation among classes to an agreed set of objectives, and by an intellectual and moral consensus regarding the means to attain those objectives. Gramscian hegemony, however, is not necessarily benign: its leadership may be misdirected, its goals inappropriate, and its preferred means counterproductive. The growth paradigm is this kind of aberrant hegemony. The expectation that social benefits will follow automatically from the free play of market forces constitutes an abnegation of political responsibility, and a dismissal of the need to specify desirable goals other than economic growth as such. Paradigmatic tension arises not only from this defection from leadership, but more specifically from the paradoxical expectation that a morally neutral economic system can effectively and consistently deliver morally positive outcomes.

The Enlightenment legacy links material progress with moral progress; historic changes driven by the steady accumulation of knowledge and its practical application have generally been perceived to be for the better. This argument is taken up by political economist and historian Benjamin J. Friedman,[498] whose broad historical perspective encompasses that span of time from the Enlightenment to the present day. He explicitly links the notion of progress to its modern instantiation as a political commitment to economic growth, and is expressly concerned to understand the moral consequences of economic growth. I examine his arguments briefly with regard to the pursuit of substantive political goals.

Friedman emphasizes that, at the Enlightenment, 'A central thrust [of religious doctrines of the time] was to lend moral support to secular activities and forms of worldly behaviour that were conducive to advance in the society's material standard of living'.[50] Reformist moral principles such as Calvinism, in other words, were originally understood to foster (what came to be called) economic growth, but Friedman's thesis attempts to close the Enlightenment circle: his argument supports the reciprocal relation, namely, that economic growth fosters moral progress. His causal lines are clearly laid out. Building from the Enlightenment foundation, a combination of market incentives and rational government policy generates economic growth, which fosters openness of opportunity, tolerance of diversity, economic and social mobility, fairness and democracy, all of which encourage enterprise and creativity, which lead to greater economic prosperity and positive feedback for the system as a whole. Friedman's thesis is defended with reference to detailed case studies of Britain, France and Germany, and its implications for the developing world are explored as well. The key question posed by Friedman, with respect to the alleged link between economic growth and moral progress within societies at large, was stated as follows: '[H]ow did the advance of knowledge and the resulting change in economic circumstances in turn [affect] the institutions and conduct of civil society more broadly?'[51] He turned first to Adam Smith to secure his historical footing with respect to this question.

Smith argued in his major eighteenth-century treatises that the evolution of economic activity was the key to understanding social evolution more generally. Scarcity drove societies, according to Smith, through a series of four stages – hunting/gathering, shepherding, agriculture and finally commerce – each of which engendered different needs and social roles, which led to the continual adaptation of political and legal institutions. Property rights, systems of weights and measures, a legal system and judiciary, enforcement mechanisms and the means for common defence, among many other 'progressive' changes, were thought to follow from the evolution of societies through these phases, or stages, of economic activity. Commerce was identified by Smith as the highest of these, characterized by specialized production, complex divisions of labour, and voluntary exchange in an open market – but including as well the civil institutions which provided social stability and an educated populace. With commerce came the new idea that individualistic, self-serving economic activity is beneficial to the common good. Private vice, as Smith's work has often been summarized, is transformed as if by an invisible hand into public virtue.

Friedman accepts the foregoing as well established in history and in practice, but raises an important question. Smith's formula for moral progress driven by economic activity was built on the premise that evolution occurs between stages. The advance, for example, from agriculture to commerce is a 'step up' which generates various social benefits. But Smith said nothing about evolution within stages; so what is it, asks Friedman, that drives economic growth now that the commerce phase has been successfully achieved? Why is the pursuit of continuous increases in GNP and an improved standard of living still 'of acute concern'.[52] To answer these questions, Friedman calls on the observation that people tend to measure the importance of changing circumstances against benchmarks, or frames of reference, which provide a context for those changes. As he puts it,

> people's satisfaction depends less on the *level* of their income than on *how it is changing* … economic growth matters because it enables the majority of a society's population to feel better off compared to benchmarks that are still recent enough to be meaningful. But once growth stops – no matter how high people's incomes have risen – it is only a question of time before habits adapt and the sense of well-being dissipates.[53]

Noting also that, in human psychology, the cost of losses tends to loom larger than the benefit of gains, Friedman concludes that stagnant economies – in which losses are more likely, and gains may be zero-sum – do not support the moral progress characteristic of growing economies. Intolerance, intensified competitiveness and the erosion of trust (and therefore democracy) are associated with periods of slowed, stalled or reversed economic activity. The lesson Friedman draws from these observations is stark: 'It is important that growth not falter',[54] even within Smithian evolutionary phases.

With respect to the developing world, it seems clear enough that economic growth fosters rising incomes and living standards, improving health, life expectancy and literacy. But Friedman notes as well that the evolution of civil institutions is also improved when economies grow. Drawing on data supplied by Freedom House, he notes that, in a survey of almost 200 countries, higher standards of living are positively correlated with improved political rights and civil liberties. And in developing economies in particular, the durability of democratic regimes is also directly related to how satisfied people say they are with their lives in general, which depends in large measure on the status of their standard of living.

Friedman's argument that economic growth can spin off positive moral consequence for societies, such as tolerance, openness, democracy and so forth, is interesting but moral arguments can easily be pushed too far by hopeful expectations. Friedman asserts, for example, that 'the majority of the total population *justly aspires* to standards more like those of industrialized countries while those countries' citizens also *rightly expect ongoing improvement* in their own living standards'.[55] It is inappropriate, in my view, to infer the existence of such rights from the moral consequences of economic growth described. If equalization and continuous socio-political improvements were rights, and if economic growth were the best way to procure them, then growth would be much more than a functionally and morally convenient objective: it would be the defining feature of a rights-based social order the deontic foundations of which would be incompatible with any non-growth alternative. Tying growth to rights effectively releases leaders from political responsibility. To meet their obligations, they need only promote more growth.

Much of Friedman's work is dedicated to illuminating the positive benefits of growth for a society's moral character, but he is sensitive as well to broader issues. He is concerned that 'moral thinking, in practically every known culture, enjoins us not to place undue emphasis on our material concerns', and that the pursuit of growth may 'compromise our moral integrity'.[56] He acknowledges that resistance to progress and growth has a lengthy pedigree – from the Romantics to Marx to the Club of Rome – and that this resistance has invariably been accompanied by a 'distinctly moral overtone'.[57] Is it wrong, Friedman asks, to use up resources indiscriminately, to inflict environmental costs on future generations, to change the climate, to extinguish species? The answer, he says, is yes, but growth as such is not the cause of these moral dilemmas; insufficiently rapid or misdirected growth is the problem. Disingenuously drawing support from Adam Smith in this regard, Friedman argues that public policy has an important role to play in economic management. 'Calling upon government to stand aside', writes Friedman, 'while the market determines our economic growth ignores the vital role of public policy: the right rate of economic growth *is greater than* the purely market-determined rate, and the role of government policy is to foster it'.[58] It is clear from this excerpt that Friedman, like the majority of contemporary economic and political leaders (that is, the upper echelon of the TMC), is of the view that problems engendered by growth are best resolved by accelerating the process of growth, providing only that it is directed by an enlightened public policy and is embedded in a kind of social morality which is itself encouraged by rising incomes.

It is thematic to the present study, however, that this reliance on 'the right kind of growth' is problematic. The Enlightenment, progress and the growth paradigm have consistently legitimated the commitment to further and more rapid economic growth, linking it to a steadily rising curve of moral evolution which maps directly onto the upward curve of technical and socio-political improvement. Contrary to this point of view, the argument developed here is that the growth paradigm has dampened the trajectory of moral evolution of human society. The linkage of economic growth to socio-political rights adds an ersatz legitimacy to the paradigm, and the defection from political responsibility in favour of economic freedom reveals the moral ineptitude of leadership with respect to the selection of major societal goals. Beyond the pursuit of growth, and beyond the generic 'peace and prosperity' rubric typical of the liberal tradition, no such goals are specified. Indeed, the particular focus on prosperity is undermining the prior and more rudimentary political responsibility to guarantee public security, and to ensure the continuity and viability of social systems through time. The paradigm's aggressive forward motion works against social stability. It has compromised the tranquillity and compressed the timeframe of civil society such that, as Friedman has discovered, dissatisfaction sets in quickly in the absence of change.

The conflicted roles of transnational civil society

Transnational civil society is the socio-cultural foundation of the growth paradigm, and the source of potentially transformative changes to it; a place of cultural compliance with the mores of paradigmatic normalcy, and a place where new social forces foment under the influence of organic intellectuals. These new forces both confront and create the contradictions and recursively dialectical tensions that mark the beginning of hegemonic transition.

One such contradiction associated with the paradigm pits monolithic neoliberalism and cultural homogenization against oppositely oriented processes of social and political fragmentation which are driven by a popular emphasis on self-reliance and individual freedom. In turn, competitive individualism corrodes the normative context, founded on trust, which is necessarily prior to a stable economy. This conflict between the global market and the global polity is manifested in civil society in the tension between the roles of citizen and consumer. The latter is fully engaged with the growth paradigm through the culture/ideology of consumerism, but the former has been effectively disenfranchised by the paradigm. Socio-political self-determination has been forfeited to the predetermined objective of universal prosperity; freedom of consumer choice has been substituted for the freedom to choose among a variety of types of polity. Transnational civil society faces a conundrum on which the viability of counter-hegemonic organization ultimately pivots, namely, which role has primacy? Each carries with it the potential for transformative change. Consumers can choose how and what they buy, and can therefore influence and shape the marketplace, and citizens in many parts of the world can form whatever political associations they see fit and elect whomever they wish. In neither instance, however, has the growth paradigm itself been targeted for change to date.

The tension between citizen and consumer is also manifested in the new need to provide global public goods versus the privatized means to produce them. The most important of these global public goods is a stable planetary environment, but here environmental stability is at odds with the consumption of natural resources.[59] Arable land is being pushed to its limits; freshwater systems around the world are being used up fast; inland and oceanic fish stocks are being harvested at unsustainable rates; the continuing loss of rainforests, wetlands and coral reefs is exacerbating a precipitous loss of biodiversity; and, in general, Earth's productive and regenerative capacities, its ability to absorb waste, and its benign climate are all being sharply tested by the sheer force of human economic activity. Moreover, these problems are being worsened by the rapid growth of human numbers, increasing at some 200,000 people per day. The planet's total stock of natural capital (and the flow of ecoservices generated by that capital) will necessarily be divided among ever more consumers and, as material living standards improve around the world, the amount consumed by each individual will increase too. These trends are opposed – available resources per capita decrease with population while consumption per capita rises – with the result that the rate of total increase of environmental load[60] rises more rapidly. Transnational civil society is confronted by the twin tasks of reclaiming its collective citizenship, then beginning to construct the foundations of an ecologically sustainable society.

To be available as a plausible and desirable alternative, and to make the transition from one to the other less disruptive, this new society must first co-exist in part with the existing hegemonic formation. The overlap in time of extant and alternative worlds is a critical feature of the process of change. 'During the transition period', writes Thomas Kuhn, 'there will be a large but never complete overlap between the problems that can be solved by the old and by the new paradigm. But there will be a decisive difference in the modes of solution'.[61] This process is a tug of war between paradigms which brings the mechanics of change into view and which emphasizes that, without overlap, change is not possible in the first place. At present, however, the growth paradigm admits no competitors. As Daly and Cobb have observed, the commitment to mathematical analysis by economists has promoted a heavy reliance on logic and abstraction to build a theoretical science. The problem with this normal economics, however, is that 'well-defined, self-identical concepts cannot capture evolutionary change. Nothing can evolve into its other if it at no stage overlaps with its other. Without admitting dialectical concepts, and a certain amount of contradiction, we cannot deal with change'.[62] The growth paradigm is well-protected behind its own logical walls. No single, compelling and desirable alternative to it has gained any purchase in the public consciousness of civil society, with the result that the escalating requirement for mitigation of environmental damage done by consumers embedded in the growth paradigm stands in stark contrast to the reduced social and political capacity to meet it.

It is not my purpose in this book to trace the contours of a utopian future in which social and environmental issues will have been resolved but it is, on the other hand, a relatively straightforward task to identify the preconditions which should be put in place in order to ensure that a range of developmental options will be available to the world's citizenry, and to future generations. For Cox, that means building an economy 'embedded in society ... and a society self-conscious of its embeddedness in the biosphere'.[63] Herman Daly too foresees a global economy providing commercial service to human society, and the human population in turn nested within Earth's ecosystem, from which a reliable stream of natural services may be drawn. He elaborates on this tripartite image by clearly identifying the three nested components of a steady-state, non-growing global economy.[64] The first, innermost, component is market capitalism itself, which successfully encourages efficient resource allocation and productivity. The market in turn is nested within a socio-political context; that is, the economy is constrained by ethico-political oversight and shaped by political intervention in order to serve the best and long-term interests of human society as a whole. The third and largest component is Earth's biosphere, the capacity of which to support aggregate economic activity will determine the ultimate limitations imposed on the capitalist core. Each of these three components draws on a different set of performance criteria. Market capitalism is defined in terms of efficiency. The socio-political system in which the market is embedded is informed by redistributive and other ethical criteria. And the overall size of the economy, and of the human population, will be determined with reference to limitations imposed by ecological criteria. The picture that emerges from this sketch is of a stable population supported by a durable set of natural and constructed artifacts, from which the elements of a good life are drawn for everyone. The artifacts in turn are maintained by a minimal throughput of material and energy, which limits resource reliance and entropic waste dispersed to the biosphere. From this secure foundation, one may imagine human society exploring its developmental options at leisure into the unforeseeable future.

The issue of an optimal scale of human society on Earth represents a key tension within the growth paradigm because Earth's carrying capacity is finite but the paradigm is open-ended, and this same tension also stresses the relationship between consumer and citizen inasmuch as it obliges the latter to constrain the former, which works against the impulse to grow. Because this issue is central to the limits to growth debate, I pursue the question of optimal scale below.

Kenneth Boulding offered a useful way of conceptualizing the idea of scale in 1966 by contrasting an open ('cowboy') economy characterized by 'reckless, exploitative, romantic and violent behaviour', and a closed ('spaceman') economy which, like a self-contained spaceship, would be a managed ecosystem 'without unlimited reserves of anything'.[65] These analogies are evocative, but they misrepresent a key issue which has subsequently been clarified by Daly and Cobb.[66] They note that the scalar issue – the problem of establishing an optimal scale of human activity relative to Earth's ecosystem – is trivialized in the cowboy economy because total human activity is minimal in a frontier context; and the issue evaporates in the spaceman economy because activity becomes coextensive with Earth's ecosystem: the global economy and ecosystem are one and the same. Neither of these analogies properly represents current reality, however, because the global economy is neither trivial nor coextensive. The first case has long since passed, and the second implies that human society can effectively and harmlessly manage the whole Earth, as a spaceship crew manages its constructed environment. Given Earth's complexity and changeability, however, this latter prospect seems unlikely.[67] It follows, then, that the human population should stabilize, and our economy settle, at a mid-range scale which is optimal both for human development and for ecosystemic viability over the long term.

The parameters of optimal scale are in fact unknown at present, but Daly and Cobb make clear that a precise predetermination of them is not necessary. We need only bear in mind that our economy, however large, should be sustainable in perpetuity at levels of per capita resource use that permit a good life for all. Knowing this,

> Our first goal therefore should be to stabilize at existing or nearby levels as soon as we reasonably can. Once we have learned to be stable at some level, then we can worry about moving to the optimal level.... If we do not know how to be stable, then identification of an optimal scale will only allow us to recognize and wave goodbye to it as we grow beyond it.... Those who argue that there is no point in talking about stability unless you can first specify the optimal scale ... have got it backwards. *Unless we are willing and able to be stable, there is no point in knowing the optimum.*[68]

This discussion regarding scale illuminates the crucial point that what needs to be managed is not Earth's ecosystem. Such an undertaking would, by any reasonable measure, exceed the reach of human abilities. What is called for instead is self-management, that is, management of human behaviour relative to the planetary environment, which implies a sense of restraint, and of respect for the life-supporting ecoservices which nature provides at no cost. Neither restraint nor respect, however, can follow easily when the role of consumer trumps that of citizen in transnational civil society.

Conclusion and prospects for change

J. K. Galbraith was among the first to identify a curious orthodoxy among states with respect to their collective perception of economic growth as a socio-political panacea. From deep within the Gramscian hegemony which was consolidated in the wake of the Second World War he observed perspicaciously, and presciently, that the commitment to growth had become monolithic and normalized and that, despite its tendency to leave in its wake 'private opulence and public squalor',[69] it admitted no alternatives. In 1958 he remarked that interrogating growth had become 'the forbidden question. Over it hangs a nearly total silence'.[70]

Increasing concerns about the social implications of economic growth and the environmental impact of industrialization, however, soon prompted a public and highly charged debate about growth which intensified in the 1960s and 1970s. E. F. Schumacher objected to the notion of unlimited expansion in the face of what he perceived to be limited human wants.[71] T. W. Hutchinson emphasized that policies for rapid economic growth 'have considerable effects on the whole politico-economic constitution of society, the nature and extent of freedom, and the distribution ... not only of income, but of power'.[72] English economist E. J. Mishan invited his readers to examine 'the blessings heaped on mankind as a result of rapid economic growth [and] to wonder whether it is really worth it; whether economic progress over the last couple of centuries has succeeded only in making life increasingly complex, frantic and wearing'.[73] Herbert Marcuse objected to the arrival of a one-dimensional society[74] in which the possibility of revolutionary change had been suppressed by affluence, the people having become a willing part of a cohesive social entity. Meadows et al. emphasized what they perceived to be the biophysical constraints on growth, and Fred Hirsch argued that the depletion of moral capital caused by capitalist competition might be even more corrosive to the social fabric than depletion of natural capital.[75]

Neither were proposed changes in short supply during that era though, for the most part, they tended to group around core issues such as stabilizing the human population, curtailing industrial investment and development, and alleviating North–South economic disparities. Massive transfers of capital and wealth, motivated by a new societal ethic and awakened concern for ecological equilibrium, were to be the main planks in a global platform of environmental sustainability and regional equity. The transition to this new world could be accomplished, according to one set of scenarios, by imperial force, by contractual arrangements secured by a world authority, or by trauma exogenously imposed by Earth's over-extended ecosystem.[76] None of these transformative changes, however, has yet occurred.

The limits to growth debate flared in the 1960s and 1970s but it had been virtually extinguished by the end of that interval, for a variety of reasons. The research done by Meadows et al., emblematic of new concerns about economic growth, was excoriated by economists, computer modellers and others as incomplete, methodologically flawed and affectively biased,[77] in the sense that prescriptions for the future were allegedly influenced by prior ideological preferences for non-material values, which moreover were being expressed by those who already enjoyed a high material standard of living. Other responses provoked by the attack on growth focused on the need for better scientific knowledge about human–nature interactions, on the alarmist tone of anti-growth stories, and on the apparent extremity of changes proposed. By the early 1980s, and in the wake of this failed assault, a new neoliberal ideology of international political economy, premised explicitly on more and faster economic growth, had begun to flourish.

Environmental concerns, though, had not been sidelined altogether. In fact, the UN Conference on the Human Environment, convened in Stockholm in 1972, provided an important institutional setting for closer consideration of issues raised, and formal international engagement with those issues grew substantially in the following years. Two landmark events during that evolutionary process were the publication in 1987 of *Our Common Future* by the World Commission on Environment and Development, and the United Nations Conference on Environment and Development (the Earth Summit) of 1992. All three of these events pressed the environmental agenda forward. They did so, however, without rejecting but instead embracing the need for continuous economic growth.

Environmental issues have clearly moved from the periphery of international relations to a much more prominent position, such that one may now speak meaningfully of a global market economy conditioned by ecological concerns, and of the development of institutions of environmental governance. Steven Bernstein has traced this movement, and the evolution of environmental norms, from 1972 to the present concluding that liberal environmentalism represents the current compromise that reflects 'the compatibility of environmental concern, economic growth, the basic tenets of a market economy, and a liberal international order'.[78] But the process of evolution and compromise uncovered by Bernstein leaves unresolved a key question posed at the beginning of his analysis. 'Why', he asks, 'when the international community finally took environmentalism seriously, was it only considered in the context of an economic program that not only encouraged growth, but actually demanded it?'[79] Answering this question would require, as I had determined at the outset of the present study, a wider historical lens and a new approach to understanding how and why an 'economic program' could dictate the terms on which environmental concerns might be considered to be legitimate, even when many of those concerns arose from within that programme itself. I have since concluded that economic growth is the non-negotiable ideological core around which a hegemonic structure has been built, so compromise may occur if and only if that core is not challenged; that concessions by rulers can be transmuted to power over the ruled; in fact, that a particular kind of transnational hegemony can co-opt and absorb the interests of subordinate social groups, or even the groups themselves as consultative partners, such that counter-hegemonic social forces are blunted. The most invasive threats to hegemony, such as those which are embodied in the norms and activism of the environmental movement, are drawn most closely to the centre of hegemonic power where they have been subsumed to the idea of sustainable development, by which growth-based economic prosperity and ecological safety can both, purportedly, be enjoyed.

This book began from the observation that modern international relations, their diversity and complexity notwithstanding, are shaped by a unique commonality the features of which led me to identify the commitment to growth as the central tenet of global governance. The characteristics of that governance include the clear intention to maximize, as far as possible, national GNPs and aggregate world economic product; a deep and broad institutionalization of the commitment to growth; the availability of coercive force to maintain compliance with the commitment; the consensual support of national governments and civil societies; and the normative stipulation that economic growth will serve the general betterment of all. I drew on Rosenau's seminal conception of governance without government in this regard, though I did not follow his empirical research because he believes 'There is no single organizing principle on which global governance rests, no emergent order around which communities and nations are likely to converge ... the world is too disaggregated for grand logics that postulate a measure of global coherence'.[80] I have disagreed profoundly with this position.

The identification of the growth paradigm as a form of governance, however, does not explain its origins or its dominant position on the world stage, and the clarification of these issues has been the major burden of this book. It seemed curious in the first instance that any form of governance whatever could ascend to dominance in the anarchic forum of international relations. Lacking an agenda imposed through an authoritative hierarchy, order is created by state leaders, among other major actors, on what amounts to, in the main, an ad hoc basis which is shaped by what Kenneth Waltz has called a 'tyranny of small decisions'.[81] How, then, did one thematic international order emerge from the disaggregation and incoherence of anarchy? I turned first to history to establish the provenance of the idea and the early processes of economic growth.

I recall from Chapter 2 that no single explanation could fully account for the pursuit of economic growth. Realists link the pursuit of wealth to the pursuit of power; liberalists point to the natural tendency of people to truck, barter and trade. Systemic forces, primarily in the form of capitalist social relations, state-level factors that inclined public policy to the functional efficacy of growth, and psychological propensities to individual gain were all examined and were all found to contribute in important ways to the spread and practice of the idea of growth. Yet none of these could account for the normative component of hegemony, for the tensions and contradictions inherent to paradigmatic hegemony, or for the pervasiveness and virtual invisibility of a form of governance in which almost everyone, over time, had begun to participate. Seeking a more holistic approach to the problem which would complement alternative explanatory schemes by illuminating these features of governance, I turned to the neo-Gramscian mode of analysis imported into IR by Robert Cox, and to the narrative protocol of interpretive explanation.

The neo-Gramscian mode of inquiry deployed here has been widened considerably in historical scope. Gramsci himself thought in terms of historic blocs and regime change within states; Cox expanded on Gramscian precepts to uncover historical structures in the domain of international relations, such as the Pax Britannica. I have in turn interpreted Coxian historical structures as conjunctural events within the broader expanse of the modern age, which I have described as being congruent with the growth paradigm. Along with this widening, I have also streamlined neo-Gramscianism by, in a sense, re-emphasizing its Marxian roots: that is, by positing a dichotomy in class relations instead of attempting to catalogue and trace the role of myriad social forces, as had been done by the empirically and inductively oriented work of both Gramsci and Cox. Using this approach, I have traced the evolution of a transnational managerial class and its counterpart, transnational civil society, in the broad strokes necessary to a discussion of class relations within the global polity as a whole. I described the TMC as that social entity which has carried forward through time the idea of progress and growth, and which has gradually incorporated the TCS into a hegemonic paradigm.

Bringing to sharper relief the respective historical roles of rulers and ruled in human society at large served the purpose of parsimony but it also, as Theodore J. Lowi had perceived, allowed a clearer attribution of political responsibility than pluralism could easily afford. My underlying interest in the long-term viability of human society on Earth, and in the duty of political leaders to meet that primordial obligation, fit well with a two-class dichotomy. Usefully for my purposes, Lowi also argued that rulers' responsibilities can in turn be expressed in terms of a duality. Material responsibility refers to the need to secure the physical requirements of social life, and moral responsibility refers to the need to provide an ethical context for that life, as embodied in mores, norms, laws and goals.

As I have discussed at length, neo-Gramscianism in IR is forged on the foundation of a similar dichotomy, namely that of its ideational and material dimensions. I have argued that the growth paradigm is an instance of hegemony in which the ideational element has become dominant and, more importantly, has been disarticulated from its material counterpart. Historical materialism and critical theory show that dominant social structures may be riven by such tensions and disharmonies from which change, and eventually transformative change, will arise. Those tensions are inevitable given the dynamic flux of human behaviour over time and the constant evolution of both material and ideational relations within human society. When they reach critical proportions, breaking points in history and tectonic shifts can occur, resulting in the emergence of a new historical structure, a new paradigm, even a new world order.

The paradigm has had, since its inception, an intrinsic element of rationality, but it has also been shaped by its consistent orientation to social betterment – to progress – and I have linked that normative aspect of the paradigm to the notion of freedom. Because the paradigm and its major social agents, namely the rulers and the ruled, have undergone a continuous process of evolution, I have observed that social betterment and freedom were only roughly hewn normative attributes of paradigmatic hegemony in its early phases. Betterment was first instantiated in practice only as the aggrandizement of powerful elites during Phase I of class evolution; and freedom meant little more than the anarchic freedom engendered by the newly formed state system, or by the *laissez-faire* approach to international trade practised during Phase II of the evolutionary process. Social betterment was only truly social at Phase III, when consensual Gramscian hegemony was achieved after the Second World War, at which time the TMC and TCS merged in an internationalized form of social democracy. By the time of this most fulsome stage of hegemony, however, the political meaning of freedom had been thoroughly distorted. The disarticulation of social consciousness from social being had allowed the mystification of the idea of economic growth, and its mutation into a disembodied and malleable ideal.

I presented the linkage between growth and freedom with reference to the commonly acknowledged distinction between freedom from constraint, and freedom to pursue desirable objectives. Regarding the former, a strong preference for faster-growing economies outpaced the notion of political intervention in socio-economic affairs. The redistributive norm, which had carried with it the political cost of having to make ethics-based decisions, was preempted by the automaticity of the market function the merits of which had been, evidently, empirically substantiated by the successful conclusion of the Cold War. Regarding the question of how the paradigm facilitates the freedom to pursue desirable objectives, I have noted that the paradigm serves up an image of the future that is equitable, cornucopian and ecologically benign. North–South issues will be resolved by integrating developing and transitional states into the global market; future generations will benefit from the production of capital goods which replace any resources exhausted in the present; and non-human species and their habitat will be protected by the moral beneficence engendered by prosperity. The power of the paradigm is proportional to the extent to which this image conforms with the hopeful expectations of civil society. And, from the point of view of the TMC, these benefits can be delivered to all social sectors – public and private, employer and employee, rich and poor – without the imposition of a redistributive burden on any sector, because economic growth promises more of everything for everybody. The growth paradigm facilitates the freedom to pursue virtually any idealized image of the future on a cost-free basis, and it is this characteristic of moral convenience that best explains its normative preeminence in international relations.

The foregoing sums up the reasons which support the normative dominance of the growth paradigm, but an evaluative assessment of it creates a tension that pulls away from the hopeful expectations outlined above. North–South disparities are widening, not decreasing; future generations are threatened not only by resource depletion, but by climate change induced by energy consumption; and species and habitat are being lost at a rate not matched in 66 million years.[82] I argued in Chapter 4 that if the resolution of these problems were truly the desired objective of political managers, then that objective would not be receding. Given the scope and probable impact of these problems on present and future generations, it strains credulity that they are worsening only because of the intractability of organizational barriers to cooperation. If those barriers were not ultimately surmountable, then one would have to conclude that human society was hard-wired for failure. A more hopeful conclusion suggests that the commitment to economic growth, exposed as disharmonious with the material world, could be superseded by a new commitment to development in the context of a steady-state global economy, and to the continuous and qualitative improvement of the socio-natural world.

The question of why this has occurred – that is, why growth is persistently pursued even as its uneconomic and immoral features come more clearly into view – has been clarified with reference to two reasons. The first of these is that politically expedient and morally convenient solutions to pressing problems flow easily from the ideational domain because that domain is divorced from its material counterpart, which would otherwise impose practical limitations on what could be done effectively.[83] Idealized solutions do not need to be accountable to reality, and in this sense they are susceptible to manipulation; they need only refer to the promise of a better future. The second reason brings to focus a related question: why does a proclivity for moral convenience, as opposed to something more ethically robust, follow from the disarticulation of the ideational domain? Here I refer back to Reinhold Niebuhr's argument that the vitality of the moral impulse diminishes from individuals to groups, and diminishes further in larger groups. Left to its own devices, human society will be incapable of generating the critical self-reflection which must precede moral judgment. The relationship between the overall size of human society and moral dissolution is mitigated somewhat by the historically consistent trend among societies to stratify – often complexly, but always at least into a basic dichotomy of leaders and led – which may tend to concentrate the resources necessary for sound decision-making in a smaller group. But in the larger context of human society as a whole the leading stratum, the TMC – the *nébuleuse* – is still a diffuse and disparate social entity with no shared consciousness (apart from its collectively held belief in economic growth) which might be employed to facilitate the ethical-rational deliberation of complex socio-economic issues. In short, the condition of anarchy in international relations works against the possibility of effective moral oversight which might be provided by a more mature form of global governance. Anarchy permits the intrusion of the amoral, and sometimes immoral, impulses of the human psyche into the shared ideational domain. Anarchy and the disengagement of the ideational domain from its socio-natural context both facilitate and help explain the dominance of the growth paradigm.

The paradigmatic hegemony of the commitment to growth has not been, and is not being, actively or coherently opposed by any organized faction of national civil societies or transnational civil society. Tensions and contradictions within the paradigm are clear and abundant, but none has been seized upon by social groups with the specific intention of opposing economic growth as such, and no evidence suggests that parallel organizations or institutions have been developed which might serve as transitional structures to a new hegemonic order. The evident stream of anomalies notwithstanding, the objective conditions for revolution, as Gramsci might have put it, are not in place. Nor are the subjective conditions propitious. The transition from one order to another requires in the first instance that an inter-subjectively shared image of the new order be widely available, but no such image exists, unless in inchoate form. The postmodern potpourri of ephemera and fragments, a product in large part of the incrementalism and change induced by ever more rapid economic growth, generates suspicion of grand narrative even when a counter-hegemonic narrative is precisely what is lacking among the disparate social forces which may potentially stand opposed to the growth paradigm.

I note with some interest that, in light of the sheer power of the growth paradigm, any such counternarrative may have to do more than merely call upon the reason of a better argument. Niebuhr makes this point by remarking that

> Contending factions in a social struggle require morale; and morale is created by the right dogmas, symbols and emotionally potent oversimplifications ... [unorganized groups] will have to believe rather more firmly in the justice and in the probable triumph of their cause, than any impartial science would give them the right to believe, if they are to have enough energy to contest the power of the strong.... The world of history, particularly in [our] collective behaviour, will never be conquered by reason, unless reason uses tools, and is itself driven by forces which are not rational.[84]

This proposal is not necessarily intended to dupe transnational civil society into an unwarranted optimism about the future through the use of 'dogmas, symbols and emotionally potent oversimplifications', but rather to call attention to the idea that optimism (or 'morale') springs from the will, which can motivate and shape behaviour independently of empirical circumstances. Will and its correlate hope can and do exist where reason would rule them illogical, whereas pessimism, a product of the intellect, sustains itself through reason and a logical assessment of the world as it is. Niebuhr's comments at least suggest, then, that the social construction of such a counternarrative may be possible given the right toolset. In fact I look with some enthusiasm to the prospect of a contest in which the proponents of a steady-state global economy, who have nothing positive to draw on but their own sense of propriety and a morally informed vision of an ecologically safe future, take on advocates of the growth paradigm with their deep commitment to a bastardized ideal. The construction of a new story about the meaning of economy will be difficult in the context of contemporary postmodernism, but the fact that a hegemonic narrative – the continuing story of progress and growth, that is – does thrive in this fragmented environment suggests that the task is not impossible;[85] that one idea has merely to be spun into its opposite.

Absent any such counter-hegemonic narrative force, and absent any organized social opposition to the growth paradigm, three inferences may be drawn from the continuing dominance of this particular form of global governance. First, no international policy or programme – even those intended to protect the long-term viability of human society on Earth – will be complied with if it significantly constrains growth options. The moribund Kyoto Protocol serves as the best example of this proposition. The Framework Convention on Climate Change obligates states to reduce greenhouse gas emissions, but Article 4(2)(a) explicitly recognizes 'the need to maintain strong and sustainable economic growth',[86] and this stipulation is part and parcel of the Kyoto negotiation process. The belief in the compatibility of growth and greenhouse gas reductions is warranted by the expectation that economies can grow out of environmental problems by, among other things, rapidly developing production efficiencies and alternative energy sources, both of which require the stimulus and revenue generated by robust growth. The challenge inherent in this approach is that the transitional process to benign energy supplies must somehow overtake the fossil-fuel dependent growth that drives it. The real-world solution to the climate change problem is to radically reduce the combustion of fossil fuels but, given that the growth paradigm induces interstate competition, no state will be prepared to blunt its competitive advantage by increasing the cost of energy, or by regulating its availability, to achieve these reductions. No state is prepared to voluntarily sacrifice growth and, under the hegemonic conditions of the paradigm, no state will sign on to or comply with any international agreement that significantly limits growth.

Second, because growth requires the capture and consumption of energy, any and all available energy resources – petrochemical, nuclear, renewable or otherwise – will be exploited. No non-economic obstacle, such as concern about climate change or the sanctity of nature preserves, will block this exploitation. It follows from this that, third, under the dominion of the growth narrative, international efforts to dampen the onset of climate change cannot succeed, nor will other environmental problems caused by excessive growth, such as species loss, be significantly mitigated. Extrapolating the trajectory of what amounts to a business-as-usual scenario suggests that the prospects for maintaining planetary ecological conditions conducive to the further evolution of human society are not bright; and, further, the need to attend to the debilitating poverty of the vast majority of our numbers, and to accommodate the imminent rapid rise of those numbers, will make any transition to a stationary state that much more challenging.

It may very well be that our common future will be common indeed. History often repeats itself and, notwithstanding the progressive teleology and open-ended forward motion of the growth paradigm, it may do so again. Instead of a linear march into the future, we may undergo the cyclical destruction and renewal which past civilizations and species have experienced. That would be regrettable – not only because of the lost potential for human development, but because of the damaged potential of Earth itself to nurture new life. Self-destruction is merely pathetic, but planetary destruction is unconscionable. The contemplation of that possibility raises the question of how one should comport oneself with respect to a future into which we grow without care.

Notes

1 What is the growth paradigm?

1 Edgar Grande and Louis W. Pauly, 'Complex Sovereignty and the Emergence of Transnational Authority', in Edgar Grande and Louis W. Pauly, eds, *Complex Sovereignty: Reconstituting Political Authority in the Twenty-first Century*, Toronto: University of Toronto Press, 2007.

2 Ibid., p. 287.

3 James N. Rosenau, 'Governance, Order and Change in World Politics', in James N. Rosenau and Ernst-Otto Czempiel, eds, *Governance without Government: Order and Change in World Politics*, Cambridge: Cambridge University Press, 1992, p. 6.

4 Ibid., p. 5.

5 Rosenau makes the point that governance is, by definition, effective. Where order is absent, so is governance. By contrast, government can exist in conditions of disorder, in which case it is simply characterized as weak.

6 Steven Bernstein, *The Compromise of Liberal Environmentalism*, New York: Columbia University Press, 2001, p. 5.

7 More formally, Rosenau defines this term as follows: '[G]lobal governance is conceived to include systems of rule at all levels of human activity – from the family to the international organization – in which the pursuit of goals through the exercise of control has transnational repercussions'. James N. Rosenau, 'Governance in the Twenty-first Century', *Global Governance*, vol. 1, no. 1, 1995, p. 13.

8 This argument was made clear in World Commission on Environment and Development, *Our Common Future*, Oxford: Oxford University Press, 1987.

9 Donella H. Meadows, Dennis L. Meadows, et al., *The Limits to Growth*, New York: New York American Library, Inc., 1972.

10 New approaches to these issues, however, have done much to reorient the discipline, and to create space for dialogue and more appropriate epistemologies. See for example Thomas Homer-Dixon, *The Upside of Down: Catastrophe, Creativity, and the Renewal of Civilization*, Toronto: Alfred A. Knopf, 2006.

11 The term 'political ecology' has no common or formalized definition, but it refers in general to the political management of the relationship between people and their natural environment.

12 Daniel Deudney, 'The Case against Linking Environmental Degradation and National Security', *Millennium*, vol. 19, no. 3, 1990, pp. 461–476. Deudney compares conventional national security with 'global habitability' along four dimensions – type of threat, source of threat, degree of intentionality, and types of organizations involved – and concludes that the two issues are substantively different on all counts.

13 Gross National Product (GNP) is a more familiar, and broader, term than Gross Domestic Product (GDP). It includes, for example, corporate profits repatriated from offshore holdings; it excludes profits exported by foreign-owned companies, and

interest payments on loans contracted abroad. In short, GNP equals GDP plus net factor earnings from abroad.

14 Sander M. de Bruyn, *Economic Growth and the Environment: An Empirical Analysis*, Dordrecht: Kluwer Academic Publishers, 2000, p. 18.
15 Herman E. Daly and John B. Cobb Jr, *For the Common Good: Redirecting the Economy toward Community, the Environment, and a Sustainable Future*, 2nd edn, Boston, MA: Beacon Press, 1994, p. 71.
16 This term is defined by Robert Cox as 'the institutions of authoritative rule in relation to the balance of social forces that can sustain or undermine them'. Robert W. Cox, *The Political Economy of a Plural World: Critical Reflections on Power, Morals and Civilization*, London: Routledge, 2002, p. 32.
17 J. Magnus Ryner, 'International Political Economy: Beyond the Poststructuralist/Historical Materialist Dichotomy', in Marieke de Goede, ed., *International Political Economy and Poststructural Politics*, New York: Palgrave Macmillan, 2006.
18 Thomas S. Kuhn, *The Structure of Scientific Revolutions*, 3rd edn, Chicago, IL: University of Chicago Press, 1996 [1962].
19 Margaret Masterman, 'The Nature of a Paradigm' in Imre Lakatos and Alan Musgrave, eds, *Criticism and the Growth of Knowledge*, New York: Cambridge University Press, 1970.
20 Kuhn, 'Postscript 1969', in *The Structure of Scientific Revolutions*, p. 175.
21 Kuhn, *The Structure of Scientific Revolutions*, p. 24.
22 Ibid., p. 36
23 Ibid., p. 52.
24 Ibid., p. 65.
25 Masterman, 'The Nature of a Paradigm', p. 83.
26 Kuhn, *The Structure of Scientific Revolutions*, p. 6.
27 For more on this, see Marieke de Goede, 'Introduction: International Political Economy and the Promises of Poststructuralism', in de Goede, *International Political Economy and Poststructural Politics*.
28 Kuhn, *The Structure of Scientific Revolutions*, p. 91.
29 Ibid., p. 65.
30 Ibid., p. 94.
31 R. J. Bernstein, *The Restructuring of Political and Social Theory*, Cambridge: Cambridge University Press, 1995, p. 88.
32 Ibid.
33 Critical theory in general refers to an entire class of political theory. Coxian critical theory is a specific, compatible subset of the wider domain. I use the term 'Coxian critical theory' to distinguish the particular version.
34 Robert W. Cox, 'Social Forces, States and World Orders: Beyond International Relations Theory', in Robert O. Keohane, ed., *Neorealism and Its Critics*, New York: Columbia University Press, 1986, p. 208.
35 Ibid., p. 209.
36 Ibid., p. 208.
37 Ibid., p. 210.
38 See ibid., pp. 217–225 for a more detailed discussion of historical structures.
39 This schematic overview is drawn primarily from Mark Neufeld, *The Restructuring of International Relations Theory*, Cambridge: Cambridge University Press, 1995, pp. 14–21, and Gerard Delanty, *Social Science: Beyond Constructivism and Realism*, Minneapolis: University of Minnesota Press, 1997, ch. 4.
40 Yosef Lapid, 'The Third Debate: On the Prospects of International Theory in a Post-Positivist Era', *International Studies Quarterly*, vol. 33, no. 3, 1989, pp. 235–254. See also Robert O. Keohane, 'International Institutions: Two Approaches', *International Studies Quarterly*, vol. 32, no. 4, 1988, pp. 379–396.

41 Jim George, *Discourses of Global Politics: A Critical (Re)Introduction to International Relations*, Boulder, CO: Lynne Rienner Publishers, 1994, p. 223.
42 For an elaboration of this, see Richard Price and Christian Reus-Smit, 'Dangerous Liaisons? Critical International Theory and Constructivism', *European Journal of International Relations*, vol. 4, no. 3, 1998, pp. 259–294.
43 For a succinct discussion of this, see Robyn Eckersley, *Environmentalism and Political Theory: Toward an Ecocentric Approach*, New York: State University of New York Press, 1992, ch. 5.
44 This pessimism was instigated by the failure of the proletarian revolution, and by the belief that the loss of 'community' was so far advanced that intellectuals could no longer present a new image of integration; they could only undermine the legitimacy of dominant social systems. Habermas attempted to redress this concern with his turn to 'communicative action', by which reasoned consensus could be reached among discursively competent social partners. For more on this, see Paul Rabinow and William M. Sullivan, 'Introduction', in P. Rabinow and W. M. Sullivan, eds, *Interpretive Social Science: A Reader*, Berkeley: University of California Press, 1979.
45 For example, Randall D. Germain and Michael Kenny, 'Engaging Gramsci: International Relations Theory and the New Gramscians', *Review of International Studies*, vol. 24, no. 1, 1998, pp. 3–21.
46 Cox, *The Political Economy of a Plural World*, p. 29.
47 Karl Marx, 'Thesis on Feuerbach', in *Karl Marx and Friedrich Engels, Collected Works (1845–1847)*, vol. 5, London: Lawrence and Wishart, 1976, p. 5.
48 Fred Halliday, *Rethinking International Relations*, Vancouver: University of British Columbia Press, 1994, p. 71.
49 Ibid., p. 60.
50 Robert W. Cox, 'Gramsci, Hegemony and International Relations: An Essay in Method', in Stephen Gill, ed., *Gramsci, Historical Materialism and International Relations*, Cambridge: Cambridge University Press, 1993, p. 56.
51 Robert W. Cox, *Production, Power and World Order: Social Forces in the Making of History*, New York: Columbia University Press, 1987, p. 1.
52 Keohane, 'International Institutions: Two Approaches'.
53 For a full discussion of the status of 'social facts' in constructivist methodologies, see John G. Ruggie, 'Introduction', in John Gerard Ruggie, *Constructing the World Polity: Essays on International Institutionalization*, London: Routledge, 1998, esp. pp. 11–22.
54 Robert W. Cox, 'Social Forces, States and World Orders: Beyond International Relations Theory/Postscript 1985', in Keohane, *Neorealism and Its Critics*, p. 242.
55 Donald E. Polkinghorne, *Narrative Knowing and the Human Sciences*, Albany: State University of New York Press, 1988.
56 John G. Ruggie, 'Epistemology, Ontology and the Study of International Regimes', in Ruggie, *Constructing the World Polity*, p. 94.
57 Polkinghorne, *Narrative Knowing*, p. 11.
58 Ibid., p. 18.
59 Ibid., p. 19.
60 Ruggie, 'Epistemology, Ontology and the Study of International Regimes', p. 94.
61 Ruggie notes the futility of employing positivist protocols to the study of international regimes, for example, which are intersubjectively constituted social phenomena that are not amenable to an approach which analytically separates subject from object.
62 A progressive, as opposed to degenerating, research programme exposes new intellectual challenges, the exploration of which increases knowledge. See Imre Lakatos and Alan Musgrave, eds, *Criticism and the Growth of Knowledge*, Cambridge: Cambridge University Press, 1970.
63 Cox, 'Social Forces, States and World Orders', p. 215.
64 This supposition is in contrast with Hegel's well-known 'thesis-antithesis-synthesis'

dialectic which was presented by him in the context of a rational/spiritual evolution of *Geist*, and which assumed a set of progressive changes that were, in the larger scheme of things, for the better. In keeping with the precepts of renovated historical materialism, I do not follow that teleology here.

65 Thomas Homer-Dixon, e-mail communication, 19 January 2007.

66 Depending upon one's preferred definition, the idea of progress could be traced much further back into history – to early Christianity within the Roman Empire, for example – which portrayed humankind's destiny as a cumulative advance toward a final state of perfection. On this, see Robert Nisbet, *History of the Idea of Progress*, New York: Basic Books, 1980.

2 Systemic-, state-, and individual-level contributions to understanding the paradigm

1 J. David Singer, 'The Levels of Analysis Problem in International Relations', in James N. Rosenau, ed., *International Politics and Foreign Policy*, New York: Free Press, 1969.

2 This definition is from Robert Gilpin, *U.S. Power and the Multinational Corporation: The Political Economy of Foreign Direct Investment*, New York: Basic Books, 1975, p. 43, as quoted in Benjamin J. Cohen, 'The Political Economy of International Trade', *International Organization*, vol. 44, no. 2, 1990, pp. 261–281. The quotation appears on p. 273.

3 Robert Gilpin, *The Political Economy of International Relations*, Princeton, NJ: Princeton University Press, 1987, pp. 10–11.

4 Ibid., p. 32.

5 Stephen Krasner was an early leader in the broadening of the realist research programme. See, for example, his 'State Power and the Structure of International Trade', *World Politics*, vol. 28, no. 3, 1976, pp. 317–346.

6 Robert O. Keohane and Joseph S. Nye, *Power and Interdependence: World Politics in Transition*, Boston, MA: Little, Brown, 1977.

7 Robert O. Keohane, *After Hegemony: Cooperation and Discord in the World Political Economy*, Princeton, NJ: Princeton University Press, 1984.

8 David A. Baldwin, ed., *Neorealism and Neoliberalism: The Contemporary Debate*, New York: Cambridge University Press, 1993.

9 Gilpin, *The Political Economy of International Relations*, p. 27.

10 Ibid., p. 30.

11 Immanuel Wallerstein, *The Modern World-System: Capitalist Agriculture and the Origins of the European World-Economy in the Sixteenth Century*, New York: Academic Press, 1974.

12 This view is explored in Richard Little, 'International Relations and the Triumph of Capitalism', in Ken Booth and Steve Smith, eds, *International Relations Theory Today*, University Park: Pennsylvania State University Press, 1995.

13 Theda Skocpol, 'Wallerstein's World Capitalist System: A Theoretical and Historical Critique', *American Journal of Sociology*, vol. 82, 1977, pp. 1075–1089.

14 A. L. Stinchcombe, 'Review Essay: The Growth of the World System', *American Journal of Sociology*, vol. 87, 1982, pp. 1389–1395.

15 This topic is taken up in detail by Susan Strange, *The Retreat of the State: The Diffusion of Power in the World Economy*, Cambridge: Cambridge University Press, 1996.

16 Michel Beaud, *A History of Capitalism, 1500–2000*, New York: Monthly Review Press, 2001, p. 8.

17 Ibid., p. 293.

18 Eric Jones, *The European Miracle: Environments, Economies and Geopolitics in the History of Europe and Asia*, Cambridge: Cambridge University Press, 2003, esp. pp. 85–103.

19 Karl Polanyi, *The Great Transformation*, New York: Farrar & Rinehart, Inc., 1944, p. 75.
20 The nature of this expansionism is discussed extensively by Beaud, *A History of Capitalism*; by Gilpin, *The Political Economy of International Relations*, ch. 2; and by Iain Wallace, *The Global Economic System*, Boston, MA: Unwin Hyman Ltd., 1990, ch. 4.
21 Douglass C. North and Robert Paul Thomas, *The Rise of the Western World: A New Economic History*, Cambridge: Cambridge University Press, 1973.
22 Hendrik Spruyt, *The Sovereign State and Its Competitors: An Analysis of Systems Change*, Princeton, NJ: Princeton University Press, 1994.
23 Joshua Cohen and Joel Rogers, *On Democracy*, New York: Penguin Books, 1984, p. 52.
24 Ibid., pp. 52–53.
25 This is so because profits may be moved offshore, applied to different productive purposes, or used to automate production, thus reducing employment. Profits may also simply be consumed.
26 Ibid., p. 71.
27 Cohen and Rogers call this the 'information problem'. Special (private) interests with a large stake in the outcome of a particular decision can supply ostensibly objective information to the decision-makers at relatively low cost. But individual citizens whose welfare may be compromised by an adverse decision have little or no incentive to seek out and deploy costly information. This puts 'the stamp of private dominance on the American public arena' (p. 64), according to these authors.
28 Their argument is supported with a detailed case study of American political economy.
29 Ibid., p. 74.
30 Ibid., p. 76.
31 David M. Andrews, 'Capital Mobility and State Autonomy: Toward a Structural Theory of International Monetary Relations', *International Studies Quarterly*, vol. 38, 1994, pp. 193–218. For the argument that mobility is not a structural feature, see Geoffrey Garret, 'Capital Mobility, Trade, and the Domestic Politics of Economic Policy', *International Organization*, vol. 49, no. 4, 1995, pp. 657–687.
32 For a good review of the capital mobility literature, see Benjamin J. Cohen, 'Phoenix Risen: The Resurrection of Global Finance', *World Politics*, vol. 48, no. 2, 1996, pp. 268–296.
33 Globalization itself is a contested term with meanings ranging from the relatively simple notion of converging interest rates to the grander vision of an emerging world society.
34 John B. Goodman and Louis W. Pauly, 'The Obsolescence of Capital Controls? Economic Management in an Age of Global Markets', *World Politics*, vol. 46, no. 1, 1993, pp. 50–82.
35 Suzanne Berger, 'Introduction', in Suzanne Berger and Ronald Dore, eds, *National Diversity and Global Capitalism*, Ithaca, NY: Cornell University Press, 1996, p. 5.
36 Martha Finnemore, 'Norms, Culture and World Politics: Insights from Sociology's Institutionalism', *International Organization*, vol. 50, no. 2, 1996, pp. 325–427.
37 Ibid., p. 326.
38 Ibid., pp. 325–326.
39 Ibid., p. 329.
40 These similarities include constitutional forms, educational institutions, welfare policies, human rights conventions, defence ministries in states that face no immediate threat, and science ministries in states that have no scientific capability.
41 These include imitation, emulation, teaching by international organizations that to be modern is to have the characteristics of rational bureaucracy, and economic pressure by developed states to modernize political and socio-economic institutions.

42 Ibid., p. 332. This point may be overstated by Finnemore. Islamic theocracies, for example, may also be 'legitimate forms of political organization' which pursue objectives other than progress and justice. Nevertheless, these cases constitute a relatively small subset of the totality of state types.

43 Ibid., p. 329.

44 This may be contrasted with non-consequentialist alternatives to rationality such as may be embodied in cultural preferences for roles, rituals, duties and obligations.

45 Martin Hollis, *The Philosophy of Social Science: An Introduction*, Cambridge: Cambridge University Press, 1994, p. 95. Original italics.

46 Lewis A. Coser, 'Functionalism', in William Outhwaite and Tom Bottomore, eds, *The Blackwell Dictionary of Twentieth-century Social Thought*, Oxford: Blackwell Publishers Ltd, 1993, pp. 236–238.

47 David Mitrany, *A Working Peace System*, Chicago, IL: Quadrangle Books, 1966, originally published with the subtitle, *An Argument for a Functional Approach to International Organization*, Royal Institute of International Affairs, 1943.

48 For a detailed explication of neofunctionalism, see Ernst Haas, *Beyond the Nation State*, Stanford, CA: Stanford University Press, 1964.

49 Anecdotally, I note that Herman Daly has from time to time criticized the common metaphor that 'a rising tide lifts all boats' by invoking the fact that a rising tide on one half of Earth is matched by a lowering tide on the other half. This corrected version of the metaphor may better represent the realities of North–South relations.

50 This point of view is arguably inherent to liberal and neoliberal doctrine, though it is not necessarily supported by empirical evidence. See, for example, Nazli Choucri and Robert C. North, *Nations in Conflict: National Growth and International Violence*, San Francisco, CA: W. H. Freeman, 1975. These authors argue that national expansion through trade and other means often evokes a violent response from rival powers, and that growth is therefore a cause of interstate violence, not a remedy for it.

51 John Kenneth Galbraith, *The Affluent Society*, London: Hamish Hamilton, 1958.

52 This theme is developed throughout Thomas Homer-Dixon, *The Upside of Down: Catastrophe, Creativity, and the Renewal of Civilization*, Toronto: Alfred A. Knopf, 2006.

53 For an elaboration of this, see Hollis, *The Philosophy of Social Science*, pp. 94–114.

54 Herman Daly uses the phrase 'uneconomic growth' to identify the condition in which the aggregated costs of growth, including especially its environmental impact, outweigh its benefits.

55 Formerly available at: www.whitehouse.gov/nsc/nss/2006/nss2006.pdf, p. 7. Viewed 3 November 2007.

56 Ibid., p. 25.

57 Ibid., p. 27. See also Milton Friedman, *Capitalism and Freedom*, Chicago, IL: University of Chicago Press, 1962.

58 Thomas C. Schelling, *Micromotives and Macrobehaviour*, New York: W. W. Norton & Company, 1978.

59 Ibid., p. 22.

60 See, for example, Donald Green and Ian Shapiro, *Pathologies of Rational Choice Theory*, New Haven, CT: Yale University Press, 1994.

61 This argument is developed by Richard Dawkins, *The Selfish Gene*, Oxford: Oxford University Press, 1989.

62 David Tilman, *Resource Competition and Community Structure*, Princeton, NJ: Princeton University Press, 1982, p. 248.

63 Edward O. Wilson, *Sociobiology: The New Synthesis*, Cambridge, MA: Belknap Press of Harvard University Press, 1975.

64 Reinhold Niebuhr, *Moral Man and Immoral Society: A Study in Ethics and Politics* [1932], New York: Charles Scribner's Sons, 1960, p. 9.

65 Ibid., p. 48.

66 Ibid., p. xii.
67 Ibid., p. 42.
68 Ibid., p. 44.
69 Mancur Olson, *The Logic of Collective Action: Public Goods and the Theory of Groups*, Cambridge, MA: Harvard University Press, 1971.
70 Niebuhr, *Moral Man and Immoral Society*, p. 88.
71 Ibid., p. 4.
72 Ibid., p. 196.
73 Ibid., p. 8.
74 Ibid., p. 15.

3 The ideational superstructure of the paradigm

1 Robert W. Cox, 'Production and Hegemony: Towards a Political Economy of World Order', in H. Jacobsen and D. Subyanski, eds, *The Emerging International Economic Order*, Newbury Park, CA: Sage, 1982, p. 38. Italics added. It is important to point out that this comment, though appropriate for my own use, was intended by Cox to apply to global structures of shorter historical duration than the growth era.
2 John S. Dryzec, *The Politics of the Earth: Environmental Discourses*, Oxford: Oxford University Press, 1997, p. 8.
3 Jim George, *Discourse of Global Politics: A Critical (Re)Introduction to International Relations*, Boulder, CO: Lynne Rienner Publishers, 1994, pp. 29–30.
4 This succinct summary was offered by Thomas Homer-Dixon, e-mail communication, 17 June 2006.
5 George, *Discourse of Global Politics*, p. 30.
6 Ibid.
7 This is a Foucauldian term.
8 Jennifer Milliken, 'The Study of Discourse in International Relations: A Critique of Research and Methods', *European Journal of International Relations*, vol. 5, no. 2, 1999, p. 229.
9 Steve Smith, 'Positivism and Beyond', in *International Theory: Positivism and Beyond*, Cambridge: Cambridge University Press, 1996, p. 13.
10 Bob Jessop and Ngai-Ling Sum, 'Towards a Cultural International Political Economy: Poststructuralism and the Italian School', in Marieke de Goede, ed., *International Political Economy and Poststructural Politics*, New York: Palgrave Macmillan, 2006, p. 159.
11 Peter Miller and Nikolas Rose, *Governing the Present: Administering Economic, Social and Personal Life*, Cambridge: Polity Press, 2008, pp. 5–6.
12 Daniel H. Deudney, 'Environmental Security: A Critique', in Daniel H. Deudney and Richard H. Matthews, eds, *Contested Grounds: Security and Conflict in the New Environmental Politics*, Albany: State University of New York Press, 1999. Quotations are from pp. 201–202.
13 Karl Marx, *Capital*, vol. 1, p. 737; quoted in Nicholas Abercrombie, Stephen Hill, and Bryan S. Turner, *The Dominant Ideology Thesis*, London: George Allen & Unwin Ltd. 1980, p. 166.
14 Abercrombie et al., *The Dominant Ideology Thesis*, p. 1. Original italics.
15 Karl Marx, 'The German Ideology', in Robert C. Tucker, ed., *The Marx-Engels Reader*, 2nd edn, New York: W. W. Norton & Company, 1972, p. 173.
16 On this, see John G. Ruggie, 'Social Time and Ecodemographic Contexts', in John Gerard Ruggie, *Constructing the World Polity: Essays on International Institutionalization*, London: Routledge, 1998.
17 Robert W. Cox, *The Political Economy of a Plural World: Critical reflections on Power, Morals and Civilization*, London: Routledge, 2002, p. 172.
18 Ruggie, Social time and ecodemographic Contexts', p. 170.

19 John G. Ruggie, 'Territoriality at Millennium's End', in Ruggie, *Constructing the World Polity*, p. 184.
20 Ibid., p. 186.
21 Cox, *The Political Economy of a Plural World*, p. 161.
22 Ibid.
23 Antonio Gramsci, *Selections from Political Writings, 1910–1920*, translated and edited by Q. Hoare, New York: International Publishers, 1977, p. 12.
24 Ronald Wright, *A Short History of Progress*, Toronto: House of Anansi Press, 2004, p. 3.
25 Ernest Tuveson, 'Progress', in William Outhwaite and Tom Bottomore, eds, *The Blackwell Dictionary of Twentieth-century Social Thought*, Oxford: Blackwell Publishers Ltd, 1993, p. 515. Original italics.
26 Cox, *The Political Economy of a Plural World*, p. 158.
27 Ibid., p. 159.
28 Wright, *A Short History of Progress*, p. 4.
29 H. W. Arndt, *Economic Development: The History of an Idea*, Chicago, IL: The University of Chicago Press, 1987, p. 11.
30 W. W. Rostow, *How It All Began: Origins of the Modern Economy*, London: Methuen, 1975, p. 7.
31 R. H. Tawney, *Religion and the Rise of Capitalism: A Historical Study*, New York: Harcourt, Brace and World, Inc., 1947, p. 31.
32 Robert L. Heilbroner, *The Making of Economic Society*, Englewood Cliffs, NJ: Prentice-Hall, 1962, p. 41.
33 Abercrombie *et al*., *The Dominant Ideology Thesis*, p. 67.
34 Max Weber, *The Protestant Ethic and the Spirit of Capitalism*, trans. Talcott Parsons, London: Routledge, [1904], 1995.
35 Abercrombie et al., *The Dominant Ideology Thesis*, p. 100.
36 David Hawkes, *Ideology*, London: Routledge, 1996, p. 142.
37 Abercrombie et al., *The Dominant Ideology Thesis*, p. 55.
38 Adam Smith, *The Wealth of Nations*, vol. 1, London: University Paperbacks, [1776], 1961, p. 91, quoted in Arndt, *Economic Development*, p. 13.
39 Heilbroner, *The Making of Economic Society*, pp. 60–62.
40 Ruggie, 'Territoriality at Mmillennium's End', p. 176.
41 Herman E. Daly and John B. Cobb, Jr, *For the Common Good: Redirecting the Economy Toward Community, the Environment, and a Sustainable Future*, 2nd edn, Boston, MA: Beacon Press, 1994, p. 5.
42 The Poor Laws were among a host of legal, social and moral strictures that were anathema to capitalist rationality. Traditionalism resisted the application of market principles to the labour force by blocking free-market wage determination, training, the development of contractual relations of employment, and hence employment opportunities for craftsmen. Similarly, labour mobility was restricted, and transactions in money and shares were inhibited, all of which impeded the growth of capital markets.
43 Abercrombie et al., *The Dominant Ideology Thesis*, pp. 96–102.
44 Heilbroner, *The Making of Economic Society*, p. 57.
45 Ibid., p. 58.
46 The early chapters of volume 1 of Marx's *Capital* (1867) trace the evolution of exchange relations from barter to capitalist circulation. Barter is readily symbolized as $C \rightarrow C^*$, where C is a commodity traded for C*. No new physical production has occurred, but the use value of both traders has increased, and both are better off. The limiting feature of barter is that there must be a coincidence of wants before any exchange will occur, but inserting money as a token of exchange into the equation eliminates this limitation, as in: $C \rightarrow M \rightarrow C^*$, where M is money. Use value for the participants has increased again, and the exchange value of money in the transaction is entirely instrumental to the acquisition of C*. In contrast to these arrangements,

capitalist circulation focuses on the expansion of exchange value, as in: M → C → M*. Here, money is used to buy labour and materials to produce a new commodity, which is then sold for a greater amount of money. The commodity itself has become instrumental, and secondary to the accumulation of wealth. In today's 'paper economy', the direct conversion of money into more money, as in M → M*, has become possible without the need to refer to commodities at all as an intermediate step in the process of expansion. Paradoxically, the modern economy, often criticized as being materialistic, is in this sense entirely removed from its material base.

47 Karl Polanyi, *The Great Transformation*, Boston, MA: Beacon Press, [1944], 1957, p. 72. Original italics.
48 Ibid., p. 73. Original italics.
49 Ibid., p. 75.
50 Heilbroner, *The Making of Economic Society*, p. 64.
51 In brief: Industrialists would be squeezed from two sides. First, increased demand for land would drive up rents, diverting a portion of national income from industrialists to the landed aristocracy. Second, increased production costs on marginal land would drive up food prices, leading to upward pressure on wages, which erodes industrial profits.
52 John S. Mill, *Principles of Political Economy: With Some of Their Applications to Social Philosophy*, London: Penguin Books, [1848], 1970, p. 111.
53 Moses Abramovitz, *Thinking about Growth*, Cambidge: Cambridge University Press, 1989, p. 8.
54 Paul Ormerod, *The Death of Economics*, New York: John Wiley & Sons, Inc., 1997, p. 45.
55 Daly and Cobb, *For the Common Good*, p. 31.
56 Also known as Walrasian general equilibrium, the model is deductive. It specifies the conditions under which supply and demand will balance, and the market will clear, that is, achieve equilibrium.
57 Daly and Cobb, *For the Common Good*, p. 111.
58 Ibid., p. 110.
59 GNP as a numerical measure of national economic activity was developed by the United States in the 1930s, as discussed in the next section of this chapter.
60 Herman Daly, 'Beyond Growth: Avoiding Uneconomic Growth', in Mohan Munsasinghe, Osvaldo Sunkel and Carlos de Miguel, eds, *The Sustainability of Long-term Growth: Socio-economic and Ecological Perspectives*, Cheltenham: Edward Elgar Publishing Limited, 2001, p. 153.
61 Ibid.
62 Ibid., p. 154.
63 Abramovitz, *Thinking about Growth*, p. 8.
64 Ibid., p. 14.
65 Thomas Homer-Dixon, *The Ingenuity Gap*, Toronto: Alfred A. Knopf, 2000, esp. ch. 9.
66 Ibid., p. 228. Original italics.
67 Ibid., p. 225.
68 Ibid., p. 246.
69 P. D. Wiles, 'The Soviet Economy Outpaces the West', *Foreign Affairs*, July 1953, quoted in H. W. Arndt, *The Rise and Fall of Economic Growth: A Study in Contemporary Thought*, Melbourne: Longman Cheshire Pty, 1978.
70 This comment by Khrushchev was made at the Twentieth Party Congress in 1956. Quoted in W. W. Heller, ed., *Perspectives on Economic Growth*, New York: Random House, 1968, p. 130.
71 Arndt, *The Rise and Fall of Economic Growth.*
72 Richard B. Norgaard, 'Growth, Globalization and an Agenda for Ecological Economics', in Munsasinghe et al. *The Sustainability of Long-term Growth*, p. 94.
73 Ibid.

74 Abramovitz, *Thinking about Growth*, p. 11.
75 Norgaard, 'Growth, Globalization and an Agenda for Ecological Economics', pp. 94–95.
76 United Nations Economic Commission for Europe, 'Economic Survey of Europe for 1949', Geneva, 1950, pp. iii-iv, quoted in Arndt, *Economic Growth*, p. 37.
77 Joint Economic Committee on Employment, Growth and Price Levels (Douglas Committee), *Report*, US Congress: Washington, 1960, p. 11; quoted in Arndt, *The Rise and Fall of Economic Growth*, p. 46.
78 R. F. Harrod, 'Monetary Policy: A Symposium', *Bulletin*, Oxford Institute of Statistics: April–May 1952, p. 170; quoted in Arndt, *The Rise and Fall of Economic Growth*, p. 42.
79 C. A. R. Crosland, *The Future of Socialism*, London: Jonathan Cape, 1956, p. 292; quoted in Arndt, *The Rise and Fall of Economic Growth*, p. 55.
80 Arndt, *The Rise and Fall of Economic Growth*, p. 56.
81 United Nations, *World Economic Survey for 1960*, New York, 1961, p. 5; quoted in Arndt, *The Rise and Fall of Economic Growth*, pp. 56–57.
82 See Leonard Silk, 'Milton Friedman', in *The Economists*, New York: Avon Books, 1974. For a fuller rendering, see David Harvey, *A Brief History of Neoliberalism*, Oxford: Oxford University Press, 2005.
83 Abercrombie et al., *The Dominant Ideology Thesis*, p. 1.
84 For more on this, see Elie Halevy, *The Growth of Philosophic Radicalism*, Boston, MA: Beacon Press, 1955.
85 Abercrombie et al., *The Dominant Ideology Thesis*, p. 122.
86 Ibid., p. 166.
87 Ibid., p. 131.
88 Ibid., p. 134.
89 Cox also draws on many other historicists in his work including, above all, Giambattista Vico. See Cox, *The Political Economy of a Plural World*, ch. 3, 'Vico then and now'.
90 Ibid., p. 26.
91 Robert W. Cox, 'Gramsci, Hegemony and International Relations: An Essay in Method', in Stephen Gill, ed., *Gramsci, Historical Materialism and International Relations*, Cambridge: Cambridge University Press, 1993, p. 128.
92 Robert W. Cox, 'Social Forces, States and World Orders: Beyond International Relations Theory', in Robert O. Keohane, ed., *Neorealism and Its Critics*, New York: Columbia University Press, 1986, p. 230.
93 Peter Burnham, 'Neo-Gramscian Hegemony and the International Order', *Capital and Class*, no. 45, 1991, p. 76.
94 Leo Panitch, 'Globalization and the State', in Leo Panitch et al., eds, *The Globalization Decade: A Critical Reader*, London: Merlin Press, 2004, p. 22.
95 Burnham, 'Neo-Gramscian Hegemony and the International Order', pp. 77–78.
96 John Kenneth Galbraith, *The Affluent Society*, London: Hamish Hamilton, 1958, pp. 86–87.
97 John Kenneth Galbraith, *The New Industrial State*, New York: The New American Library, Inc., 1968, p. 183.
98 Such, at least, was the prevalent sentiment engendered by the utilitarianism, and instrumentalism, bequeathed by the Enlightenment, and by the classical economists.

4 The class structure and normative foundations of the paradigm

1 Theodore J. Lowi, 'Foreword', in Kenneth Prewitt and Alan Stone, *The Ruling Elites: Elite Theory, Power, and American Democracy*, New York: Harper & Row, 1973, p. ix.
2 Robert W. Cox, 'Social Forces, States and World Orders: Beyond International Relations Theory', in Robert O. Keohane, ed., *Neorealism and Its Critics*, New York: Columbia University Press, 1986, p. 225. Original italics.

3 Robert W. Cox, *The Political Economy of a Plural World: Critical Reflections on Power, Morals and Civilization*, London: Routledge, 2002, pp. 31–32.
4 Ibid., p. 32.
5 Cox offers a succinct definition of class:

> [P]eople who are members of a social class … know themselves to be members and they recognize others as members of their own or another social class. Class involves awareness of sharing common experiences of life and work, common perceptions of the cleavages in society (of being distinguished from and opposed to another class), and most likely of expressing this sense of community in collective action and shared aspirations.

Robert W. Cox, *Production, Power and World Order: Social Forces in the Making of History*, New York: Columbia University Press, 1986, fn. 8, p. 407. I adopt this definition as well.
6 David B. Grusky, 'Social Stratification', in William Outhwaite and Tom Bottomore, eds, *The Blackwell Dictionary of Twentieth-century Social Thought*, Oxford: Blackwell Publishers Ltd, 1993, p. 610.
7 These variables are used as stratification identifiers for familiar divisions such as, for example, 'middle class', comprising managers, professionals, white-collar workers, artisans, etc.
8 Cox, *Production, Power and World Order*, p. 2.
9 Prewitt and Stone, *The Ruling Elites*, pp. 8–9.
10 'Without tried and talented leaders', said Lenin, '…no class in modern society is capable of conducting a determined struggle'. V. Lenin, 'What Is to Be Done', (1902), reprinted in Henry M. Christman, ed., *Essential Works of Lenin*, New York: Bantam, 1966, p. 145.
11 For a useful survey, see Anthony Brewer, *Marxist Theories of Imperialism: A Critical Survey*, 2nd edn, New York: Routledge, 1989.
12 Nicholas Greenwood Onuf, *World of our Making: Rules and Rule in Social Theory and International Relations*, Columbia: University of South Carolina Press, 1989, p. 288. It is important to note that, as a constructivist, Onuf does not find the origins of classes in production relations. He looks instead to the notion of 'rules' that provide a guide to human conduct and give it social meaning. Rules are also key to the distribution of influence and rewards in society. Rule and the generation of classes is the result of the unequal distribution of these advantages.
13 Worldwatch Institute, *Vital Signs 2003: The Trends That Are Shaping Our Future*, New York: W. W. Norton & Company, 2003, pp. 88–89.
14 David Morley and Kuan-Hsing Chen, *Stuart Hall: Critical Dialogues in Cultural Studies*, London: Routledge, 1996, p. 432. Hall is the founder and chief intellectual force behind the Birmingham School at the Open University in Birmingham, England, which has been largely responsible for the formation and development of cultural studies as an international discipline.
15 Gramsci defines a subaltern group as one 'which has not yet gained consciousness of its strength, its possibilities, of how it is to develop, and which therefore does not know how to escape from the primitivist phase'. David Forgacs, ed., *An Antonio Gramsci Reader: Selected Writings 1916–1935*, New York: Schocken Books, 1988, p. 210.
16 Morley and Chen, *Stuart Hall*, p. 432.
17 Walter L. Adamson, *Hegemony and Revolution: A Study of Antonio Gramsci's Political and Cultural Theory*, Berkeley: University of California Press, 1991, p. 176.
18 Morley and Chen, *Stuart Hall*, p. 424.
19 Ibid., p. 423.
20 Ibid.
21 Antonio Gramsci, 'Analysis of Situations: Relations of Force', in Forgacs, *An Antonio Gramsci Reader*, p. 205.

22 Morley and Chen, *Stuart Hall*, p. 423.
23 Cox, *Production, Power and World Order*, p. 113.
24 Ibid., p. 144.
25 Robert L. Heilbroner, *The Making of Economic Society*, Englewood Cliffs, NJ: Prentice-Hall, 1962, p. 71.
26 H. W. Arndt, *The Rise and Fall of Economic Growth: A Study in Contemporary Thought*, Melbourne: Longman Cheshire Pty Limited, 1978, p. 6.
27 Heilbroner, *The Making of Economic Society*, p. 27.
28 Ibid., p. 98.
29 Cox, *Production, Power and World Order*, p. 118.
30 Ibid., p. 119.
31 Ibid., pp. 122–123.
32 Ibid., p. 125.
33 Ibid., p. 127.
34 Ibid., p. 128.
35 Ibid.
36 Ibid., p. 144.
37 Ibid.
38 Technology played an important role in this change. For example, the British navy developed the Dreadnought, a new steel-hulled warship that tilted power relations in her favour immediately. However, this new shipbuilding technology simultaneously rendered the preexisting British fleet obsolete, just as it did those of her naval opponents. That change effectively levelled the playing field, and in fact rendered a significant advantage to Germany, whose steel production had been rapidly increased.
39 Cox, *Production, Power and World Order*, p. 155.
40 Ibid., p. 156.
41 Ibid., p. 214.
42 Ibid., p. 217.
43 On this, see John G. Ruggie, 'Embedded Liberalism and Postwar Regimes', in John Gerard Ruggie, *Constructing the World Polity: Essays on International Institutionalization*, New York: Routledge, 1998.
44 Production-line specialization was originally developed by F. W. Taylor at the Bethlehem Steel Company in the 1880s and subsequently adapted by Ford to the construction of automobiles.
45 Alain Lipietz, 'Fordism and Post-Fordism', in Outhwaite and Bottomore, *The Blackwell Dictionary of Twentieth-century Social Thought*, p. 230.
46 Cox, *Production, Power and World Order*, p. 168.
47 Ibid., p. 210.
48 Michael Adams, *American Backlash: The Untold Story of Social Change in the United States*, Toronto: Penguin Group, 2005.
49 See, for example, Stephen R. Gill, 'Neo-liberalism and the Shift towards a US-centred Transnational Hegemony', in Henk Overbeek, ed., *Restructuring Hegemony in the Global Political Economy: The Rise of Transnational Neo-liberalism in the 1980s*, London: Routledge, 1993.
50 Stephen Gill, 'Globalization, Market Civilization, and Disciplinary Neoliberalism', *Millennium*, vol. 24, no. 4, 1995, p. 400.
51 Adams, *American Backlash*, p. 134.
52 For a detailed look at the social construction of the consumer from a Foucauldain/poststructuralist point of view, see Peter Miller and Nikolas Rose, 'Mobilizing the Consumer: Assembling the Subject of Consumption', in Peter Miller and Nikolas Rose, *Governing the Present*, Cambridge: Polity Press, 2008.
53 On this, see Leslie Sklair, 'Social Movements for Global Capitalism: The Transnational Capitalist Class in Action', *Review of International Political Economy*, vol. 4, no. 3, 1997, esp. pp. 521–524.

54 Robert W. Cox, 'Gramsci, Hegemony and International Relations: an Essay in Method', in Stephen Gill, ed., *Gramsci, Historical Materialism and International Relations*, Cambridge: Cambridge University Press, 1993, p. 137.
55 Kees van der Pijl, *Transnational Classes and International Relations*, London: Routledge, 1998.
56 Leslie Sklair, *Sociology of the Global System*, Baltimore, MD: Johns Hopkins University Press, 1991.
57 Ibid., p. 53.
58 By most accounts of class formation, self-identification as a class is an important prerequisite for qualification as a social group of this nature.
59 Cox, *The Political Economy of a Plural World*, p. 12. The *nébuleuse* is not, according to Cox, a fully fledged transnational class, but it does indicate the presence of what he calls a nascent global historic bloc.
60 Ibid., p. 36.
61 Lowi, 'Foreword', p. 16.
62 Ibid., p. 18.
63 Ibid., p. 16.
64 This definition is drawn from Avital Simhony, 'Beyond Negative and Positive Freedom: T. H. Green's View of Freedom', *Political Theory*, vol. 21, no. 1, 1993, pp. 28–54.
65 This stark dichotomy may seem simplistic, especially in light of Cox's propensity to study political change in terms of myriad social forces, which in their various combinations produce many different modes of development, forms of state and world orders. I read this dichotomy as an expression of boundary conditions, distinguished by the extent and objectives of political intervention in society. Capitalist and redistributive systems are, on the interpretation adopted here, two poles – defined in terms of 'no intervention' and 'full intervention' – that bracket a spectrum of intermediate modes. Cox's discussion of the historical evolution of capitalist and redistributive modes can be found in Chapters 2 and 3 respectively in Cox, *Production, Power and World Order*.
66 Cox, *Production, Power and World Order*, p. 398.
67 Ibid., fn. 7, pp. 406–407.
68 A notable exception to this trend was the Soviet economy during its phase of rapid industrialization after the Second World War and through the 1950s. During that interval, the Soviet GNP was consistently higher than its American counterpart.
69 World Commission on Environment and Development, *Our Common Future*, Oxford: Oxford University Press, 1987, p. 8.
70 This decline is documented in Philippe G. Le Prestre, 'Studying the Effectiveness of the CBD', in Philippe G. Le Prestre, ed., *Governing Global Biodiversity: The Evolution and Implementation of the Convention on Biological Diversity*, Burlington, VT: Ashgate, 2002.
71 These activities include, primarily, overconsumption of useful species (e.g. hardwood forests, or the marine fishery), and the destruction of non-human habitat. Both these categories are directly related to economic growth.
72 Ruggie has recommended the use of (among other tools) counterfactual evidence to bolster interpretive analysis which, absent such support, may be vulnerable to criticism as idiosyncratic. See John G. Ruggie, 'Epistemology, Ontology, and the Study ofInternational Regimes', in Ruggie, *Constructing the World Polity*, p. 94.
73 This admonishment is from WCED, *Our Common Future*, p. 8.

5 Tensions in the paradigm and prospects for change

1 David Forgacs, ed., *An Antonio Gramsci Reader: Selected Writings, 1916–1935*, New York: Schocken Books, 1988, pp. 222–230.
2 Robert W. Cox, *The Political Economy of a Plural World: Critical Reflections on Power, Morals and Civilization*, London: Routledge, 2002, p. 106.

3 For historical overviews, see Ronnie D. Lipschutz, 'Reconstructing World Politics: The Emergence of Global Civil Society', *Millennium*, vol. 21, no. 3, 1992, pp. 389–420; Ray Kiely, *The Clash of Globalizations: Neo-Liberalism, the Third Way and Anti-Globalization*, Leiden: Koninklijke Brill NV, 2005; and Cox, *The Political Economy of a Plural World*, esp. ch. 8.
4 Cox, *The Political Economy of a Plural World*, p. 104.
5 Ibid.
6 Srilatha Batliwala and L. David Brown, eds, *Transnational Civil Society: An Introduction*, Bloomfield, CT: Kumarian Press, Inc., 2006, p. xi.
7 Cox, *Political Economy of a Plural World*, p. 97.
8 Lipschutz, 'Reconstructing World Politics', esp. pp. 390–400.
9 Ibid., p. 399.
10 Peter Smith, 'The World Social Forum – A New Space of Politics?', paper presented at the Conference on Contemporary Governance and the Question of the Social, University of Alberta, Edmonton, June, 2004.
11 Ibid., p. 1.
12 This charter is available at www.wsfindia.org.
13 Smith, 'The World Social Forum', p. 8.
14 Cox, *The Political Economy of a Plural World*, ch. 6.
15 Tanja A. Börzel and Thomas Risse, 'Private-public Partnerships: Effective and Legitimate Tools of International Governance?', in Edgar Grande and Louis W. Pauly, *Complex Sovereignty: Reconstituting Political Authority in the Twenty-first Century*, Toronto: University of Toronto Press, 2007, p. 198.
16 Ibid., p. 208.
17 Paul Wapner, *Environmental Activism and World Civic Politics*, Albany: State University of New York Press, 1997.
18 For more on this, see www.unglobalcompact.org.
19 United Nations General Assembly, *United Nations Millennium Declaration*, UN Resolution A/RES/55/S, New York: United Nations, 18 September 2000.
20 United Nations General Assembly, *Monterrey Consensus: Draft Outcome of the International Conference on Financing for Development*, New York: United Nations, 30 January 2002.
21 Jean-Philippe Thérien, 'The Politics of International Development: Approaching a New Grand Compromise?', in Steven Bernstein and Louis W. Pauly, eds, *Global Liberalism and Political Order: Toward a New Grand Compromise?*, Albany: State University of New York Press, 2007, p. 83.
22 Bron Raymond Taylor, ed., *Ecological Resistance Movements: The Global Emergence of Radical and Popular Environmentalism*, Albany: State University of New York Press, 1995, p. 340.
23 Ibid., p. 341.
24 Stephen Gill, 'Transformation and Innovation in the Study of World Order', in Stephen Gill and James H. Mittelman, eds, *Innovation and Transformation in International Studies*, Cambridge: Cambridge University Press, 1997, p. 20.
25 For more on this, see Thomas Homer-Dixon, *The Ingenuity Gap*, Toronto: Alfred A. Knopf, 2000, esp. ch. 3.
26 The familiar 'hockey stick' image is often derided as simplistically Malthusian, but I reject that complaint. In fact the woodenness and perceptible boundaries of the hockey-stick metaphor fail to capture the most dangerous feature of exponential curves, namely their extraordinarily dynamic expansionary power.
27 John G. Ruggie, 'Social Time and Ecodemographic Contexts', in John Gerard Ruggie, *Constructing the World Polity: Essays on International Institutionalization*, London: Routledge, 1998, p. 169.
28 Ibid.
29 Ibid.

30 For an instructive analysis of how neoliberal capitalism and economic globalization can be made more socially and ecologically responsible, see Richard Sandbrook, ed., *Civilizing Globalization: A Survival Guide*, Albany: State University of New York Press, 2003.
31 The full text is at www.reagan.utexas.edu/archives/speeches/1983/92083c.htm.
32 Cox, *The Political Economy of a Plural World*, p. 107.
33 Herman E. Daly and John B. Cobb, Jr, *For the Common Good: Redirecting the Economy Toward Community, the Environment, and a Sustainable Future*, 2nd edn, Boston, MA: Beacon Press, 1994, p. 37.
34 Another notable author in this regard is Oran R. Young, whose recent work on environmental governance examines the benefits of adapting the attributes of institutional structures to match the properties of the ecosystems they are intended to manage. See Oran R. Young, *The Institutional Dimensions of Environmental Change: Fit, Interplay and Scale*, Cambridge: MIT Press, 2002.
35 Daniel H. Deudney, 'Bringing Nature Back In: Geopolitical Theory from the Greeks to the Global Era', in Daniel H. Deudney and Richard A. Matthew, eds, *Contested Grounds: Security and Conflict in the New International Politics*, Albany: State University of New York Press, 1999, p. 29.
36 See, for example, J. L. Simon, *The Economics of Population Growth*, Princeton, NJ: Princeton University Press, 1977; J. L. Simon, *The Ultimate Resource*, Princeton, NJ: Princeton University Press, 1981; and W. B. Beckerman, 'Economic Development and the Environment: A False Dilemma', in W. B. Beckerman, ed., *Growth, the Environment and the Distribution of Incomes: Essays by a Sceptical Optimist*, Brookfield, VT: Edward Elgar Publishing, 1995.
37 T. M. Seldon and D. S. Song, 'Environmental Quality and Development: Is There a Kuznet's Curve for Air Pollution Emissions?', *Journal of Environmental Economics and Management*, vol. 27, 1994, pp. 147–162.
38 An inverted-U curve was postulated much earlier, in 1955, by Simon Kuznets, which reflected a possible relationship between per capita income and income distribution. See Simon Kuznets, 'Economic Growth and Income Inequality', *American Economic Review*, vol. 49, pp. 1–28. Kuznets's original work had nothing to do with the environment.
39 Sander M. de Bruyn, *Economic Growth and the Environment: An Empirical Analysis*, Dordrecht: Kluwer Academic Publishers, 2000, p. 77.
40 De Bruyn, *Economic Growth and the Environment*, p. 227.
41 J. B. Opschoor, *Economic Incentives and Environmental Policies*, Dordrecht: Kluwer Academic Publishers, 1994, p. 78.
42 de Bruyn, *Economic Growth and the Environment*, p. 222.
43 Ibid., p. 227.
44 Per Kågeson, *Growth versus the Environment: Is There a Trade-off?*, Dordrecht: Kluwer Academic Publishers, 1998.
45 Ibid., p. 9.
46 Ibid., p. 266.
47 This follows necessarily from the first and second laws of thermodynamics. See Nicholas Georgescu-Roegen, 'The Entropy Law and the Economic Problem', in Herman E. Daly and Kenneth N. Townsend, eds, *Valuing the Earth: Economics, Ecology, Ethics*, Cambridge, MA: MIT Press, 1993. This issue is also discussed in Thomas Homer-Dixon, *The Upside of Down: Catastrophe, Creativity, and the Renewal of Civilization*, Toronto: Alfred A. Knopf Canada, 2006. See esp. pp. 38–42, and pp. 198–203.
48 As previously discussed, this sort of hegemony also includes the tacit availability of coercive force which may be required from time to time to actively support or reproduce the social consensus.
49 Benjamin J. Friedman, *The Moral Consequences of Economic Growth*, New York: Alfred A. Knopf, 2005.

50 Ibid., p. 47.
51 Ibid., p. 26.
52 Ibid., p. 3.
53 Ibid., p. 82. Original italics.
54 Ibid., p. 309.
55 Ibid., p. 394. Italics added.
56 Ibid., p. 4.
57 Ibid., p. 13.
58 Ibid., p. 15. Italics added.
59 For a look at the rising consumption of food in particular, and its environmental impact, see Lester R. Brown, *Outgrowing the Earth: The Food Security Challenge in an Age of Falling Water tables and Rising Temperatures*, London: W. W. Norton & Company, Ltd, 2004.
60 Environmental load is defined by Wakernagel and Rees as population times per capita resource use. See M. Wackernagel and W. Rees, *Our Ecological Footprint: Reducing Human Impact on the Earth*, Gabriola Island, BC: New Society Publishers, 1996, p. 53.
61 Thomas S. Kuhn, *The Structure of Scientific Revolutions*, 3rd edn, Chicago, IL: University of Chicago Press, [1962], 1996, p. 85.
62 Daly and Cobb, *For the Common Good*, p. 130.
63 Cox, *The Political Economy of a Plural World*, p. 38.
64 For a detailed discussion of a steady-state global economy, see Herman E. Daly, *Beyond Growth: The Economics of Sustainable Development*, , MA: Beacon Press, 1996.
65 K. E. Boulding, 'The Economics of the Coming Spaceship Earth', in H. Jarrett, ed., *Environmental Quality in a Growing Economy*, Baltimore, MD: Johns Hopkins University Press, 1966, p. 9.
66 Daly and Cobb, *For the Common Good*, p. 60.
67 An attempt in 1993 to construct an enclosed ecosystem to support eight people failed completely, and quickly. See Homer-Dixon, *The Ingenuity Gap*, pp. 134–136.
68 Ibid., pp. 241–242. Italics added.
69 John Kenneth Galbraith, *The Affluent Society*, London: Hamish Hamilton, 1958, p. 211.
70 J. K. Galbraith, 'How Much Should a Country Consume?', in H. Jarret, ed., *Perspectives on Conservation*, Baltimore, MD: Johns Hopkins University Press, 1958, pp. 91–92.
71 E. F. Schumacher, *Roots of Economic Growth*, Varanasi: Gandhian Institute of Studies, 1962.
72 T. W. Hutchinson, *'Positive' Economics and Policy Objectives*, London: Allen & Unwin, 1964, p. 12.
73 E. J. Mishan, *The Costs of Economic Growth*, London: Staples, 1967, p. x.
74 Herbert Marcuse, *One-dimensional Man*, London: Routledge & Kegan Paul, 1964.
75 Fred Hirsch, *The Social Limits to Growth*, Cambridge, MA: Harvard University Press, 1976.
76 These transition scenarios were proposed by Richard A. Falk, *A Study of Future Worlds*, New York: The Free Press, 1975. Other solution sets and futurist scenarios are offered by Dennis Pirages and Paul Ehrlich, *Ark II*, San Francisco, CA: W. H. Freeman and Company, 1974; Jay Forrester, *World Dynamics*, Cambridge: Wright-Allen Press, 1971; and Lester R. Brown, *World without Borders*, New York: Random House, 1972.
77 Luke Martel has ably compiled a full inventory of complaints levelled against Meadows et al. See Luke Martel, *Ecology and Society: An Introduction*, Cambridge: Polity Press, 1994.

78 Steven F. Bernstein, *The Compromise of Liberal Environmentalism*, New York: Columbia University Press, 2001, p. 3.
79 Ibid.
80 James N. Rosenau, 'Governance in the Twenty-first Century', *Global Governance*, vol. 1, no. 1, 1995, p. 13.
81 Kenneth Waltz, *Theory of International Politics*, New York: McGraw-Hill, Inc., p. 108.
82 Edward O. Wilson, *The Diversity of Life*, Cambridge, MA: Belknap Press of Harvard University Press, 1992, p. 282.
83 Braudel called this constrained solution set the 'terrain of the possible'.
84 Reinhold Niebuhr, *Moral Man and Immoral Society: A Study in Ethics and Politics*, New York: Charles Scribner's Sons, [1932], 1960, pp. xv–xvi.
85 It is certainly possible that the postmodern environment may be more conducive to the social construction of multiple narratives, each telling a local story of non-growth-oriented sustainable development – but even these local stories would ultimately have to be consistent with each other with respect to, for example, planetary ecological principles. Such consistency implies a conjoining of stories into a mother document, which again suggests the need for a metanarrative. A project of this nature (one central and multiple satellite stories) was undertaken in the 1990s with the construction of the NGO-sponsored Earth Charter.
86 The full text is available at www.unfccc,int/resource/docs/convkp/conveng.pdf.

Index

For Product Safety Concerns and Information please contact our EU
representative GPSR@taylorandfrancis.com
Taylor & Francis Verlag GmbH, Kaufingerstraße 24, 80331 München, Germany

www.ingramcontent.com/pod-product-compliance
Ingram Content Group UK Ltd.
Pitfield, Milton Keynes, MK11 3LW, UK
UKHW022125190926
475702UK00013B/1653

* 9 7 8 0 4 1 5 5 0 3 5 0 1 *